FROM
Bannockburn
TO
Flodden

1

Tales of a Scottish Grandfather

FROM
Bannockburn
TO
Flodden

Wallace, Bruce & the Heroes
of Medieval Scotland

Sir Walter Scott

Introduction by
GEORGE GRANT

CUMBERLAND HOUSE
NASHVILLE, TENNESSEE

FROM BANNOCKBURN TO FLODDEN
PUBLISHED BY CUMBERLAND HOUSE PUBLISHING INC.
431 Harding Industrial Drive
Nashville, Tennessee 37211

Cover design by Unlikely Suburban Design, Nashville, Tennessee

Library of Congress Cataloging-in-Publication Data

Scott, Walter, Sir, 1771–1832.
 [Tales of a grandfather]
 Tales of a Scottish grandfather / Sir Walter Scott ; introduction by George Grant.
     p. cm.
 Includes index.
 Originally published: London : Routledge, 1828.
 Contents: v. 1. From Bannockburn to Flodden : Wallace, Bruce & the heroes of
medieval Scotland.
 ISBN-13 978-1-58182-127-7 (v. 1 : pbk. : alk. paper)
 ISBN-10 1-58182-127-1 (v. 1 : pbk. : alk. paper)
 1. Scotland—History. I. Title.
DA761.S55 2001
941.1—dc21   00-065775

Printed in the United States of America

2 3 4 5 6 7 8—12 11 10 09 08

CONTENTS

INTRODUCTION

I N 1828, the world's greatest storyteller sat down to weave yet another yarn. Over the past dozen years or so he had almost single-handedly revived Scottish pride—he had recovered the Royal Honors of Crown in Edinburgh Castle in 1818, more than a century after they had been locked away after the Union of Parliaments in 1707. And of course, his novels had fanned the flames of passion for the kilts, the bagpipes, and the highland burr of the Scots. He had become the world's spokesman for all things Celtic.

But now he had something entirely different in mind. His *Tales of a Scottish Grandfather* proved to be his most intimate, most accessible, and most dramatic stories of all. The reason was simple: He was no longer telling his stories to the world; he was telling them to his grandson.

Sir Walter Scott (1771–1832) was the most popular writer of the nineteenth century. Often mentioned in the same breath with Geoffrey Chaucer, William Shakespeare, and John Milton, his output was prodigious: twenty-seven novels, five epic poems, three biographies, fourteen histories, and half a dozen collections of tales, legends, and ballads. All remain classics. But it was for his popularization of his native Scotland that he is best remembered. Scott created and popularized historical fiction in a series called the Waverley Novels—which included such works as *Old Mortality* (1816), *Rob Roy* (1817), *The Heart of Midlothian* (1819), *Quentin Dunward* (1823), and *St Ronan's Well* (1824). In these stories Scott arranged the plots and characters so that the readers entered into the lives of both great and ordinary people caught up in violent, dramatic changes in history. These writings included romance, adventure, action, and an incredibly vivid eye and ear for detail.

Scott was proud of his work, and rightly so. Novels such as *Ivanhoe* (1819) and *The Chronicles of Canongate* (1827) are marvels of the literary craft. But he was especially proud of these volumes of stories for his grandson. In Tales of a Scottish Grandfather he recovered the whole story of his beloved Scotland—its history, not some fictionalized approximation. From William Wallace and Robert the Bruce to John Knox and Mary Queen of Scots, from the subjugation of Rob Roy and the rising of the Jacobites to the crusade of Bonnie Prince Charlie and the quest of the Duke of Cumberland, the entire romantic story is told—not as a historian would tell it, but as a grandfather would.

He began this work shortly after finishing the difficult task of writing the comprehensive Life of Napoleon. The biography had been completed on June 9, 1828, and the very next morning Scott recorded in his journal that "the good thought came into my head to write stories for little Johnny Lockhart from the history of Scotland." The idea had been sparked by the immense popularity of J. W. Croker's *Stories from the History of England,* but he determined not to write quite so simply as Croker had done, because he felt a conviction that children "hate books which are written down to their capacity, and love those that are composed more for their betters and elders." He aspired to write "a book that a child shall understand, yet a man will feel some temptation to peruse should he chance to take it up. It will require, however, a simplicity of style not quite my own. The grand and interesting consists in ideas, not in words."

Scott was by no means disappointed in his expectations. This first volume—which is followed by three more—retells the heroic stories of William Wallace, Robert the Bruce, and the foundations of the Stewart monarchy through the medieval history of Scotland. It was met with great success. Indeed, his son-in-law, J. G. Lockhart, remarked that its reception "was more rapturous than that of any of his other books since *Ivanhoe.*"

In each of the four volumes Scott marshaled all his narrative power. But he did it for the sake of love—love of family, love of place, and love of legacy.

George Grant

PREFACE

THESE Tales were written in the interval of other avocations, for the use of the young relative to whom they are inscribed. They embrace at the same time some attempt at a general view of Scottish History, with a selection of its more picturesque and prominent points. Having been found useful to the young person for whom the compilation was made, they are now given to the public, in the hope that they may be a source of instruction for others. The compilation, though professing to be only a collection of Tales, or Narratives from the Scottish Chronicles, will nevertheless be found to contain a general view of the History of that country, from the period when it begins to possess general interest.

The Author may here mention that, after commencing his task in a manner obvious to the most limited capacity, of which the Tale of Macbeth is an example, he was led to take a different view of the subject, by finding that a style considerably more elevated was more interesting to his juvenile reader. There is no harm, but, on the contrary, there is benefit, in presenting a child with ideas somewhat beyond his easy and immediate comprehension. The difficulties thus offered, if not too great or too frequent, stimulate curiosity and encourage exertion.

The Author has carefully revised the present (second) edition, corrected several errors and inaccuracies, and made numerous and large additions, so as to bring the little book nearer its proper character, of an abridged History of Scotland, for the use of young persons. The reigns of Malcolm Canmore, and of his immediate successors, have been given in some detail, instead of passing at once from the defeat and death of Macbeth to the wars of Bruce and Baliol.

It is the Author's purpose to carry this little work down to the period of 1748, when the two sister nations became blended together in manners as well as by political ties. The task will afford an opportunity to show the slow and interrupted progress by which England and

Scotland, ostensibly united by the accession of James the First of England, gradually approximated to each other, until the last shades of national difference may be almost said to have disappeared.

W. S.

Abbotsford, *February* 1828.

DEDICATION

To Hugh Littlejohn, Esq.

MUCH Respected Sir,
Although I have not yet arrived at the reverend period of life which may put me once more on a level with yours, yet I find myself already better pleased to seek an auditor of your age, who is usually contented to hear the same story repeated twenty times over, than to attempt instructing the more critical hearers among my contemporaries, who are apt to object to any tale twice told. It is, therefore, probable that had we been to remain near to each other I should have repeated to you many of the stories contained in this book more than once. But, since that has ceased to be the case, I have nothing remaining save to put them in this shape, in which you may read them as often as you have a mind.

I have in this little book imitated one with which you are well acquainted,—I mean the collection of Stories taken from the *History of England*, and which has been so deservedly popular.[1]

As you, however, happen to be a person of quick study, and great penetration, it is my purpose to write a little work, which may not only be useful to you at the age of five or six years, which I think may be about your worship's present period of life, but which may not be beneath your attention, either for style or matter, at the graver term of eight, or even ten years old. When, therefore, you find anything a little too hard for you to understand at this moment, you must consider that you will be better able to make out the sense a year or two afterwards; or perhaps you may make a great exertion, and get at the meaning, just as you might contrive to reach something placed upon a high shelf by

---

[1] *Stories from the History of England for Children,* by the Right Hon. J. W. Croker.

standing on your tiptoes, instead of waiting till you grow a little taller. Or who knows but Papa will give you some assistance, and that will be the same as if he set you upon a stool that you might reach down what you wanted.

And so farewell, my dear Hugh Littlejohn.[1]

If you should grow wiser and better from what you read in this book, it will give great pleasure to your very affectionate

Grandfather
Abbotsford, *December* 1827.

---

[1] [John Hugh Lockhart, nicknamed as above by his grandfather, was the son of J. G. Lockhart and Sophia, eldest daughter of Sir Walter Scott. John Hugh was born in 1821, and, after a precarious existence, died in 1831.]

FROM
Bannockburn
TO
Flodden

I

How Scotland and England Came to Be Separate Kingdoms

ENGLAND is the southern, and Scotland is the northern part of the celebrated island called Great Britain. England is greatly larger than Scotland, and the land is much richer, and produces better crops. There are also a great many more men in England, and both the gentlemen and the country people are more wealthy, and have better food and clothing there than in Scotland. The towns, also, are much more numerous, and more populous.

Scotland, on the contrary, is full of hills, and huge moors and wildernesses, which bear no corn, and afford but little food for flocks of sheep or herds of cattle. But the level ground that lies along the great rivers is more fertile, and produces good crops. The natives of Scotland are accustomed to live more hardily in general than those of England. The cities and towns are fewer, smaller, and less full of inhabitants than in England. But as Scotland possesses great quarries of stone, the houses are commonly built of that material, which is more lasting, and has a grander effect to the eye than the bricks used in England.

Now, as these two nations live in the different ends of the same island, and are separated by large and stormy seas from all other parts of the world, it seems natural that they should have been friendly to each other, and that they should have lived as one people under the same government. Accordingly, above two hundred years ago, the King of Scotland becoming King of England, as I shall tell you in another part of this book, the two nations have ever since then been joined in one great kingdom, which is called Great Britain.

But, before this happy union of England and Scotland, there were many long, cruel, and bloody wars, between the two nations; and, far from helping or assisting each other, as became good neighbours and friends, they did each other all the harm and injury that they possibly could, by invading each other's territories, killing their subjects, burning their towns, and taking their wives and children prisoners. This lasted for many many hundred years; and I am about to tell you the reason why the land was so divided.

A long time since, eighteen hundred years ago and more, there was a brave and warlike people, called the Romans, who undertook to conquer the whole world, and subdue all countries, so as to make their own city of Rome the head of all the nations upon the face of the earth. And after conquering far and near, at last they came to Britain, and made a great war upon the inhabitants, called the British, or Britons, whom they found living there. The Romans, who were a very brave people, and well armed, beat the British, and took possession of almost all the flat part of the island, which is now called England, and also of a part of the south of Scotland. But they could not make their way into the high northern mountains of Scotland, where they could hardly get anything to feed their soldiers, and where they met with much opposition from the inhabitants. The Romans, therefore, gave up all attempts to subdue this impenetrable country, and resolved to remain satisfied with that level ground, of which they had already possessed themselves.[1]

Then the wild people of Scotland, whom the Romans had not been able to subdue, began to come down from their mountains, and make inroads upon that part of the country which had been conquered by the Romans.

These people of the northern parts of Scotland were not one nation, but divided in two, called the Scots and the Picts; they often fought against each other, but they always joined together against the Romans, and the Britons who had been subdued by them. At length,

---

[1] The first invasion of England by the Romans, under Julius Caesar, was in the 55th year before the Christian Era; that of Scotland, under Agricola, A.D. 40.

the Romans thought they would prevent these Picts and Scots from coming into the southern part of Britain, and laying it waste. For this purpose, they built a very long wall between the one side of the island and the other, so that none of the Scots or Picts should come into the country on the south side of the wall; and they made towers on the wall, and camps, with soldiers, from place to place; so that, at the least alarm, the soldiers might hasten to defend any part of the wall which was attacked. This first Roman wall was built[1] between the two great Firths of the Clyde and the Forth, just where the island of Britain is at the narrowest, and some parts of it are to be seen at this day. You can see it on the map.

This wall defended the Britons for a time, and the Scots and Picts were shut out from the fine rich land, and enclosed within their own mountains. But they were very much displeased with this, and assembled in great numbers, and climbed over the wall, in spite of all that the Romans could do to oppose them. A man, named Grahame, is said to have been the first soldier who got over; and the common people still call the remains of the wall Grahame's dike.

Now the Romans, finding that this first wall could not keep out the barbarians (for so they termed the Picts and the Scots), thought they would give up a large portion of the country to them, and perhaps it might make them quiet. So they built a new wall, and a much stronger one than the first, sixty miles farther back from the Picts and Scots.[2] Yet the barbarians made as many furious attacks to get over this second wall, as ever they had done to break through the former. But the Roman soldiers defended the second wall so well, that the Scots and Picts could not break through it; though they often came round the end of the wall by sea, in boats made of ox hides, stretched upon hoops, landed on the other side, and did very much mischief. In the meantime, the poor Britons led a very unhappy life; for the Romans, when they subdued their country, having taken away all their arms, they lost the habit of using them, or of defending themselves, and trusted entirely to the protection of their conquerors.

But at this time great quarrels, and confusions, and civil wars, took place at Rome. So the Roman Emperor sent to the soldiers whom he

---

[1] During the invasion of Agricola, A.D. 81—and rebuilt by Antoninus in 140.

[2] The wall of Adrian, built A.D. 120. It extended quite across the island, from the river Tyne at Newcastle to the Solway Firth at Carlisle.

had maintained in Britain, and ordered that they should immediately return to their own country, and leave the Britons to defend their wall as well as they could, against their unruly and warlike neighbours the Picts and Scots. The Roman soldiers were very sorry for the poor Britons, but they could do no more to help them than by repairing the wall of defence. They therefore built it all up, and made it as if it were quite new. And then they took to their ships, and left the island.[1]

After the departure of the Romans, the Britons were quite unable to protect the wall against the barbarians; for, since their conquest by the Romans, they had become a weak and cowardly people. So the Picts and Scots broke through the wall at several points, wasted and destroyed the country, and took away the boys and girls to be slaves, seized upon the sheep, and upon the cattle, and burnt the houses, and did the inhabitants every sort of mischief. Thus at last the Britons, finding themselves no longer able to resist these barbarous people, invited into Britain to their assistance a number of men from the north of Germany who were called Anglo-Saxons. Now, these were a very brave and warlike people, and they came in their ships from Germany, and landed in the south part of Britain, and helped the Britons to fight with the Scots and Picts [A.D. 449], and drove these nations again into the hills and fastnesses of their own country, to the north of the wall which the Romans built; and they were never afterwards so troublesome to their neighbours.

But the Britons were not much the better for the defeat of their northern enemies; for the Saxons, when they had come into Britain, and saw what a beautiful rich country it was, and that the people were not able to defend it, resolved to take the land to themselves, and to make the Britons their slaves and servants. The Britons were very unwilling to have their country taken from them by the people they had called in to help them, and so strove to oppose them; but the Saxons were stronger and more warlike than they, and defeated them so often, that they at last got possession of all the level and flat land in the south part of Britain. However, the bravest part of the Britons fled into a very hilly part of the country, which is called Wales, and there they defended themselves against the Saxons for a great many years; and their descendants still speak the ancient British language, called

---

[1] After the partial occupation of Great Britain by the Romans during a period of 500 years, they finally abdicated the island A.D. 446.

Welsh. In the meantime, the Anglo-Saxons spread themselves throughout all the south part of Britain, and the name of the country was
changed, and it was no longer called Britain, but England; which
means the land of the Anglo-Saxons who had conquered it.

While the Saxons and Britons were thus fighting together, the
Scots and the Picts, after they had been driven back behind the
Roman wall, also quarrelled and fought between themselves; and at
last, after a great many battles, the Scots got completely the better of
the Picts. The common people say that the Scots destroyed them
entirely; but I think it is not likely that they could kill such great numbers of people. Yet it is certain they must have slain many, and driven
others out of the country, and made the rest their servants and slaves;
at least the Picts were never heard of in history after these great
defeats, and the Scots gave their own name to the north part of
Britain, as the Angles, or Anglo-Saxons, did to the south part; and so
came the name of Scotland, the land of the Scots; and England, the
land of the English. The two kingdoms were divided from each other,
on the east by the river Tweed; then, as you proceed westward, by a
great range of hills and wildernesses, and at length by a branch of the
sea called the Firth of Solway. The division is not very far from the old
Roman wall. The wall itself has been long suffered to go to ruins; but,
as I have already said, there are some parts of it still standing, and it is
curious to see how it runs as straight as an arrow over high hills, and
through great bogs and morasses.

You see, therefore, that Britain was divided between three different nations, who were enemies to each other.—There was England,
which was the richest and best part of the island, and which was
inhabited by the English. Then there was Scotland, full of hills and
great lakes, and difficult and dangerous precipices, wild heaths, and
great morasses. This country was inhabited by the Scots, or Scottish
men. And there was Wales, also a very wild and mountainous country,
whither the remains of the ancient Britons had fled, to obtain safety
from the Saxons.

The Welsh defended their country for a long time, and lived under
their own government and laws; yet the English got possession of it at
last. But they were not able to become masters of Scotland, though
they tried it frequently. The two countries were under different kings,
who fought together very often and very desperately; and thus you see
the reason why England and Scotland, though making parts of the

same island, were for a long time great enemies to each other. Papa will show you the two countries on the map, and you must take notice that Scotland is all full of hills, and wild moors covered with heather.—But now I think upon it, Mr. Hugh Littlejohn is a traveller, and has seen Scotland, and England too, with his own eyes. However, it will do no harm to look at the map.

The English are very fond of their fine country; they call it "Old England," and "Merry England," and think it the finest land that the sun shines upon. And the Scots are also very proud of their own country, with its great lakes and mountains; and, in the old language of the country, they call it "The land of the lakes and mountains; and of the brave men;" and often, also, "The Land of Cakes," because the people live a good deal upon cakes made of oatmeal, instead of wheaten bread. But both England and Scotland are now parts of the same kingdom, and there is no use in asking which is the best country, or has the bravest men.[1]

This is but a dull chapter, Mr. Littlejohn. But as we are to tell many stories about Scotland and England, it is best to learn what sort of countries we are talking about. The next story shall be more entertaining.

---

[1] "From the time of Kenneth MacAlpine to that of Macbeth—that is, from 841 to 1040, a space of about two centuries—we have a line of fifteen kings of Scots, of whom it is easy to perceive that, in spite of the absurd prejudices concerning the inferiority of the Gaelic race, they sustained successfully the sceptre of Kenneth, and, by repeated battles both with the English and the Danes, not only repelled the attacks of their neighbours, but consolidated the strength of their kingdom, gradually modelling an association of barbarous, and in part wandering tribes, into the consistence of a regular state. It is true that, through the mist of years, these sceptered shades are seen but indistinctly and dimly; yet, as we catch a glimpse, we see them occupied always in battle, and often in conquest."—*Miscellaneous Prose Works.*

II

The Story of Macbeth

1033-1056

S OON after the Scots and Picts had become one people, as I told you before, there was a King of Scotland called Duncan, a very good old man. He had two sons; one was called Malcolm, and the other Donald-bane. But King Duncan was too old to lead out his army to battle, and his sons were too young to help him.

At this time Scotland, and indeed France and England, and all the other countries of Europe, were much harassed by the Danes. These were a very fierce, warlike people, who sailed from one place to another, and landed their armies on the coast, burning and destroying everything wherever they came. They were heathens, and did not believe in the Bible, but thought of nothing but battle and slaughter, and making plunder. When they came to countries where the inhabitants were cowardly, they took possession of the land, as I told you the Saxons took possession of Britain. At other times, they landed with their soldiers, took what spoil they could find, burned the houses, and then got on board, hoisted sails, and away again. They did so much mischief, that people put up prayers to God in the churches, to deliver them from the rage of the Danes.

Now, it happened in King Duncan's time, that a great fleet of these Danes came to Scotland and landed their men in Fife,[1] and threatened to take possession of that province. So a numerous Scottish army was levied to go to fight against them. The King, as I told you, was too old to command his army, and his sons were too young. He therefore sent out one of his near relations, who was called Macbeth; he was son of Finel, who was Thane, as it was called, of Glammis. The governors of provinces were at that time, in Scotland, called thanes; they were afterwards termed earls.

This Macbeth, who was a brave soldier, put himself at the head of the Scottish army, and marched against the Danes. And he carried with him a relation of his own, called Banquo, who was Thane of Lochaber, and was also a very brave man. So there was a great battle fought between the Danes and the Scots; and Macbeth and Banquo, the Scottish generals, defeated the Danes, and drove them back to their ships, leaving a great many of their soldiers both killed and wounded. Then Macbeth and his army marched back to a town in the north of Scotland, called Forres, rejoicing on account of their victory.

Now there lived at this time three old women in the town of Forres, whom people looked upon as witches, and supposed they could tell what was to come to pass. Nobody would believe such folly nowadays, except low and ignorant creatures, such as those who consult gipsies in order to have their fortunes told; but in those early times the people were much more ignorant, and even great men, like Macbeth, believed that such persons as these witches of Forres could tell what was to come to pass afterwards, and listen to the nonsense they told them, as if the old women had really been prophetesses. The old women saw that they were respected and feared, so that they were tempted to impose upon people, by pretending to tell what was to happen to them; and they got presents for doing so.

So the three old women went and stood by the wayside, in a great moor or heath near Forres, and waited till Macbeth came up. And then, stepping before him as he was marching at the head of his soldiers, the first woman said, "All hail, Macbeth—hail to thee, Thane of Glammis." The second said, "All hail, Macbeth—hail to thee, Thane of Cawdor." Then the third, wishing to pay him a higher compliment than the other two, said, "All hail, Macbeth, that shalt be King of Scot-

---

[1] Under the command of Sueno, King of Denmark and Norway.

land." Macbeth was very much surprised to hear them give him these titles; and while he was wondering what they could mean, Banquo stepped forward, and asked them whether they had nothing to tell about him as well as about Macbeth. And they said that be should not be so great as Macbeth, but that, though he himself should never be a king, yet his children should succeed to the throne of Scotland, and be kings for a great number of years.

Before Macbeth recovered from his surprise, there came a messenger to tell him that his father was dead, so that he was become Thane of Glammis by inheritance. And there came a second messenger, from the King, to thank Macbeth for the great victory over the Danes, and tell him that the Thane of Cawdor had rebelled against the King, and that the King had taken his office from him, and had sent to make Macbeth Thane of Cawdor as well as of Glammis. Thus the two first old women seemed to be right in giving him those two titles. I daresay they knew something of the death of Macbeth's father, and that the government of Cawdor was intended for Macbeth, though he had not heard of it.

However, Macbeth, seeing a part of their words come to be true, began to think how he was to bring the rest to pass, and make himself king, as well as Thane of Glammis and Cawdor. Now Macbeth had a wife, who was a very ambitious, wicked woman, and when she found out that her husband thought of raising himself up to be King of Scotland, she encouraged him in his wicked purpose, by all the means in her power, and persuaded him that the only way to get possession of the crown was to kill the good old King, Duncan. Macbeth was very unwilling to commit so great a crime, for he knew what a good sovereign Duncan had been; and he recollected that he was his relation, and had been always very kind to him, and had entrusted him with the command of his army, and had bestowed on him the government or thanedom of Cawdor. But his wife continued telling him what a foolish, cowardly thing it was in him not to take the opportunity of making himself King, when it was in his power to gain what the witches promised him. So the wicked advice of his wife, and the prophecy of these wretched old women, at last brought Macbeth to think of murdering his King and his friend. The way in which he accomplished his crime, made it still more abominable.

Macbeth invited Duncan to come to visit him, at a great castle near Inverness; and the good King, who had no suspicions of his kinsman, accepted the invitation very willingly. Macbeth and his lady received the King and all his retinue with much appearance of joy, and made a great feast, as a subject would do to make his King welcome. About the middle of the night, the King desired to go to his apartment, and Macbeth conducted him to a fine room which had been prepared for him. Now, it was the custom, in those barbarous times, that wherever the King slept, two armed men slept in the same chamber, in order to defend his person in case he should be attacked by any one during the night. But the wicked Lady Macbeth had made these two watchmen drink a great deal of wine, and had besides put some drugs into the liquor; so that when they went to the King's apartment they both fell asleep, and slept so soundly, that nothing could awaken them.

Then the cruel Macbeth came into King Duncan's bedroom about two in the morning. It was a terrible stormy night; but the noise of the wind and of the thunder did not awaken the King, for he was old, and weary with his journey; neither could it awaken the two sentinels, who were stupefied with the liquor and the drugs they had swallowed. They all slept soundly. So Macbeth having come into the room, and stepped gently over the floor, he took the two dirks which belonged to the sentinels, and stabbed poor old King Duncan to the heart, and that so effectually, that he died without giving even a groan. Then Macbeth put the bloody daggers into the hands of the sentinels, and daubed their faces over with blood, that it might appear as if they had committed the murder. Macbeth was, however, greatly frightened at what he had done, but his wife made him wash his hands and go to bed.

Early in the morning, the nobles and gentlemen who attended on the King assembled in the great hall of the castle, and there they began to talk of what a dreadful storm it had been the night before. But Macbeth could scarcely understand what they said, for he was thinking on something much worse and more frightful than the storm, and was wondering what would be said when they heard of the murder. They waited for some time, but finding the King did not come from his apartment, one of the noblemen went to see whether he was well or not. But when he came into the room, he found poor King Duncan lying stiff, and cold, and bloody, and the two sentinels both fast asleep, with their dirks or daggers covered with blood. As soon as the Scottish nobles saw this terrible sight, they were greatly astonished and enraged; and Macbeth made believe as if he were more enraged than any of them, and, drawing, his sword before any one could prevent him, he killed the two attendants of the King who slept in the bedchamber, pretending to think they had been guilty of murdering King Duncan.

When Malcolm and Donaldbane, the two sons of the good King, saw their father slain in this strange manner within Macbeth's castle, they became afraid that they might be put to death likewise, and fled away out of Scotland; for, notwithstanding all the excuses which he could make, they still believed that Macbeth had killed their father. Donaldbane fled into some distant islands, but Malcolm, the eldest son of Duncan, went to the Court of England, where he begged for assistance from the English King, to place him on the throne of Scotland as his father's successor.

In the meantime, Macbeth took possession of the kingdom of Scotland, and thus all his wicked wishes seemed to be fulfilled. But he was not happy. He began to reflect how wicked he had been in killing his friend and benefactor, and how some other person, as ambitious as he was himself, might do the same thing to him. He remembered, too, that the old women had said, that the children of Banquo should succeed to the throne after his death, and therefore he concluded that Banquo might be tempted to conspire against him, as he had himself done against King Duncan. The wicked always think other people are as bad as themselves. In order to prevent this supposed danger, Macbeth hired ruffians to watch in a wood, where Banquo and his son Fleance sometimes used to walk in the evening, with instructions to attack them, and kill both father and son. The villains did as they were ordered by Macbeth; but while they were killing Banquo, the boy Fleance made his escape from their wicked hands, and fled from Scotland into Wales. And it is said, that, long afterwards, his children came to possess the Scottish crown.[1]

Macbeth was not the more happy that he had slain his brave friend and cousin, Banquo. He knew that men began to suspect the wicked deeds which he had done, and he was constantly afraid that some one would put him to death as he had done his old sovereign, or that Malcolm would obtain assistance from the King of England, and come to make war against him, and take from him the Scottish kingdom. So, in this great perplexity of mind, he thought he would go to the old women, whose words had first put into his mind the desire

---

[1] Stewart family.

of becoming a king. It is to be supposed that he offered them presents, and that they were cunning enough to study how to give him some answer, which should make him continue in the belief that they could prophesy what was to happen in future times. So they answered him that he should not be conquered, or lose the crown of Scotland, until a great forest, called Birnam Wood, should come to attack a strong castle situated on a high hill called Dunsinane,[1] in which castle Macbeth commonly resided. Now, the hill of Dunsinane is upon the one side of a great valley, and the forest of Birnam is upon the other. There are twelve miles' distance betwixt them; and besides that, Macbeth thought it was impossible that the trees could ever come to the assault of the castle. He therefore resolved to fortify his castle on the hill of Dunsinane very strongly, as being a place in which he would always be sure to be safe. For this purpose he caused all his great nobility and thanes to send in stones, and wood, and other things wanted in building, and to drag them with oxen up to the top of the steep hill where he was building the castle.

Now, among other nobles who were obliged to send oxen, and horses, and materials to this laborious work, was one called Macduff, the Thane of Fife. Macbeth was afraid of this Thane, for he was very powerful, and was accounted both brave and wise; and Macbeth thought he would most probably join with Prince Malcolm, if ever he should come from England with an army. The King, therefore, had a private hatred against the Thane of Fife, which he kept concealed from all men, until he should have some opportunity of putting him to death, as he had done Duncan and Banquo. Macduff, on his part, kept upon his guard, and went to the King's court as seldom as he could, thinking himself never safe unless while in his own castle of Kennoway, which is on the coast of Fife, near to the mouth of the Firth of Forth.

It happened, however, that the King had summoned several of his nobles, and Macduff, the Thane of Fife, amongst others, to attend him at his new castle of Dunsinane; and they were all obliged to come— none dared stay behind. Now, the King was to give the nobles a great entertainment, and preparations were made for it. In the meantime, Macbeth rode out with a few attendants, to see the oxen drag the wood and the stones up the hill, for enlarging and strengthening the castle. So they saw most of the oxen trudging up the hill with great difficulty

---

[1] In Scotland pronounced Dunsinnan

(for the ascent is very steep), and the burdens were heavy, and the weather was extremely hot. At length Macbeth saw a pair of oxen so tired that they could go no farther up the hill, but fell down under their load. Then the King was very angry, and demanded to know who it was among his Thanes that had sent oxen so weak and so unfit for labour, when he had so much work for them to do. Some one replied that the oxen belonged to Macduff, the Thane of Fife. "Then," said the King, in great anger, "since the Thane of Fife sends such worthless cattle as these to do my labour, I will put his own neck into the yoke, and make him drag the burdens himself."

There was a friend of Macduff who heard these angry expressions of the King, and hastened to communicate them to the Thane of Fife, who was walking in the hall of the King's castle while dinner was preparing. The instant that Macduff heard what the King had said, he knew he had no time to lose in making his escape; for whenever Macbeth threatened to do mischief to any one, he was sure to keep his word.

So Macduff snatched up from the table a loaf of bread, called for his horses and his servants, and was galloping back to his own province of Fife, before Macbeth and the rest of the nobility were returned to the castle. The first question which the King asked was, what had become of Macduff? and being informed that he had fled from Dunsinane, he ordered a body of his guards to attend him, and mounted on horseback himself to pursue the Thane, with the purpose of putting him to death.

Macduff, in the meantime, fled as fast as horses' feet could carry him; but he was so ill provided with money for his expenses, that, when he came to the great ferry over the river Tay, he had nothing to give to the boatmen who took him across, excepting the loaf of bread which he had taken from the King's table. The place was called, for a long time afterwards, the Ferry of the Loaf.

When Macduff got into his province of Fife, which is on the other side of the Tay, he rode on faster than before, towards his own castle of Kennoway, which, as I told you, stands close by the seaside; and when he reached it, the King and his guards were not far behind him. Macduff ordered his wife to shut the gates of the castle, draw up the drawbridge, and on no account to permit the King or any of his soldiers to enter. In the meantime, he went to the small harbour belonging to the castle, and caused a ship which was lying there to be fitted out for sea in all haste, and got on board himself, in order to escape from Macbeth.

In the meantime, Macbeth summoned the lady to surrender the castle, and to deliver up her husband. But Lady Macduff, who was a wise and a brave woman, made many excuses and delays, until she knew that her husband was safely on board the ship, and had sailed from the harbour. Then she spoke boldly from the wall of the castle to the King, who was standing before the gate still demanding entrance, with many threats of what he would do if Macduff was not given up to him.

"Do you see," she said, "yon white sail upon the sea? Yonder goes Macduff to the Court of England. You will never see him again, till he comes back with young Prince Malcolm, to pull you down from the throne, and to put you to death. You will never be able to put your yoke, as you threatened, on the Thane of Fife's neck."

Some say that Macbeth was so much incensed at this bold answer, that he and his guards attacked the castle and took it, killing the brave lady and all whom they found there. But others say, and I believe more truly, that the King, seeing that the fortress of Kennoway was very strong, and that Macduff had escaped from him, and was embarked for England, returned to Dunsinane without attempting to take the castle. The ruins are still to be seen, and are called the Thane's Castle.

There reigned at that time in England a very good king, called Edward the Confessor. I told you that Prince Malcolm, the son of Duncan, was at his court, soliciting assistance to recover the Scottish throne. The arrival of Macduff greatly aided the success of his petition; for the English King knew that Macduff was a brave and a wise man. As he assured Edward that the Scots were tired of the cruel Macbeth, and would join Prince Malcolm if he were to return to his country at the head of an army, the King ordered a great warrior, called Siward, Earl of Northumberland, to enter Scotland with a large force [A.D. 1054], and assist Prince Malcolm in the recovery of his father's crown.

Then it happened just as Macduff had said; for the Scottish thanes and nobles would not fight for Macbeth, but joined Prince Malcolm and Macduff against him; so that at length he shut himself up in his castle of Dunsinane, where he thought himself safe, according to the old women's prophecy, until Birnam Wood should come against him. He boasted of this to his followers, and encouraged them to make a valiant defence, assuring them of certain victory. At this time Malcolm and Macduff were come as far as Birnam Wood, and lay encamped there with their army. The next morning, when they were to march across the broad valley to attack the castle of Dunsinane, Macduff advised that every soldier should cut down a bough of a tree and carry it in his hand, that the enemy might not be able to see how many men were coming against them.

Now, the sentinel who stood on Macbeth's castle-wall, when he saw all these branches, which the soldiers of Prince Malcolm carried, ran to the King, and informed him that the wood of Birnam was moving towards the castle of Dunsinane. The King at first called him a liar, and threatened to put him to death; but when he looked from the walls himself, and saw the appearance of a forest approaching from Birnam, he knew the hour of his destruction was come. His followers, too, began to be disheartened and to fly from the castle, seeing their master had lost all hopes.

Macbeth, however, recollected his own bravery, and sallied desperately out at the head of the few followers who remained faithful to him. He was killed, after a furious resistance, fighting hand to hand with Macduff in the thick of the battle. Prince Malcolm mounted the throne of Scotland, and reigned long and prosperously. He rewarded Macduff by declaring that his descendants should lead the vanguard of the Scottish army in battle, and place the crown on the King's head at the ceremony of coronation. King Malcolm also created the Thanes of Scotland earls, after the title of dignity adopted in the court of England.[1]

---

[1] The preceding traditional story of *Macbeth* has been adopted by Holingshed, dignified by the classical Latinity of Buchanan, and dramatised by Shakspeare. For its variation from ascertained historical facts, see Hailes's *Annals,* 8vo, vol. i. pp. 1-4; Chalmers's *Caledonia,* vol. i. pp. 404-414.

"Malcolm died peaceably in 1033, and was succeeded by 'The gracious Duncan,' the same who fell by the poniard of Macbeth. On reading these names every reader must feel as if brought from darkness into the blaze of noonday; so familiar are we with the personages whom we last named, and so clearly and distinctly we recall the events in which they are interested, in comparison with any doubtful and misty views which we can form of the twilight times before and after that fortunate period. But we must not be blinded by our poetical enthusiasm, nor add more than due importance to legends because they have been woven into the most striking tale of ambition and remorse that ever struck awe into a human bosom. The genius of Shakspeare having found the tale of Macbeth in the Scottish chronicles of Holingshed, adorned it with a lustre similar to that with which a level beam of the sun often invests some fragment of glass, which, though shining at a distance with the lustre of a diamond, is by a near investigation, discovered to be of no worth or estimation.

"Duncan, by his mother Beatrice a grandson of Malcolm II., succeeded to the throne on his grandfather's death, in 1033: he reigned only six years. Macbeth, his near relation, also a grandchild of Malcolm II., though by the mother's side, was stirred up by ambition to contest the throne with the possessor. The lady of Macbeth also, whose real name was Graoch, had deadly injuries to avenge, on the reigning prince. She was the grand-daughter of Kenneth IV., killed in 1003, fighting against Malcolm II.; and other causes for revenge animated the mind of her who has been since painted as the sternest of women. The old annalists add some instigations of a supernatural kind to the influence of a vindictive woman over an ambitious husband. Three women, of more than human stature and beauty, appeared to Macbeth in a dream or vision, and hailed him successively by the titles of Thane of Cromarty, Thane of Moray, which the King afterwards bestowed on him, and finally by that of King of Scots; this dream, it is said, inspired him with the seductive hopes so well expressed in the drama.

"Macbeth broke no law of hospitality in his attempt on Duncan's life. He attacked and slew the King at a place called Bothgowan, or the Smith's House, near Elgin, in 1039, and not, as has been supposed, in his own castle of Inverness. The act was bloody, as was the complexion of the times; but, in very truth, the claim of Macbeth to the throne, according to the rule of Scottish succession, was better than that of Duncan. As a king, the tyrant so much exclaimed against was, in reality, a firm, just, and equitable prince. Apprehensions of danger from a party which Malcolm, the eldest son of the slaughtered Duncan, had set on foot in Northumberland, and still main-tained in Scotland, seems, in process of time, to have soured the temper of Macbeth, and rendered him formidable to his nobility. Against Macduff, in particular, the power-ful Maormor of Fife, he had uttered some threats which occasioned that chief to fly from the Court of Scotland. Urged by this new counsellor, Siward, the Danish Earl of Northumberland, invaded Scotland in the year 1054, displaying his banner in behalf of the banished Malcolm. Macbeth engaged the foe in the neighbourbood of his cele-brated castle of Dunsinane. He was defeated, but escaped from the battle, and was slain at Lumphanan in 1056.

"Very slight observation will enable us to recollect how much this simple statement differs from that of the drama, though the plot of the latter is consistent enough with the inaccurate historians from whom Shakspeare drew his materials. It might be added, that early authorities show us no such persons as Banquo and his son Fleance, nor have we reason to think that the latter ever fled farther from Macbeth than across the flat scene, according to the stage direction. Neither were Banquo or his son ancestors of the house of Stewart. All these things are now known: but the mind retains pertinaciously the impression made by the impositions of genius. While the works of Shakspeare are read, and the English language subsists, History may say what she will, but the general reader will only recollect Macbeth as a sacrilegious usurper, and Richard as a deformed mur-therer."—Lardner's *Cyclopaedia.*

III

The Feudal System and the Norman Conquest

1057–1066

THE conduct of Edward the Confessor, King of England, in the story of Macbeth, was very generous and noble. He sent a large army and his General Siward to assist in dethroning the tyrant Macbeth, and placing Malcolm, the son of the murdered King Duncan, upon the throne; and we have seen how, with the assistance of Macduff, they fortunately succeeded. But King Edward never thought of taking any part of Scotland to himself in the confusion occasioned by the invasion; for he was a good man, and was not ambitious or covetous of what did not belong to him. It had been well both for England and Scotland that there had been more such good and moderate kings, as it would have prevented many great quarrels, long wars, and terrible bloodshed.

But good King Edward the Confessor did not leave any children to succeed him on the throne. He was succeeded by a king called Harold, who was the last monarch of the Saxon race that ever reigned in England. The Saxons, you recollect, had conquered the Britons, and now there came a new enemy to attack the Saxons. These were the Normans, a people who came from France, but were not originally Frenchmen. Their forefathers were a colony of those Northern pirates, whom we mentioned before as plundering all the sea-coasts which promised them any booty. They were frequently called Northmen or Normans, as they came from Denmark, Sweden, Norway, and the other Northern regions. A large body of them landed on the north part of France, and compelled the king of that country to yield up to them the possession of a large territory, or province, called Neustria, the name of which was changed to Normandy, when it became the property of these Northmen, or Normans. This province was governed by the Norman chief, who was called a duke, from a Latin word signifying a general. He exercised all the powers of a king within his dominions of Normandy, but, in consideration of his being possessed of a part of the territories of France, he acknowledged the king of that country for his sovereign, and became what was called his vassal.

This connection of a king as *sovereign,* with his princes and great men as *vassals,* must be attended to and understood, in order that you may comprehend the history which follows. A great king, or sovereign prince, gave large provinces, or grants of land, to his dukes, earls, and noblemen; and each of these possessed nearly as much power, within his own district, as the king did in the rest of his dominions. But then the vassal, whether duke, earl, or lord, or whatever he was, was obliged to come with a certain number of men to assist the sovereign, when he was engaged in war; and in time of peace, he was bound to attend on his court when summoned, and do homage to him—that is, acknowledge that he was his master and liege lord. In like manner, the vassals of the crown, as they were called, divided the lands which the king had given them into estates, which they bestowed on knights and gentlemen, whom they thought fitted to follow them in war, and to attend them in peace; for they, too, held courts, and administered justice, each in his own province. Then the knights and gentlemen, who had these estates from the great nobles, distributed the property among an inferior class of proprietors, some of whom cultivated the land themselves, and others by means of husbandmen and peasants, who were treated as a sort of slaves, being bought and sold like brute beasts, along with the farms which they laboured.

Thus, when a great king, like that of France or England, went to war, he summoned all his crown vassals to attend him, with the number of armed men corresponding to his fief, as it was called; that is, the territory which had been granted to each of them. The prince, duke, or earl, in order to obey the summons, called upon all the gentlemen to whom he had given estates, to attend his standard with their followers in arms. The gentlemen, in their turn, called on the franklins, a lower order of gentry, and upon the peasants; and thus the whole force of the kingdom was assembled in one array. This system of holding lands for military service, that is, for fighting for the sovereign when called upon, was called the FEUDAL SYSTEM. It was general throughout all Europe for a great many ages.

But as many of these great crown vassals, as, for example, the Dukes of Normandy, became extremely powerful, they were in the custom of making peace and war at their own hand, without the knowledge or consent of the King of France, their sovereign. In the same manner, the vassals of those great dukes and princes frequently made war on each other, for war was the business of every one; while the poor bondsman, who cultivated the ground, was subjected to the greatest hardships, and plundered and ill-treated by whichever side had the better. The nobles and gentlemen fought on horseback, arrayed in armour of steel, richly ornamented with gold and silver, and were called knights or squires. They used long lances, with which they rode fiercely against each other, and heavy swords, or clubs or maces, to fight hand to hand, when the lance was broken. Inferior persons fought on foot, and were armed with bows and arrows, which, according to their form, were called longbows, or cross-bows, and served to kill men at a distance, instead of guns and cannon, which were not then invented. The poor husbandmen were obliged to come to the field of battle with such arms as they had: and it was no uncommon thing to see a few of these knights and squires ride over and put to flight many hundreds of them; for the gentry were clothed in complete armour, so that they could receive little hurt, and the poor peasants had scarce clothes sufficient to cover them. You may see coats of the ancient armour preserved in the Tower of London and elsewhere, as matters of curiosity.

It was not a very happy time this, when there was scarcely any law, but the strong took everything from the weak at their pleasure; for as almost all the inhabitants of the country were obliged to be soldiers, it naturally followed that they were engaged in continual fighting.

The great crown-vassals, in particular, made constant war upon one another, and sometimes upon the sovereign himself, though to do so was to incur the forfeiture of their fiefs, or the territories which he had bestowed upon them, and which he was enabled by law to recall when they became his enemies. But they took the opportunity, when they were tolerably certain that their prince would not have strength sufficient to punish them. In short, no one could maintain his right longer than he had the power of defending it; and this induced the more poor and helpless to throw themselves under the protection of the brave and powerful—acknowledge themselves their vassals and subjects, and do homage to them, in order that they might obtain their safeguard and patronage.

While things were in this state, William, the Duke of Normandy, and the leader of that valiant people whose ancestors had conquered that province, began, upon the death of good King Edward the Confessor, to consider the time as favourable for an attempt to conquer the wealthy kingdom of England. He pretended King Edward had named him his heir; but his surest reliance was upon a strong army of his brave Normans, to whom were joined many knights and squires from distant countries, who hoped, by assisting this Duke William in his proposed conquest, to obtain from him good English estates, under the regulations which I have described.

The Duke of Normandy landed [on the 28th of September, at Pevensey] in Sussex, in the year one thousand and sixty-six after the birth of our blessed Saviour. He had an army of sixty thousand chosen men, for accomplishing his bold enterprise. Harold, who had succeeded Edward the Confessor on the throne of England, had been just engaged in repelling an attack upon England by the Norwegians, and was now called upon to oppose this new and more formidable invasion. He was, therefore, taken at considerable disadvantage.

The armies of England and Normandy engaged in a desperate battle near Hastings, and the victory was long obstinately contested. The Normans had a great advantage, from having amongst them large bands of archers, who used the long-bow, and greatly annoyed the English, who had but few bow-men to oppose them, and only short darts called javelins, which they threw from their hands, and which could do little hurt at a distance. Yet the victory remained doubtful, though the battle had lasted from nine in the morning until the close of the day, when an arrow pierced through King Harold's head, and he fell dead on the spot.[1] The English then retreated from the field, and Duke William used his advantage with so much skill and dexterity, that he made himself master of all England, and reigned there under the title of William the Conqueror. He divided great part of the rich country of England among his

---

[1] The battle of Hastings was fought 14th October 1066.

Norman followers, who held their estates of him for military service, according to the rules of the Feudal System, of which I gave you some account. The Anglo-Saxons, you may well suppose, were angry at this, and attempted several times to rise against King William, and drive him and his soldiers back to Normandy. But they were always defeated; and so King William became more severe towards these Anglo-Saxons, and took away their lands, and their high rank and appointments, until he left scarce any of them in possession of great estates, or offices of rank, but put his Normans above them, as masters, in every situation.

Thus the Saxons who had conquered the British, as you have before read, were in their turn conquered by the Normans, deprived of their property, and reduced to be the servants of those proud foreigners. To this day, though several of the ancient nobility of England claim to be descended from the Normans, there is scarcely a nobleman, and very few of the gentry, who can show that they are descended of the Saxon blood; William the Conqueror took so much care to deprive the conquered people of all power and importance.

It must have been a sad state of matters in England, when the Normans were turning the Saxons out of their estates and habitations, and degrading them from being freemen into slaves. But good came out of it in the end; for these Normans were not only one of the bravest people that ever lived, but they were possessed of more learning and skill in the arts than the Saxons. They brought with them the art of building large and beautiful castles and churches composed of stone, whereas the Saxons had only miserable houses made of wood. The Normans introduced the use of the long-bow also, which became so general, that the English were afterwards accounted the best archers in the world, and gained many battles by their superiority in that military art. Besides these advantages, the Normans lived in a more civilised manner than the Saxons, and observed among each other the rules of civility and good-breeding, of which the Saxons were ignorant. The Norman barons were also great friends to national liberty, and would not allow their kings to do anything contrary to their privileges, but resisted them whenever they attempted anything beyond the power which was given to them by law. Schools were set up in various places by the Norman princes, and learning was encouraged. Large towns were founded in different places of the kingdom, and received favour from the Norman kings, who desired to have the assistance of the townsmen in case of any dispute with their nobility.

Thus the Norman Conquest, though a most unhappy and disastrous event at the time it took place, rendered England, in the end, a more wise, more civilised, and more powerful country than it had been before; and you will find many such cases in history, my dear child, in which it has pleased the providence of God to bring great good out of what seems, at first sight, to be unmixed evil.

IV

From Malcolm Canmore to William the Lion

1067-1214

THE last chapter may seem to have little to do with Scottish history, yet the Norman Conquest of England produced a great effect upon their neighbours. In the first place, a very great number of the Saxons who fled from the cruelty of William the Conqueror, retired into Scotland, and this had a considerable effect in civilising the southern parts of that country; for if the Saxons were inferior to the Normans in arts and in learning, they were, on the other hand, much superior to the Scots who were a rude and very ignorant people.

These exiles were headed and accompanied by what remained of the Saxon royal family, and particularly by a young prince named Edgar Etheling, who was a near kinsman of Edward the Confessor, and the heir of his throne, but dispossessed by the Norman Conqueror.

This prince brought with him to Scotland two sisters, named Margaret and Christian. They were received with much kindness by Malcolm III., called Canmore (or Great Head), who remembered the assistance which he had received from Edward the Confessor, and felt himself obliged to behave generously towards his family in their misfortunes. He himself married the Princess Margaret [1068], and made her the Queen of Scotland. She was an excellent woman, and of such a gentle, amiable disposition, that she often prevailed upon her husband,

who was a fierce, passionate man, to lay aside his resentment, and forgive those who had offended him.

When Malcolm, King of Scotland, was thus connected with the
Saxon royal family of England, he began to think of chasing away the
Normans, and of restoring Edgar Etheling to the English throne. This
was an enterprise for which he had not sufficient strength; but he made
deep and bloody inroads into the northern parts of England, and
brought away so many captives, that they were to be found for many
years afterwards in every Scottish village, nay, in every Scottish hovel.
No doubt, the number of the Saxons thus introduced into Scotland
tended much to improve and civilise the manners of the people; for, as
I have already said, the Scots were inferior to the Saxons in all branches
of useful knowledge.

Not only the Saxons, but afterwards a number of the Normans
themselves, came to settle in Scotland. King William could not satisfy
the whole of them, and some, who were discontented, and thought
they could mend their fortunes, repaired to the Scottish court, and
were welcomed by King Malcolm.[1] He was desirous to retain these
brave men in his service, and for that purpose he gave them great
grants of land, to be held for military services; and most of the Scottish
nobility are of Norman descent. And thus the Feudal System was introduced into Scotland as well as England, and went on gradually gaining
strength, till it became the general law of the country, as indeed it was
that of Europe at large.

Malcolm Canmore, thus increasing in power, and obtaining rein-
forcements of warlike and civilised subjects, began greatly to enlarge
his dominions. At first he had resided almost entirely in the province of
Fife, and at the town of Dunfermline, where there are still the ruins of a
small tower which served him for a palace. But as he found his power
increase, he ventured across the Firth of Forth, and took possession of

---

[1] "During this reign a great change was introduced into the manners of Scotland. Malcolm had passed his youth at the English court; he married an Anglo-Saxon princess;
he afforded an asylum in his dominions to many English and Norman malecontents.
The king appeared in public with a state and retinue unknown in more rude and
simple times, and affected to give frequent and sumptuous entertainments to his
nobles. The natives of Scotland, tenacious of their ancient customs, viewed with dis-
gust the introduction of foreign manners, and secretly censured the favour shown to
the English and Norman adventurers, as proceeding from injurious partiality."—
Hailes's *Annals of Scotland*.

Edinburgh and the surrounding country, which had hitherto been accounted part of England. The great strength of the castle of Edinburgh, situated upon a lofty rock, led him to choose that town frequently for his residence, so that in time it became the metropolis, or chief city of Scotland.

This King Malcolm was a brave and wise prince, though without education.[1] He often made war upon King William the Conqueror of England, and upon his son and successor William, who, from his complexion, was called William Rufus, that is, Red William. Malcolm was sometimes beaten in these wars, but he was more frequently successful; and not only made a complete conquest of Lothian, but threatened also to possess himself of the great English province of Northumberland, which he frequently invaded. In Cumberland, also, he held many possessions. But in the year 1093, having assembled a large army for the purpose, Malcolm besieged the Border fortress of Alnwick, where he was unexpectedly attacked by a great Norman baron, called Robert de Moubray, who defeated the Scottish army completely. Malcolm Canmore was killed in the action, and his eldest son fell by his side.

There is a silly story told of Malcolm being killed by one of the garrison of Alnwick, who, pretending to surrender the keys of the castle on the point of a spear, thrust the lance-point into the eye of the King of Scotland, and so killed him. They pretend that this soldier took the name of Pierce-eye, and that the great family of the Percies of Northumberland were descended from him. But this is all a fable. The Percies are descended from a great Norman baron, who came over with William, and who took his name from his castle and estate in Normandy.

Queen Margaret of Scotland was extremely ill at the time her husband marched against England. When she was lying on her death-bed,

---

[1] "In the introduction of the Saxon language into his kingdom," it has been said, "Malcolm himself was a considerable agent. As frequently happens, he caught the flame of religion from the pure torch of conjugal affection. His love of his consort led him to engage in the devotional services which afterwards procured for her the title of a saint. Totally illiterate, the King was unable to peruse his wife's missals and prayer-books; but he had them gorgeously bound, and frequently, by kissing them, expressed his veneration for what he could not understand. When the Queen undertook to correct some alleged abuses of the church, Malcolm stood interpreter betwixt the fair and royal reformer and such of the Scottish clergy as did not understand English, which Malcolm loved because it was the native tongue of Margaret. Such pictures occurring in history delight by their beauty and simplicity."—*Miscellaneous Prose Works.*

she saw her second son, who had escaped from the fatal battle, approach her bed. "How fares it," said the expiring Queen, "with your father, and with your brother Edward?—The young man stood silent.— "I conjure you," she added, "by the Holy Cross, and by the duty you owe me, to tell me the truth."

"Your husband and your son are both slain."

"The will of God be done!" answered the Queen, and expired, with expressions of devout resignation to the pleasure of Heaven. This good princess was esteemed a saint by those of the period in which she lived, and was called Saint Margaret.

After the death of Malcolm Canmore, the Scottish crown was occupied successively by three princes of little power or talent, who seized on the supreme authority because the children of the deceased sovereign were under age. After these had ended their short reigns, the sons of Malcolm came to the throne in succession, by name Edgar; Alexander, called the First; and David, also called the First of that name. These two last princes were men of great ability. David, in particular, was a wise, religious, and powerful prince. He had many furious wars with England, and made dreadful incursions into the neighbouring provinces, which were the more easy that the country of England was then disunited by civil war. The cause was this:—

Henry I., the youngest son of William the Conqueror, had died, leaving only one child, a daughter, named Matilda, or Maud, whose mother was a daughter of Malcolm Canmore, and a sister, consequently, of David, King of Scotland. During Henry's life, all the English barons had agreed that his daughter should succeed him in the throne. Upon the King's death [1135], however, Stephen, Earl of Montague, a great Norman lord, usurped the government, to the exclusion of the Empress Matilda (so called because she had married the Emperor of Germany), and caused himself to be proclaimed king. Many of the English barons took arms against Stephen, with the purpose of doing justice to the Empress Maud, and her son Henry. It was natural that David, King of Scotland, should join the party which favoured his niece. But he also took the opportunity to attempt an extension of his own dominions.

He assembled from the different provinces of Scotland a large but ill-disciplined army, consisting of troops of different nations and languages, who had only one common principle—the love of plunder. There were Normans, and Germans, and English; there were the Danes of Northumberland, and the British of Cumberland, and of the valley of Clyde; there were the men of Teviotdale, who were chiefly Britons, and those of Lothian, who were Saxons; and there were also the people of Galloway. These last were almost a separate and independent people, of peculiarly wild and ferocious habits. Some historians say they came of the race of the ancient Picts; some call them the wild Scots of Galloway; all agree that they were a fierce, ungovernable race of men, who fought half naked, and committed great cruelty upon the inhabitants of the invaded country. These men of Galloway were commanded by several chiefs. Amongst others, was a chief leader called William MacDonochy, that is, William the son of Duncan.

The barons of the northern parts of England, hearing that the King of Scotland was advancing at the head of this formidable army, resolved to assemble their forces to give him battle. Thurstan, the Archbishop of York, joined with them. They hoisted a banner, which they called that of Saint Peter, upon a carriage mounted on wheels;[1] from which circumstance the war took the name of the Battle of the Standard. The two armies came in sight of each other at Cuton Moor, near Northallerton, and prepared to fight on the next morning. It was a contest of great importance; for if David should prove able to defeat the army now opposed to him, there seemed little to prevent him from conquering England as far as the Humber.

There was in the English army an aged baron named Robert Bruce, father of a race afterwards very famous in Scottish history. He had great estates both in England and Scotland. He loved King David, because he had been formerly his companion in arms, and he resolved to make an effort to preserve peace.

He went, therefore, to the Scottish camp, and endeavoured to persuade King David to retreat, and to make peace—remonstrated with him on the excesses which his army had committed—exaggerated the danger in which he was placed; and finally burst into tears when he declared his own purpose of relinquishing his allegiance to the King of Scotland, and fighting against him in battle, if he persevered in his invasion. The King shed tears at this exhortation; but William Mac-Donochy exclaimed, "Bruce, thou art a false traitor!" Bruce, incensed at

---

[1] "It was the mast of a ship, fitted into the perch of a high four-wheeled carriage; from it were displayed the banners of St. Peter of York, of St. John of Beverly, and of St. Wilfred of Rippon. On the top of this mast there was a little casket, containing a consecrated host."—*Hailes.*

this insult, left the camp of the Scots, renouncing for ever all obedience to David, and giving up the lands he held of him in Scotland.

A dispute arose in the Scottish council of war. The Galloway men, who had gained a considerable battle in their advance into England, were intoxicated with their own success, and demanded peremptorily that they should lead the van in the battle of the next day. King David would fain have eluded the request. He had more confidence in the disciplined valour of the men-at-arms in his service, than in those brave, but tumultuous barbarians. A chief, called Malise, Earl of Strathearn, saw and was angry at David's hesitation. "Why so much confidence in a plate of steel, or in rings of iron?" said he. "I who wear no armour, will go as far to-morrow with a bare breast, as any one who wears a cuirass."

"Rude earl, "said Allan de Percy, a Norman knight, "you brag of what you dare not do."

The King interposed, and with difficulty appeased the dispute. He granted with reluctance the request of the men of Galloway.

In the morning, David prepared for the eventful contest. He drew his army up in three lines. The first, according to his promise, consisted of the Galloway men, who were commanded by William Mac-Donochy, and Ulrick, and Dovenald. The second line consisted of the men-at-arms, the Borderers of Teviotdale, with the archers of Cumberland and Strathclyde. They were headed by Henry, Prince of Scotland, a brave and amiable youth. The King himself, surrounded by a guard consisting of English and Norman men-at-arms, commanded the third body of troops, who were the men of Lothian, with the Northern Scots, properly so called.

The English were formed into one compact and firm battalion, in the midst of which the consecrated Standard was displayed. The bishop of Orkney, as deputed by the aged Thurstan, mounted the carriage of St. Peter's Standard, and proclaiming the war was a holy one, assured each English soldier that those who fell should immediately pass into Paradise. The English barons grasped each other's hands, and swore to be victorious, or die in the field.[1]

---

[1] "The aged and venerable Walter L'Espec (also) ascended the carriage in which the holy standard was fixed, and harangued the surrounding multitude. He reminded them of the glory of their ancestors, and described the barbarities of the Scottish invaders. 'Your cause is just; it is for your all that you combat; I swear, said he, grasping the hand of the Earl of Albemarle, "I swear," that on this day I will overcome the Scots, or perish.' 'So swear we all,' cried the barons assembled around him."—*Hailes*.

The armies being now near each other, the men of Galloway charged, with cries which resembled the roar of a tempest. They fought for two hours with the greatest fury, and made such slaughter amongst the English spearmen that they began to give way. But the archers supported them, and showered their arrows so thick upon the Galloway men, that, having no defensive armour to resist the shot, they became dismayed, and began to retreat. Prince Henry of Scotland advanced to their support with the men-at-arms. He rushed at full gallop on that part of the English line which was opposed to him, and broke through it, says a historian, as if it had been a spider's web. He then attacked the rear of the English; the men of Galloway rallied, and were about to renew the contest, when an English soldier showed the head of a slain man on a spear, and called out it was the King of Scots. The falsehood was believed by the Scottish army who fell into confusion and fled. The King in vain threw his helmet from his head, and rode barefaced among the soldiers, to show that he still lived. The alarm and panic were general, and the Scots lost a battle which, if they had won, must have given them a great part of England, and eventually, it may be, the whole of that kingdom, distracted as it was with civil war. Such was the famous battle of the Standard.[1] It forced David to make peace with England, but it was upon the most favourable terms; since, excepting the fortresses of Newcastle and Bamborough, the whole of Northumberland and Durham was surrendered by Stephen to the Scottish monarch.

David died in the year 1153. His brave and amiable son, Henry, had died two or three years before his father. David was a most excellent sovereign. He would leave his sport of hunting, or anything in which he was engaged at the time, if the meanest of his subjects came to complain of any wrong which he had received; nor would he resume his amusement till he had seen the poor man redressed. He is also much praised by historians, who, in those times, were chiefly clergymen, for his great bounty to the church. He founded bishoprics, and

---

[1] "The Galwegians cast away their arms; the troops of Lothian, the Islanders, and all who composed the third body, fled without show of resistance. The King leapt from his horse, and brought up the reserve to support the infantry of the second body; but the Scots, abandoned by so many of their companions, were now dispirited and feeble. The nobles who attended on the person of the King, saw that the day was irrecoverably lost; they urged and even compelled him to retreat. The fugitives, perceiving the royal ensign displayed, rallied around it, opposed a formidable body to the conquerors, and checked their pursuit. This memorable battle was fought on the 22d August 1138."—*Hailes.*

built and endowed many monasteries, which he vested with large grants of lands out of the patrimony of the kings. Amongst these were the Abbeys of Holyrood, near Edinburgh; of Melrose, in Roxburghshire; of Dryburgh, in Berwickshire; of Newbattle, in Lothian; of Cambuskenneth, in Stirlingshire; also those of Kelso and Jedburgh, and many ecclesiastical houses of less note.

It was, perhaps, as much from his munificence to the church, as from his private virtues and public deeds, that this monarch was received into the catalogue of holy persons, and called Saint David.[1] One of his successors, James I., who esteemed his liberality to the church rather excessive, said, "St. David had proved a sore saint for the crown." But we ought to recollect that the church lands were frequently spared, out of veneration to religion, when, in those restless times, all the rest of the country was burned and plundered. David, therefore, by putting these large estates under the protection of the church, may be considered as having done his best to secure them against devastation; and we may observe that most of his monasteries were founded in provinces peculiarly exposed to the dangers of war. The monks, it must be also remembered, were the only persons possessed of the most ordinary branches of knowledge. They were able to read and write; they understood French and Latin; they were excellent architects, as their magnificent buildings still testify; they possessed the art of gardening,

---

[1] "Aldred," says Lord Hailes, "has recorded many curious, although minute particulars, of the manners and private life of David. At the condemnation of the worst of criminals his strong emotions of sympathy were visible to the spectators; yet, resisting the seduction of his tender nature, he constantly maintained the just severity of a magistrate. His apartments were always open to suitors; for he had nothing secret but his counsels. On certain days he sat at the gate of his palace, to hear and to decide the causes of the poor. This he did, probably, with the view of restraining the enormities of inferior judges, so prevalent in loose times. To suppose that *he regarded the poor in judgment,* would be to impute ostentatious injustice to a wise and good man. While deciding against the poor, he attempted to make them understand and acknowledge the equity of his decisions: an attempt equally benevolent and vain! At sunset he dismissed all his attendants, and retired to meditate on his duty to God and the people. At daybreak he resumed his labours. He used hunting as an exercise; yet so as never to encroach on the hours of business. 'I have seen him,' says Aldred, 'quit his horse and dismiss his hunting equipage, when any, even of the meanest of his subjects, implored an audience.' He sometimes employed his leisure hours in the culture of his garden, and in the philosophic amusement of budding and ingrafting trees." Buchanan, whose principles are esteemed unfavourable to monarchy, says, "A more perfect exemplar of *a good king* is to be found in the reign of David I. than in all the theories of the learned and ingenious."

and of forming plantations; and it appears that the children of the gentry were often educated in these monasteries. It was, therefore, no wonder that David should have desired to encourage communities so nearly connected with arts and learning, although be certainly carried to excess the patronage which he was disposed to afford them.

It was during the reigns of Malcolm Canmore and his successors, that a dispute arose, grounded upon the feudal law, which occasioned a most dreadful quarrel between England and Scotland; and though Master Littlejohn be no great lawyer, it is necessary he should try all he can to understand it, for it is a very material point in history.

While the English were fighting among themselves, and afterwards with the Normans, the Scottish Kings, as I have repeatedly told you, had been enlarging their dominions at the expense of their neighbours, and had possessed themselves, in a great measure, of the northern provinces of England, called Lothian, Northumberland, Cumberland, and Westmoreland. After much fighting and disputing, it was agreed that the King of Scotland should keep these English provinces, or such parts of them as he possessed, not as an independent sovereign, however, but as a vassal of the King of England; and that he should do homage for the same to the English King, and attend him to the field of battle when summoned. But this homage, and this military service, were not paid on account of the kingdom of Scotland, which had never since the beginning of the world been under the dominion of an English King, but was, and had always remained independent, a free state, having sovereigns and monarchs of its own. It may seem strange to Master Littlejohn, how a King of Scotland should be vassal for that part of his dominions which lay in England, and an independent prince when he was considered as King of Scotland; but this might easily happen, according to the regulations of the Feudal System. William the Conqueror himself stood in the same situation; for he held his great dukedom of Normandy, and his other possessions, in France, as a vassal of the King of France, by whom it had been granted as a fief to his ancestor Rollo; but he was, at the same time, the independent Sovereign of England, of which he had gained possession by his victory at Hastings.

The English Kings, however, occasionally took opportunities to insinuate that the homage paid by the Scottish Kings was not only for the provinces which they at this time possessed in England, but also for the kingdom of Scotland. The Scottish Kings, on the contrary, although they rendered the homage and services demanded, as holding large possessions within the boundaries of England, uniformly and positively refused to permit it to be said or supposed, that they were subject to any claim of homage on account of the kingdom of Scotland. This was one cause of the frequent wars which took place betwixt the countries, in which the Scots maintained their national independence, and though frequently defeated, were often victorious, and threatened, upon more than one occasion, to make extensive acquisitions of territory at the expense of their neighbours.

At the death of David the First of Scotland, that monarch was in full possession of Lothian, which began to be considered as a part of Scotland, and which still continues to be so; as also of Northumberland and of Cumberland, with great part of Westmoreland, of which his sovereignty was less secure.

David was succeeded by his grandson, named Malcolm [1153, in his twelfth year], the eldest son of the brave and generous Prince Henry. Malcolm did homage to the King of England for the possessions which he had in England. He was so kind and gentle in his disposition that he was usually called Malcolm the Maiden. Malcolm attached himself particularly to Henry II., King of England, who was indeed a very wise and able prince. The Scottish King at one time went the length of resigning to Henry the possessions he held in the north of England; nay, he followed that prince into France, and acted as a volunteer in his army. This partiality to the English King disgusted the Scottish nation, who were afraid of the influence which Henry possessed over the mind of their youthful sovereign. They sent a message to France to upbraid Malcolm with his folly and to declare they would not have Henry of England to rule over them. Malcolm returned to Scotland with all speed, and reconciled himself to his subjects. He died at Jedburgh in the year 1165.

Malcolm the Maiden was succeeded by his brother William [crowned 24th December 1165,] a son of Prince Henry, and grandson of the good King David. In his time, warriors and men of consequence began to assume what are called armorial bearings, which you may very often see cut upon seals, engraved on silver plate, and painted upon gentlemen's carriages. Now, Master Littlejohn, it is as well, to know the meaning of this ancient custom.

In the time of which I am speaking, the warriors went into battle clad in complete armour, which covered them from top to toe. On their head they wore iron caps, called helmets, with visors, which came down and protected the face, so that nothing could be seen of the countenance except the eyes peeping through bars of iron. You have seen such helmets in grandpapa's entrance-hall. But as it was necessary that a king, lord, or knight, should be known to his followers in battle, they adopted two ways of distinguishing themselves. The one was by a crest, that is, a figure of some kind or other, as a lion, a wolf, a hand holding a sword, or some such decoration, which they wore on the top of the helmet, as we talk of a cock's comb being the crest of that bird. But besides this mark of distinction, these warriors were accustomed to paint emblematical figures, sometimes of a very whimsical kind, upon their shields. These emblems became general; and at length no one was permitted to bear any such armorial device, excepting he either had right to carry it by inheritance, or that such right had been conferred upon him by some sovereign prince. To assume the crest or armorial emblems of another man was a high offence, and often mortally resented; and to adopt armorial bearings for yourself, was punished as a misdemeanour by a peculiar court, composed of men called Heralds, who gave their name to the science called Heraldry. As men disused the wearing of armour, the original purpose of heraldry fell into neglect, but still persons of ancient descent remained tenacious of the armorial distinctions of their ancestors; and, as I told you before, they are now painted on carriages, or placed above the principal door of country-houses, or frequently engraved on seals. But there is much less attention paid to heraldry now than there was formerly, although the College of Heralds still exists.

Now, William King of Scotland having chosen for his armorial bearing a Red Lion, *rampant* (that is, standing on its hind legs, as if it were going to climb), he acquired the name of William the Lion. And this Rampant Lion still constitutes the arms of Scotland, and the President of the Heralds' Court in that country, who is always a person of high rank, is called Lord Lion King-at-Arms.

William, though a brave man, and though he had a lion for his emblem, was unfortunate in war. In the year 1174 he invaded England, for the purpose of demanding and compelling restoration of the portion of Northumberland which had been possessed by his ancestors. He himself, with a small body of men, lay in careless security near Alnwick, while his numerous, but barbarous and undisciplined army, were spread throughout the country, burning and destroying wherever they came. Some gallant Yorkshire barons marched to the aid of their neighbours of Northumberland. They assembled four hundred men-at-arms, and made a forced march of twenty-four miles from Newcastle towards Alnwick, without being discovered. On the morning a thick mist fell—they became uncertain of their road—and some proposed to turn back. "If you should all turn back," said one of their leaders, named Bernard de Baliol, "I would go forward alone." The others adopted the same resolution, and, concealed by the mist, they rode forward towards Alnwick. In their way they suddenly encountered the Scottish King, at the head of a small party of only sixty men. William so little expected a sudden attack of this nature that at first he thought the body of cavalry which he saw advancing was a part of his own army. When he was undeceived, he had too much of the lion about him to fear. "Now shall we see," he said, "which of us are good knights;" and instantly charged the Yorkshire barons, with the handful of men who attended him. But sixty men at arms could make no impression on four hundred, and as the rest of William's army were too distant to give him assistance, he was, after defending himself with the utmost gallantry, unhorsed and made prisoner. The English immediately retreated with their royal captive, after this bold and successful adventure. They carried William to Newcastle, and from that town to Northampton, where he was conducted to the presence of Henry II., King of England, with his legs tied under his horse's belly, as if he had been a common malefactor or felon.[1]

This was a great abuse of the advantage which fortune had given to Henry, and was in fact more disgraceful to himself than to his prisoner. But the English King's subsequent conduct was equally harsh and ungenerous. He would not release his unfortunate captive until he had agreed to do homage to the King of England, not only for his English possessions, but also for Scotland, and all his other dominions. The Scottish parliament were brought to acquiesce in this treaty, and thus, in order to recover the liberty of their King, they sacrificed the independence of their country, which remained for a time subject to the English claim of paramount sovereignty. This dishonourable treaty was made on the 8th of December 1174.

Thus the great national question of supremacy was for a time abandoned by the Scots; but this state of things did not last long. In 1189 Henry II. died, and was succeeded by his son, Richard the First, one of the most remarkable men in English history. He was so brave that he

---

[1] "William was at first confined to the castle of Richmond, but Henry, sensible of the value of this unexpected acquisition, secured him beyond seas at Falaise in Normandy."—*Hailes*.

was generally known by the name of Coeur de Lion, that is, the Lion-hearted; and he was as generous as he was brave. Nothing was so much at his heart as what was then called the Holy War, that is, a war undertaken to drive the Saracens out of Palestine. For this he resolved to go to Palestine with a large army: but it was first necessary that he should place his affairs at home in such condition as might ensure the quiet of his dominions during his absence upon the expedition. This point could not be accomplished without his making a solid peace with Scotland; and in order to obtain it, King Richard resolved to renounce the claim for homage, which had been extorted from William the Lion. By a charter, dated 5th December of the same year (1189), he restored to the King of Scots the castles of Berwick and Roxburgh, and granted an acquittance to him of all obligations which Henry II. had extorted from him in consequence of his captivity, reserving only Richard's title to such homage as was anciently rendered by Malcolm Canmore. For this renunciation William paid ten thousand merks; a sum which probably assisted in furnishing the expenses of Richard's expedition to Palestine.

Thus was Scotland again restored to the dignity of an independent nation, and her monarchs were declared liable only to the homage due for the lands which the King of Scotland held beyond the boundaries of his own kingdom, and within those of England. The period of Scottish subjection lasted only fifteen years.

This generous behaviour of Richard of England was attended with such good effects that it almost put an end to all wars and quarrels betwixt England and Scotland for more than a hundred years, during which time, with one or two brief interruptions, the nations lived in great harmony together. This was much to the happiness of both, and might in time have led to their becoming one people, for which Nature, which placed them both in the same island, seemed to have designed them. Intercourse for the purpose of traffic became more frequent. Some of the Scottish and English families formed marriages and friendships together, and several powerful lords and barons had lands both in England and Scotland. All seemed to promise peace and tranquillity betwixt the two kingdoms, until a course of melancholy accidents having nearly extinguished the Scottish royal family, tempted the English monarch again to set up his unjust pretensions to be sovereign of Scotland, and gave occasion to a series of wars, fiercer and more bloody than any which had ever before taken place betwixt the countries.

V

The Reigns of Alexander II. and Alexander III.

1214-1266

WILLIAM THE LION died at Stirling in December 1214, and was succeeded by his son, Alexander II., a youth in years, but remarkable for prudence and for firmness. In his days there was some war with England, as he espoused the cause of the disaffected barons, against King John. But no disastrous consequences having arisen, the peace betwixt the two kingdoms was so effectually restored that Henry III. of England, having occasion to visit his French dominions, committed the care of the northern frontiers of his kingdom to Alexander of Scotland, the prince who was most likely to have seized the opportunity of disturbing them. Alexander II. repaid with fidelity the great and honourable trust which his brother sovereign had reposed in him.

Relieved from the cares of an English war, Alexander endeavoured to civilise the savage manners of his own people. These were disorderly to a great degree.

For example, one Adam, Bishop of Caithness, proved extremely rigorous in enforcing the demand of tithes,—the tenth part, that is, of the produce of the ground, which the church claimed for support of the clergy. The people of Caithness assembled to consider what should be done in this dilemma, when one of them exclaimed, "Short rede, good rede, slay, we the bishop!" which means, "Few words are best, let us kill the bishop." They ran instantly to the bishop's house, assaulted it with fury, set it on fire, and burned the prelate alive in his own palace (A.D. 1222)

While this tragedy was going on, some of the bishop's servants applied for protection for their master to the Earl of Orkney and Caithness. This nobleman, who probably favoured the conspiracy, answered hypocritically, that the bishop had only to come to him, and he would assure him of protection; —as if it had been possible for the unhappy bishop to escape from his blazing palace, and through his raging enemies, and to make his way to the earl's residence.

The tidings of this cruel action were brought to Alexander II. when he was upon a journey towards England. He immediately turned back, marched into Caithness with an army, and put to death four hundred of those who had been concerned in the murder of the bishop. The hard-hearted earl was soon afterwards slain, and his castle burned, in revenge of that odious crime.

By the prompt administration of justice, Alexander both became obeyed and dreaded. He was a sovereign of considerable power, beloved both by English and Scots. He had a brave and not ill-disciplined army; but his cavalry, which amounted only to a thousand spears, were not very well mounted, and bore no proportion to one hundred thousand of infantry, strong, good, and resolute men.

ALEXANDER III., then only in his eighth year, succeeded to his father in 1249. Yet, when only two years older, he went to York to meet with the English King, and to marry his daughter, the Princess Margaret. On this occasion Henry endeavoured to revive the old claim of homage, which he insisted should be rendered to him by the boy-bridegroom for all his dominions. Alexander answered, with wisdom beyond his years, that he was come to marry the Princess of England, and not to treat of affairs of state; and that he could not, and would not, enter upon the subject proposed, without advice of his Parliament.

Upon another occasion, when visiting his father-in-law at London, Alexander made it a condition of his journey, that he should not be called upon to discuss any state affairs. In this, and on other occasions, Alexander showed great willingness to be on good terms with England, qualified by a sincere resolution that he would not sacrifice any part of the rights and independence of his dominions.

In the days of Alexander III. Scotland was threatened with a great danger, from the invasion of the Danes and the Norwegians. I have told you before, that these northern people were at this time wont to scour the seas with their vessels, and to make descents and conquests where it suited them to settle. England had been at one time conquered by them, and France had been compelled to yield up to them the fine provinces which, after their name, were called Normandy. The Scots, whose country was at once poor and mountainous, had hitherto held these rovers at defiance. But in the year 1263 Haco, King of Norway, at the head of a powerful fleet and army, came to invade and conquer the kingdom of Scotland. Alexander, on his part, lost no time in assembling a great army, and preparing for the defence of the country, in which he was zealously seconded by most of his nobles. They were not all, however, equally faithful, some of them had encouraged the attempt of the invaders.

On the 1st October 1263 Haco, having arrived on the western coast, commenced hostilities by making himself master of the Islands of Bute and Arran, lying in the mouth of the Firth of Clyde, and then appeared with his great navy off the village of Largs, in Cunninghame. The Scots were in arms to defend the shore, but Haco disembarked a great part of his troops, and obtained some advantages over them. On the next day, more Scottish troops having come up, the battle was renewed with great fury. Alexander, fighting in person at the head of his troops, was wounded in the face by an arrow. Alexander the Steward, a high officer in the Scottish court, was killed. But the Danes lost the nephew of their king, one of the most renowned champions in their host. While the battle was still raging on shore, a furious tempest arose, which drove the ships of the Danes and Norwegians from their anchorage; many were shipwrecked on the coast, and the crews were destroyed by the Scots, when they attempted to get upon land. The soldiers, who had been disembarked, lost courage, and retired before the Scots, who were hourly reinforced by their countrymen coming from all quarters. It was with the utmost difficulty that Haco got the remnant of his scattered forces on board of such vessels as remained. He retired to the Orkney Islands, and there died, full of shame and sorrow for the loss of his army, and the inglorious conclusion of his formidable invasion.

The consequence of this victory was, that the King of the Island of Man, who had been tributary to Haco, now submitted himself to the

King of Scotland; and negotiations took place betwixt Alexander III. and Magnus, who had succeeded Haco in the throne of Norway, by which the latter resigned to the King of Scotland (1266) all right to the islands on the western side of Scotland, called the Hebrides.

The traces of the battle of Largs, a victory of so much consequence to Scotland, are still to be found on the shores where the action was fought. There are visible great rocks and heaps of stones, beneath which lie interred the remains of the slain. Human bones are found in great quantities, and also warlike weapons, particularly axes, and swords, which being made of brass, remain longer unconsumed than if they had been of iron or steel like those now used.

Thus you see, Master Littlejohn, that down to the period of which we speak, Scotland had been a powerful and victorious nation, maintaining a more equal rank with England than could have been expected from the different size and strength of the two kingdoms, and repelling by force of arms those northern people who had so long been the terror of Europe.

VI

The Interregnum and Longshanks

1266-1296

SEVEN kings of Scotland, omitting one or two temporary occupants of the throne, had reigned in succession after Malcolm Canmore, the son of Duncan, who recovered the kingdom from Macbeth. Their reigns occupied a period of nearly two hundred years. Some of them were very able men; all of them were well-disposed, good sovereigns, and inclined to discharge their duty towards their subjects. They made good laws; and, considering the barbarous and ignorant times they lived in, they appear to have been men as deserving of praise as any race of kings who reigned in Europe during that period. Alexander, the third of that name, and the last of these seven princes, was an excellent sovereign. He married, as I told you in the last chapter, Margaret, daughter of Henry III. of England; but unhappily all the children who were born of that marriage died before their father. After the death of Queen Margaret, Alexander married another wife; but he did not live to have any family by her. As he was riding in the dusk of the evening, along the sea-coast of Fife, betwixt Burnt-island and Kinghorn, he approached too near the brink of the precipice, and his horse starting or stumbling, he was thrown over the rock, and killed on the spot. It is now no less than five hundred and forty-two years since Alexander's death, yet the people of the country still point out the very spot where it happened, and which is called the King's Crag. The very melancholy consequences which followed Alexander's decease made the manner of it long remembered. A sort of elegy is also preserved, in which his virtues, and the misfortunes that followed his death, are recorded. It is the oldest specimen of the Scottish language which is known to remain in existence; but as you would not understand it, I am obliged to alter it a little:—

> When Alexander our king was dead,
>> Who Scotland led in love and le,
> Away was wealth of ale and bread,
>> Of wine and wax, of game and glee.
> Then pray to God, since only he
> Can succour Scotland in her need,
>> That placed is in perplexity!

Another legend says, that a wise man, who is called Thomas the Rhymer, and about whom many stories are told, had said to a great Scottish nobleman, called the Earl of March, that the sixteenth day of March should be the stormiest day that ever was witnessed in Scotland. The day came, and was remarkably clear, mild, and temperate. But while they were all laughing at Thomas the Rhymer on account of his false prophecy, an express brought the news of the King's death. "There," said Thomas, "that is the storm which I meant; and there was never tempest which will bring more ill luck to Scotland." This story may very possibly be false; but the general belief in it serves to show that the death of Alexander the Third was looked upon as an event of the most threatening and calamitous nature.

The full consequences of the evil were not visible at first; for, although all Alexander's children had, as we have already said, died before him, yet one of them, who had been married to Eric, King of Norway, had left a daughter named Margaret, upon whom, as the grand-daughter and nearest heir of the deceased prince, the crown of Scotland devolved. The young princess, called by our historians, the Maid of Norway, was residing at her father's court.

While the crown of Scotland thus passed to a young girl, the King of England began to consider by what means he could so avail himself of circumstances, as to unite it with his own. This king was Edward, called the First, because he was the first of the Norman line of princes so named. He was a very brave man, and a good soldier,—wise, skilful, and prudent, but unhappily very ambitious, and desirous of extending his royal authority, without caring much whether he did so by right means or by those which were unjust. And although it is a great sin to covet that which does not belong to you, and a still greater to endeavour to possess yourself of it by any unfair practices, yet his desire of adding the kingdom of Scotland to that of England was so great, that Edward was unable to resist it.

The mode by which the English King at first endeavoured to accomplish his object was a very just one. He proposed a marriage betwixt the Maiden of Norway, the young Queen of Scotland, and his own eldest son, called Edward, after himself. A treaty was entered into for this purpose; and had the marriage been effected, and been followed by children, the union of England and Scotland might have taken place more than three hundred years sooner than it did, and an immeasurable quantity of money and bloodshed would probably have been saved. But it was not the will of Heaven that this desirable union should be accomplished till many long years of war and distress had afflicted both these nations. The young Queen of Scotland sickened and died, and the treaty for the marriage was ended with her life.[1]

The kingdom of Scotland was troubled, and its inhabitants sunk into despair, at the death of their young princess. There was not any descendant of Alexander III. remaining, who could be considered as his direct and undeniable heir: and many of the great nobles, who were more or less distantly related to the royal family, prepared each of them to assert a right to the crown, began to assemble forces and form parties, and threatened the country with a civil war, which is the greatest of all misfortunes. The number of persons who set up claims to the crown was no fewer than twelve, all of them forming pretensions on some relationship, more or less distant, to the royal family. These claimants were most of them powerful, from their rank and the number of their followers; and, if they should dispute the question of right by the sword, it was evident that the whole country would be at war from one sea to the other.

To prevent this great dilemma, it is said the Scottish nobility resolved to submit the question respecting the succession of their kingdom to Edward I. of England, who was one of the wisest princes of his

---

[1] She landed in Orkney, on her way to take possession of her crown, and died there, Sept. 1290.

time, and to request of him to settle, as umpire, which of the persons claiming the throne of Scotland had best right to be preferred to the others. The people of Scotland are said to have sent ambassadors to Edward, to request his interference as judge; but he had already determined to regulate the succession of the kingdom, not as a mere umpire, having no authority but from the desire of the parties, but as himself a person principally concerned; and for this purpose he resolved to revive the old pretext of his having right to the feudal sovereignty of Scotland, which, as we have before seen, had been deliberately renounced by his generous predecessor, Richard I.

With this secret and unjust purpose, Edward of England summoned the nobility and clergy of Scotland to meet him at the castle of Norham, a large and strong fortress, which stands on the English side of the Tweed, on the line where that river divides England from Scotland. They met there on the 10th May 1291, and were presented to the King of England, who received them in great state, surrounded by the high officers of his court. He was a very handsome man, and so tall, that he was popularly known by the name of Longshanks, that is, long legs. The Justiciary of England then informed the nobility and clergy of Scotland, in King Edward's name, that before he could proceed to decide who should be the vassal King of Scotland, it was necessary that they should acknowledge the King of England's right as lord paramount, or sovereign of that kingdom.

The nobles and churchmen of Scotland were surprised to hear the King of England propose a claim which had never been admitted, except for a short time, in order to procure the freedom of King William the Lion, and which had been afterwards renounced for ever by Richard I. They refused to give any answer until they should consult together by themselves. "By St. Edward!" said the King, "whose crown I wear, I will make good my just rights, or perish in the attempt!" He then dismissed the assembly, allowing the Scots a delay of three weeks, however, to accede to his terms.

The Scottish nobility being thus made aware of King Edward's selfish and ambitious designs, ought to have assembled their forces together and declared that they would defend the rights and independence of their country. But they were much divided among themselves, and without any leader; and the competitors, who laid claim to the crown were mean-spirited enough to desire to make favour with King Edward, in expectation that he would raise to the throne him whom he should find most willing to subscribe to his own claims of paramount superiority.

Accordingly, the second assembly of the Scottish nobility and clergy took place without any one having dared to state any objection to what the King of England proposed, however unreasonable they knew his pretensions to be. They were assembled in a large open plain, called Upsettlington, opposite to the castle of Norham, but on the northern or Scottish side of the river. The Chancellor of England then demanded of such of the candidates as were present, whether they acknowledged the King of England as Lord Paramount of Scotland, and whether they were willing to receive and hold the crown of Scotland as awarded by Edward in that character. They all answered that they were willing to do so; and thus, rather than hazard their own claims by offending King Edward, these unworthy candidates consented to resign the independence of their country, which had been so long and so bravely defended.

Upon examining the claims of the candidates, the right of succession to the throne of Scotland was found to lie chiefly betwixt Robert Bruce, the Lord of Annandale, and John Baliol, who was the Lord of Galloway. Both were great and powerful barons; both were of Norman descent, and had great estates in England as well as Scotland; lastly, both were descended from the Scottish royal family, and each by a daughter of David, Earl of Huntingdon, brother of William the Lion. Edward, upon due consideration, declared Baliol to be King of Scotland, as being son of Margaret, the eldest of the two sisters. But he declared that the kingdom was always to be held under him as the lord paramount, or sovereign thereof. John Baliol closed the disgraceful scene by doing homage to the King of England, and acknowledging that he was his liege vassal and subject. This remarkable event took place on 20th November 1292.

Soon after this remarkable, and to Scotland most shameful transaction, King Edward began to show to Baliol that it was not his purpose to be satisfied with a bare acknowledgment of his right of sovereignty, but that he was determined to exercise it with severity on every possible occasion. He did this, no doubt, on purpose to provoke the dependent king to some act of resistance which should give him a pretext for depriving him of the kingdom altogether as a disobedient subject, and taking it under his own government in his usurped character of lord paramount. The King of England, therefore, encouraged the Scottish subjects to appeal from the courts of Baliol to his own; and as Baliol declined making appearance in the English tribunals, or answering there for the sentences which he had pronounced in his capacity of King of Scotland, Edward insisted upon having possession of three principal fortresses of Scotland—Berwick, Roxburgh, and Jedburgh.

Baliol surrendered, or at least agreed to surrender, these castles; but the people murmured against this base compliance, and Baliol himself, perceiving that it was Edward's intention gradually to destroy his power, was stung at once with shame and fear, and entering into a league with France, raised a great army, for the purpose of invading England, the dominions of the prince whom he had so lately acknowledged his lord paramount, or sovereign. At the same time he sent a letter to Edward, formally renouncing his dependence upon him.[1] Edward replied in Norman-French, "Ha!—dares this idiot commit such folly? Since he will not attend on us, as is his duty, we will go to him."

The King of England accordingly assembled a powerful army, amongst which came Bruce, who had formerly contended for the crown of Scotland with Baliol, and who now hoped to gain it upon his forfeiture. Edward defeated the Scottish army in a great battle near Dunbar, and Baliol, who appears to have been a mean-spirited man, gave up the contest. He came before Edward in the castle of Roxburgh, and there made a most humiliating submission. He appeared in a mean dress, without sword, royal robes, or arms of any kind, and bearing in his hand a white wand. He there confessed that through bad counsel and folly he had rebelled against his liege lord, and, in atonement, he resigned the kingdom of Scotland, with the inhabitants, and all right which he possessed to their obedience and duty, to their liege lord, King Edward. He was then permitted to retire uninjured.

Baliol being thus removed, Bruce expressed his hopes of being allowed to supply his place, as tributary or dependent King of Scotland. But Edward answered him sternly, "Have we nothing, think you, to do, but to conquer kingdoms for you?" By which words the English King plainly expressed that he intended to keep Scotland to himself;

---

[1] "The reasons assigned by Baliol were:—1. That Edward had wantonly, and upon slight suggestions, summoned Baliol to his courts. 2. Had seized his English estates. 3. Had seized his goods and the goods of his subjects. 4. Had forcibly carried off, and still detained, certain natives of Scotland." (April 1296).—*Hailes.*

and he proceeded to take such measures as made his purpose still more evident.

Edward marched through Scotland at the head of a powerful army, compelling all ranks of people to submit to him. He removed to London the records of the kingdom of Scotland, and was at the pains to transport to the Abbey Church at Westminster a great stone, upon which it had been the national custom to place the King of Scotland when he was crowned for the first time. He did this to show that he was absolute master of Scotland, and that the country was in future to have no other king but himself, and his descendants the Kings of England. The stone is still preserved, and to this day the King's throne is placed upon it at the time when he is crowned.[1] Last of all, King Edward placed the government of Scotland in the hands of John de Warenne, Earl of Surrey, a brave nobleman; of Hugh Cressingham, a clergyman, whom he named chief treasurer; and of William Ormesby, whom he appointed the chief judge of the kingdom. He placed English soldiers in all the castles and strongholds of Scotland, from the one end of the kingdom to the other; and not trusting the Scots themselves, he appointed English governors in most of the provinces of the kingdom.

We may here remark, my dear child, that a little before he thus subdued Scotland, this same Edward I. had made conquest of Wales, that mountainous part of the island of Britain into which the Britons

---

[1] "This fatal stone was said to have been brought from Ireland by Fergus, the son of Eric, who led the Dalriads to the shores of Argyleshire. Its virtues are preserved in the celebrated leonine verse—

'Ni fallat fatum, Scoti quocunque locatum
Invenient lapidem, regnare tenentur ibidem.

Which may be rendered thus:—

Unless the fates are faithless found,
And prophets' voice be vain.
Where'er this monument is found
The Scottish race shall reign.

There were Scots who hailed the accomplishment of this prophecy at the accession of James VI. to the crown of England, and exulted, that in removing this palladium, the policy of Edward resembled that which brought the Trojan horse in triumph within their walls, and which occasioned the destruction of their royal family. The stone is still preserved, and forms the support of King Edward the Confessor's chair, which the Sovereign occupies at his coronation, and, independent of the divination so long in being accomplished, is in itself a very curious remnant of extreme antiquity."—Sir Walter Scott, *Lardner's Cyclopaedia*.

had retreated from the Saxons, and where, until the reign of this artful and ambitious prince, they had been able to maintain their independence. In subduing Wales, Edward had acted as treacherously, and more cruelly, than he had done in Scotland; since he had hanged the last Prince of Wales, when he became his prisoner, for no other crime than because he defended his country against the English, who had no right to it. Perhaps Edward thought to himself that, by uniting the whole island of Britain under one king and one government, he would do so much good by preventing future wars, as might be an excuse for the force and fraud which he made use of to bring about his purpose. But, my dear child, God, who sees into our hearts, will not bless those measures which are wicked in themselves, because they are used under a pretence of bringing about that which is good. We must not do evil even that good may come of it; and the happy prospect that England and Scotland would be united under one government, was so far from being brought nearer by Edward's unprincipled usurpation, that the hatred and violence of national antipathy which arose betwixt the sister countries, removed to a distance almost incalculable, the prospect of their becoming one people, for which nature seemed to design them.

VII

William Wallace

1296-1305

I TOLD you, my dear Hugh, that Edward I. of England had reduced Scotland almost entirely to the condition of a conquered country, although he had obtained possession of the kingdom, less by his bravery, than by cunningly taking advantage of the disputes and divisions that followed amongst the Scots themselves after the death of Alexander III.

The English, however, had in point of fact obtained possession of the country, and governed it with much rigour. The Lord High Justice Ormesby called all men to account, who would not take the oath of allegiance to King Edward. Many of the Scots refused this, as what the English King had no right to demand from them. Such persons were called into the courts of justice, fined, deprived of their estates, and otherwise severely punished. Then Hugh Cressingham, the English treasurer, tormented the Scottish nation by collecting money from them under various pretexts. The Scots were always a poor people, and their native kings had treated them with much kindness, and seldom required them to pay any taxes. They were, therefore, extremely enraged at finding themselves obliged to pay to the English treasurer much larger sums of money than their own good kings had ever demanded from them; and they became exceedingly dissatisfied.

Besides these modes of oppression, the English soldiers, who, I told you, had been placed in garrison in the different castles of Scotland, thought themselves masters of the country, treated the Scots with great contempt, took from them by main force whatever they had a fancy to, and if the owners offered to resist, abused them, beat and wounded, and sometimes killed them; for which acts of violence the English officers did not check or punish their soldiers. Scotland was, therefore, in great distress, and the inhabitants, exceedingly enraged, only wanted some leader to command them, to rise up in a body against the English or *Southern* men, as they called them, and recover the liberty and independence of their country, which had been destroyed by Edward the First.

Such a leader arose in the person of William Wallace, whose name is still so often mentioned in Scotland. It is a great pity we do not know exactly the history of this brave man; for at the time when he lived, every one was so busy fighting, that there was no person to write down the history of what took place; and afterwards, when there was more leisure for composition, the truths that were collected were greatly mingled with falsehood. What I shall tell you of him is generally believed to be true.

William Wallace was none of the high nobles of Scotland, but the son of a private gentleman, called Wallace of Ellerslie, in Renfrewshire, near Paisley. He was very tall and handsome, and one of the strongest and bravest men that ever lived. He had a very fine countenance, with a quantity of fair hair, and was particularly dexterous in the use of all weapons which were then employed in battle. Wallace, like all Scotsmen of high spirit, had looked with great indignation upon the usurpation of the crown by Edward, and upon the insolences which the English soldiers committed on his countrymen. It is said, that when he was very young, he went a-fishing for sport in the river of Irvine, near Ayr. He had caught a good many trouts, which were carried by a boy, who attended him with a fishing-basket, as is usual with anglers. Two or three English soldiers who belonged to the garrison of Ayr came up to Wallace, and insisted, with their usual insolence, on taking the fish from the boy. Wallace was contented to allow them a part of the trouts, but he refused to part with the whole basketful. The soldiers insisted, and from words came to blows. Wallace had no better weapon than the butt-end of his fishingrod; but he struck the foremost of the Englishmen so hard under the ear with it, that he killed him on the spot; and getting possession of the slain man's sword, he fought with so much fury that he put the others to flight, and brought home his fish safe and sound. The English governor of Ayr sought for him, to punish him with death for this action; but Wallace lay concealed among the hills and great woods till the matter was forgotten, and then appeared in another part of the country. He is said to have had other adventures of the same kind, in which he gallantly defended himself, sometimes when alone, sometimes with very few companions, against superior numbers of the English, until at last his name became generally known as a terror to them.

But the action which occasioned his finally rising in arms is believed to have happened in the town of Lanark. Wallace was at this time married to a lady of that place, and residing there with his wife. It chanced, as he walked in the market place, dressed in a green garment, with a rich dagger by his side, that an Englishman came up and insulted him on account of his finery, saying, a Scotsman had no business to wear so gay a dress, or carry so handsome a weapon. It soon came to a quarrel, as on many former occasions; and Wallace, having killed the Englishman, fled to his own house, which was speedily assaulted by all the English soldiers. While they were endeavouring to force their way in at the front of the house Wallace escaped by a backdoor, and got in safety to a rugged and rocky glen, near Lanark, called the Cartland crags, all covered with bushes and trees, and full of high precipices, where he knew he should be safe from the pursuit of the English soldiers.[1] In the meantime the governor of Lanark, whose name was Hazelrigg, burned Wallace's house, and put his wife and servants to death; and by committing this cruelty increased to the highest pitch, as you may well believe, the hatred which the champion had always borne against the English usurper. Hazelrigg also proclaimed Wallace an outlaw, and offered a reward to anyone who should bring him to an English garrison, alive or dead.

On the other hand, Wallace soon collected a body of men, outlawed like himself, or willing to become so, rather than any longer endure the oppression of the English. One of his earliest expeditions was directed against Hazelrigg, whom be killed, and thus avenged the death of his wife. He fought skirmishes with the soldiers who were sent against him, and often defeated them; and in time became so well

---

[1] In the western face of the chasm of Cartland crags, a few yards above the new bridge, a cave in the rock is pointed out by tradition as having been the hiding-place of Wallace.

known and so formidable that multitudes began to resort to his standard, until at length he was at the head of a considerable army, with
which he proposed to restore his country to independence.

About this time is said to have taken place a memorable event,
which the Scottish people called the Barns of Ayr. It is alleged that the
English governor of Ayr had invited the greater part of the Scottish
nobility and gentry in the western parts to meet him at some large
buildings called the Barns of Ayr, for the purpose of friendly conference
upon the affairs of the nation. But the English earl entertained the
treacherous purpose of putting the Scottish gentlemen to death. The
English soldiers had halters with running nooses ready prepared, and
hung upon the beams which supported the roof; and, as the Scottish
gentlemen were admitted by two and two at a time, the nooses were
thrown over their heads, and they were pulled up by the neck, and
thus hanged or strangled to death. Among those who were slain in this
base and treacherous manner was, it is said, Sir Reginald Crawford,
Sheriff of the county of Ayr, and uncle to William Wallace.

When Wallace heard of what had befallen he was dreadfully
enraged, and collecting his men in a wood near the town of Ayr, he
resolved to be revenged on the authors of this great crime. The English
in the meanwhile made much feasting, and when they had eaten and
drunk plentifully, they lay down to sleep in the same large barns in
which they had murdered the Scottish gentlemen. But Wallace, learning that they kept no guard or watch, not suspecting there were any
enemies so near them, directed a woman who knew the place to mark
with chalk the doors of the lodgings where the Englishmen lay. Then
he sent a party of men, who, with strong ropes, made all the doors so
fast on the outside that those within could not open them. On the outside the Scots had prepared heaps of straw, to which they set fire, and
the barns of Ayr, being themselves made of wood, were soon burning
in a bright flame. Then the English were awakened, and endeavoured
to get out to save their lives. But the doors, as I told you, were secured
on the outside, and bound fast with ropes; and, besides, the blazing
houses were surrounded by the Scots, who forced those who got out to
run back into the fire, or else put them to death on the spot; and thus
great numbers perished miserably. Many of the English were lodged in
a convent, but they had no better fortune than the others; for the prior
of the convent caused all the friars to arm themselves, and, attacking,
the English guests, they put most of them to the sword. This was called

the "Friar of Ayr's blessing." We cannot tell if this story of the *Barns of Ayr* be exactly true; but it is probable there is some foundation for it, as it is universally believed in that country.

Thus Wallace's party grew daily stronger and stronger, and many of the Scottish nobles joined with him. Among these were Sir William Douglas, the Lord of Douglas-dale, and the head of a great family often mentioned in Scottish history. There was also Sir John the Grahame, who became Wallace's bosom friend and greatest confident. Many of these great noblemen, however, deserted the cause of the country on the approach of John de Warenne, Earl of Surrey, the English governor, at the head of a numerous and well-appointed army. They thought that Wallace would be unable to withstand the attack of so many disciplined soldiers, and hastened to submit themselves to the English, for fear of losing their estates. Wallace, however, remained undismayed, and at the head of a considerable army. He had taken up his camp upon the northern side of the river Forth, near the town of Stirling. The river was there crossed by a long wooden bridge, about a mile above the spot where the present bridge is situated.

The English general approached the banks of the river on the southern side. He sent two clergymen to offer a pardon to Wallace and his followers, on condition that they should lay down their arms. But such was not the purpose of the high-minded champion of Scotland.

"Go back to Warenne," said Wallace, "and tell him we value not the pardon of the King of England. We are not here for the purpose of treating of peace, but of abiding battle, and restoring freedom to our country. Let the English come on;—we defy them to their very beards!"

The English, upon hearing this haughty answer, called loudly to be led to the attack. Their leader, Sir Richard Lundin, a Scottish knight, who had gone over to the enemy at Irvine, hesitated, for he was a skilful soldier, and he saw that, to approach the Scottish army, his troops must pass over the long, narrow wooden bridge; so that those who should get over first might be attacked by Wallace with all his forces, before those who remained behind could possibly come to their assistance. He therefore inclined to delay the battle. But Cressingham the treasurer, who was ignorant and presumptuous, insisted that it was their duty to fight, and put an end to the war at once; and Lundin gave way to his opinion, although Cressingham, being a churchman, could not be so good a judge of what was fitting as he himself, an experienced officer.

The English army began to cross the bridge, Cressingham leading the van, or foremost division of the army; for, in those military days, even clergymen wore armour and fought in battle. That took place which Lundin had foreseen. Wallace suffered a considerable part of the English army to pass the bridge, without offering any opposition; but when about one-half were over, and the bridge was crowded with those who were following, he charged those who had crossed with his whole strength, slew a very great number, and drove the rest into the river Forth, where the greater part were drowned. The remainder of the English army, who were left on the southern bank of the river, fled in great confusion, having first set fire to the wooden bridge that the Scots might not pursue them. Cressingham was killed in the very beginning of the battle; and the Scots detested him so much, that they flayed the skin from his dead body, and kept pieces of it, in memory of the revenge they had taken upon the English treasurer. Some say they made saddle-girths of this same skin; a purpose for which I do not think it could be very fit. It must be owned to have been a dishonourable thing of the Scots to insult thus the dead body of their enemy, and shows that they must have been then a ferocious and barbarous people.

The remains of Surrey's great army fled out of Scotland after this defeat; and the Scots, taking arms on all sides, attacked the castles in which the English soldiers continued to shelter themselves, and took most of them by force or stratagem. Many wonderful stories are told of Wallace's exploits on these occasions; some of which are no doubt true, while others are either invented, or very much exaggerated. It seems certain, however, that he defeated the English in several combats, chased them almost entirely out of Scotland, regained the towns and castles of which they had possessed themselves, and recovered for a time the complete freedom of the country. He even marched into England, and laid Cumberland and Northumberland waste, where the Scottish soldiers, in revenge for the mischief which the English had done in their country, committed great cruelties. Wallace did not approve of their killing the people who were not in arms, and he endeavoured to protect the clergymen and others, who were not able to defend themselves. "Remain with me," he said to the priests of Hexham, a large town in Northumberland, "or I cannot protect you from my soldiers when you are out of my presence." The troops who followed Wallace received no pay, because he had no money to give them; and that was one great reason why be could not keep them under restraint, or prevent their doing much harm to the defenceless country people. He remained in England more than three weeks, and did a great deal of mischief to the country.

Indeed, it appears, that, though Wallace disapproved of slaying priests, women, and children, he partook of the ferocity of the times so much as to put to death without quarter all whom he found in arms. In the north of Scotland, the English had placed a garrison in the strong castle of Dunnottar, which, built on a large and precipitous rock, overhangs the raging sea. Though the place is almost inaccessible, Wallace and his followers found their way into the castle, while the garrison in great terror fled into the church or chapel, which was built on the very verge of the precipice. This did not save them, for Wallace caused the church to be set on fire. The terrified garrison, involved in the flames, ran some of them upon the points of the Scottish swords, while others threw themselves from the precipice into the sea, and swam along to the cliffs, where they hung like sea-fowl, screaming in vain for mercy and assistance.

The followers of Wallace were frightened at this dreadful scene, and falling on their knees before the priests who chanced to be in the army, they asked forgiveness for having committed so much slaughter within the limits of a church dedicated to the service of God. But Wallace had so deep a sense of the injuries which the English had done to his country, that he only laughed at the contrition of his soldiers—"I will absolve you all myself," he said. "Are you Scottish soldiers, and do you repent for a trifle like this, which is not half what the invaders deserved at our hands?" So deep-seated was Wallace's feeling of national resentment, that it seems to have overcome, in such instances, the scruples of a temper which was naturally humane.

Edward I. was in Flanders when all these events took place. You may suppose he was very angry when he learned that Scotland, which he thought completely subdued, had risen into a great insurrection against him, defeated his armies, killed his treasurer, chased his soldiers out of their country, and invaded England with a great force. He came back from Flanders in a mighty rage, and determined not to leave that rebellious country until it was finally conquered; for which purpose he assembled a very fine army, and marched into Scotland.

In the meantime the Scots prepared to defend themselves, and chose Wallace to be Governor, or Protector of the kingdom, because they had no King at the time. He was now titled Sir William Wallace,

Protector, or Governor of the Scottish nation. But although Wallace, as we have seen, was the best soldier and bravest man in Scotland, and therefore the most fit to be placed in command at this critical period, when the King of England was coming against them with such great forces, yet the nobles of Scotland envied him this important situation, because he was not a man born in high rank, or enjoying a large estate. So great was their jealousy of Sir William Wallace, that many of these great barons did not seem very willing to bring forward their forces, or fight against the English, because they would not have a man of inferior condition to be general. This was base and mean conduct, and it was attended with great disasters to Scotland.[1] Yet, notwithstanding this unwillingness of the great nobility to support him, Wallace assembled a large army; for the middling, but especially the lower classes, were very much attached to him. He marched boldly against the King of England, and met him near the town of Falkirk. Most of the Scottish army were on foot, because, as I already told you, in those days only the nobility and great men of Scotland fought on horseback. The English King, on the contrary, had a very large body of the finest cavalry in the world, Normans and English, all clothed in complete armour. He had also the celebrated archers of England, each of whom was said to carry twelve Scotsmen's lives under his girdle; because every archer had twelve arrows stuck in his belt, and was expected to kill a man with every arrow.

The Scots had some good archers from the Forest of Ettrick, who fought under command of Sir John Stewart of Bonkill; but they were not nearly equal in number to the English. The greater part of the Scottish army were on foot, armed with long spears; they were placed thick and close together, and laid all their spears so close, point over point, that it seemed as difficult to break through them as through the wall of a strong castle. When the two armies were drawn up facing each other, Wallace said to his soldiers, "I have brought you to the ring, let me see how you can dance;" meaning, I have brought you to the decisive field of battle, let me see how bravely you can fight.

---

[1] "These mean and selfish jealousies were increased by the terror of Edward's military renown, and in many by the fear of losing their English estates; so that at the very time when an honest love of liberty, and a simultaneous spirit of resistance, could alone have saved Scotland, its nobility deserted it at its utmost need, and refused to act with the only man whose military talents and prosperity were equal to the emergency."—Tytler's *History of Scotland.*

The English made the attack. King Edward, though he saw the close ranks and undaunted appearance of the Scottish infantry, resolved nevertheless to try whether he could not ride them down with his fine cavalry. He therefore gave his horsemen orders to advance. They charged accordingly, at full gallop. It must have been a terrible thing to have seen these fine horses riding as hard as they could against the long lances, which were held out by the Scots to keep them back; and a dreadful cry arose when they came against each other.

The first line of cavalry was commanded by the Earl Marshal of England, whose progress was checked by a morass. The second line of English horse was commanded by Antony Beck, the Bishop of Durham, who, nevertheless, wore armour, and fought like a lay baron. He wheeled round the morass; but when he saw the deep and firm order of the Scots, his heart failed, and he proposed to Sir Ralph Basset of Drayton, who commanded under him, to halt till Edward himself brought up the reserve. "Go say your mass, bishop," answered Basset contemptuously, and advanced at full gallop with the second line. However, the Scots stood their ground with their long spears; many of the foremost of the English horses were thrown down, and the riders were killed as they lay rolling, unable to rise, owing to the weight of their heavy armour. But the Scottish horse did not come to the assistance of their infantry, but, on the contrary, fled away from the battle. It is supposed that this was owing to the treachery or ill-will of the nobility, who were jealous of Wallace. But it must be considered that the Scottish cavalry were few in number; and that they had much worse arms, and weaker horses, than their enemies. The English cavalry attempted again and again to disperse the deep and solid ranks in which Wallace had stationed his foot soldiers. But they were repeatedly beaten off with loss, nor could they make their way through that wood of spears, as it is called by one of the English historians. King Edward then commanded his archers to advance; and these approaching within arrow-shot of the Scottish ranks, poured on them such close and dreadful volleys of arrows that it was impossible to sustain the discharge. It happened at the same time, that Sir John Stewart was killed by a fall from his horse; and the archers of Ettrick Forest, whom he was bringing forward to oppose those of King Edward, were slain in great numbers around him. Their bodies were afterwards distinguished among the slain, as being the tallest and handsomest men of the army.

The Scottish spearmen being thus thrown into some degree of confusion, by the loss of those who were slain by the arrows of the English, the heavy cavalry of Edward again charged with more success than formerly, and broke through the ranks, which were already disordered. Sir John Grahame, Wallace's great friend and companion, was slain, with many other brave soldiers; and the Scots, having lost a very great number of men were at length obliged to take to flight.

This fatal battle was fought upon 22d July 1298. Sir John the Grahame lies buried in the churchyard of Falkirk. A tombstone was laid over him, which has been three times renewed since his death. The inscription bears, "That Sir John the Grahame, equally remarkable for wisdom and courage, and the faithful friend of Wallace, being slain in battle by the English, lies buried in this place." A large oak-tree in the adjoining forest was long shown as marking the spot where Wallace slept before the battle, or, as others said, in which he hid himself after the defeat. Nearly forty years ago Grandpapa saw some of its roots; but the body of the tree was even then entirely decayed, and there is not now, and has not been for many years, the least vestige of it to be seen.

After this fatal defeat of Falkirk, Sir William Wallace seems to have resigned his office of Governor of Scotland. Several nobles were named guardians in his place, and continued to make resistance to the English armies; and they gained some advantages, particularly near Roslin, where a body of Scots, commanded by John Comyn of Badenoch, who was one of the guardians of the kingdom, and another distinguished commander, called Simon Fraser, defeated three armies, or detachments, of English in one day.

Nevertheless, the King of England possessed so much wealth, and so many means of raising soldiers, that he sent army after army into the poor oppressed country of Scotland, and obliged all its nobles and great men, one after another, to submit themselves once more to his yoke. Sir William Wallace, alone, or with a very small band of followers, refused either to acknowledge the usurper Edward or to lay down his arms. He continued to maintain himself among the woods, and mountains of his native country for no less than seven years after his defeat at Falkirk, and for more than one year after all the other defenders of Scottish liberty had laid down their arms. Many proclamations were sent out against him by the English, and a great reward was set upon his head; for Edward did not think he could have any secure possession of his usurped kingdom of Scotland while Wallace lived. At

length he was taken prisoner; and, shame it is to say, a Scotsman, called
Sir John Menteith, was the person by whom he was seized and delivered to the English. It is generally said that he was made prisoner at
Robroyston, near Glasgow; and the tradition of the country bears that
the signal made for rushing upon him and taking him at unawares was,
when one of his pretended friends, who betrayed him, should turn a
loaf, which was placed upon the table, with its bottom or flat side
uppermost. And in after times it was reckoned ill-breeding to turn a
loaf in that manner if there was a person named Menteith in company;
since it was as much as to remind him that his namesake had betrayed
Sir William Wallace, the Champion of Scotland.

Whether Sir John Menteith was actually the person by whom Wallace was betrayed is not perfectly certain. He was, however, the individual by whom the patriot was made prisoner, and delivered up to the
English, for which his name and his memory have been long loaded
with disgrace.

Edward having thus obtained possession of the person whom he
considered as the greatest obstacle to his complete conquest of Scotland, resolved to make Wallace an example to all Scottish patriots who
should in future venture to oppose his ambitious projects. He caused
this gallant defender of his country to be brought to trial in Westminster hall, before the English judges, and produced him there, crowned,
in mockery, with a green garland, because they said he had been king
of outlaws and robbers among the Scottish woods. Wallace was
accused of having been a traitor to the English crown; to which he
answered, "I could not be a traitor to Edward, for I was never his subject." He was then charged with having taken and burnt towns and castles, with having killed many men and done much violence. He replied
with the same calm resolution, "That it was true he had killed very
many Englishmen, but it was because they had come to subdue and
oppress his native country of Scotland; and far from repenting what he
had done, he declared he was only sorry that he had not put to death
many more of them."

Notwithstanding that Wallace's defence was a good one, both in
law and in common sense (for surely every one has not only a right to
fight in defence of his native country, but is bound in duty to do so),
the English judges condemned him to be executed. So this brave
patriot was dragged upon a sledge to the place of execution, where his
head was struck off, and his body divided into four quarters, which,

according to the cruel custom of the time, were exposed upon spikes of iron on London Bridge, and were termed the limbs of a traitor.

No doubt King Edward thought, that by exercising this great severity towards so distinguished a patriot as Sir William Wallace he should terrify all the Scots into obedience, and so be able in future to reign over their country without resistance. But though Edward was a powerful, a brave, and a wise king, and though he took the most cautious, as well as the most strict measures, to preserve the obedience of Scotland, yet his claim being founded in injustice and usurpation, was not permitted by Providence to be established in security or peace. Sir William Wallace, that immortal supporter of the independence of his country, was no sooner deprived of his life, in the cruel and unjust manner I have told you, than other patriots arose to assert the cause of Scottish liberty.

VIII

Robert the Bruce

1305-1314

I HOPE, my dear child, that you have not forgotten that all the cruel
wars in Scotland arose out of the debate between the great lords who
claimed the throne after King Alexander the Third's death, which
induced the Scottish nobility rashly to submit the decision of that
matter to King Edward of England, and thus opened the way to his
endeavouring to seize the kingdom of Scotland to himself. You recollect also, that Edward had dethroned John Baliol, on account of his
attempting to restore the independence of Scotland, and that Baliol had
resigned the crown of Scotland into the hands of Edward as lord paramount. This John Baliol, therefore, was very little respected in Scotland; he had renounced the kingdom, and had been absent from it for
fifteen years, during the greater part of which time he remained a prisoner in the hands of the King of England.

It was therefore natural that such of the people of Scotland as were
still determined to fight for the deliverance of their country from the
English yoke should look around for some other king, under whom
they might unite themselves, to combat the power of England. The
feeling was universal in Scotland that they would not any longer
endure the English government; and therefore such great Scottish

nobles as believed they had right to the crown began to think of standing forward to claim it.

Amongst these, the principal candidates (supposing John Baliol, by his renunciation and captivity to have lost all right to the kingdom) were two powerful noblemen. The first was Robert Bruce, Earl of Carrick, the grandson of that elder Robert Bruce who, as you have heard, disputed the throne with John Baliol. The other was John Comyn, or Cuming, of Badenoch,[1] usually called the Red Comyn, to distinguish him from his kinsman, the Black Comyn, so named from his swarthy complexion. These two great and powerful barons had taken part with Sir William Wallace in the wars against England; but, after the defeat of Falkirk, being fearful of losing their great estates, and considering the freedom of Scotland as beyond the possibility of being recovered, both Bruce and Comyn had not only submitted themselves to Edward, and acknowledged his title as king of Scotland, but even borne arms, along with the English against such of their countrymen as still continued to resist the usurper. But the feelings of Bruce concerning the baseness of this conduct are said, by the old traditions of Scotland, to have been awakened by the following incident. In one of the numerous battles, or skirmishes, which took place at the time between the English and their adherents on the one side, and the insurgent or patriotic Scots upon the other, Robert the Bruce was present, and assisted the English to gain the victory. After the battle was over, he sat down to dinner among his southern friends and allies without washing his hands, on which there still remained spots of the blood which he had shed during the action. The English lords, observing this, whispered to each other in mockery, "Look at that Scotsman, who is eating his own blood!" Bruce heard what they said, and began to reflect that the blood upon his hands might be indeed called his own, since it was that of his brave countrymen, who were fighting for the independence of Scotland, whilst he was assisting its oppressors, who only laughed at and mocked him for his unnatural conduct. He was so much shocked and disgusted that he arose from table, and, going into a neighbouring chapel, shed many tears, and, asking pardon of God for the great crime he had been guilty of, made a solemn vow that he would atone for it by doing all in his

---

[1] He was the son of Marjory, sister of King John Baliol, by her marriage with John Comyn of Badenoch, one of the competitors with Baliol for the crown, but who afterwards withdrew his pretensions and supported the claim and the government of Baliol."—Wood's *Peerage*.

power to deliver Scotland from the foreign yoke. Accordingly, he left, it is said, the English army, and never joined it again, but remained watching an opportunity for restoring the freedom of his country.

Now, this Robert the Bruce was a remarkably brave and strong man: there was no man in Scotland that was thought a match for him except Sir William Wallace; and now that Wallace was dead, Bruce was held the best warrior in Scotland. He was very wise and prudent, and an excellent general: that is, he knew how to conduct an army, and place them in order for battle, as well or better than any great man of his time. He was generous, too, and courteous by nature; but he had some faults, which perhaps belonged as much to the fierce period in which he lived as to his own character. He was rash and passionate, and in his passion he was sometimes relentless and cruel.

Robert the Bruce had fixed his purpose, as I told you, to attempt once again to drive the English out of Scotland, and he desired to prevail upon Sir John the Red Comyn, who was his rival in his pretensions to the throne, to join with him in expelling the foreign enemy by their common efforts. With this purpose, Bruce posted down from London to Dumfries, on the borders of Scotland, and requested an interview with John Comyn. They met in the church of the Minorites in that town, before the high altar. What passed betwixt them is not known with certainty; but they quarrelled, either concerning their mutual pretensions to the crown, or because Comyn refused to join Bruce in the proposed insurrection against the English; or, as many writers say, because Bruce charged Comyn with having betrayed to the English his purpose of rising up against King Edward. It is, however, certain that these two haughty barons came to high and abusive words, until at length Bruce, who, I told you, was extremely passionate, forgot the sacred character of the place in which they stood, and struck Comyn a blow with his dagger. Having done this rash deed, he instantly ran out of the church and called for his horse. Two gentlemen of the country, Lindesay and Kirkpatrick, friends of Bruce, were then in attendance on him. Seeing him pale, bloody, and in much agitation, they eagerly inquired what was the matter.

"I doubt," said Bruce, "that I have slain the Red Comyn."

"Do you leave such a matter in doubt?" said Kirkpatrick. "I will make sicker!"—that is, I will make certain.

Accordingly, he and his companion Lindesay rushed into the church, and made the matter certain with a vengeance, by despatching the wounded Comyn with their daggers. His uncle, Sir Robert Comyn, was slain at the same time.

This slaughter of Comyn was a rash and cruel action; and the historian of Bruce observes that it was followed by the displeasure of Heaven; for no man ever went through more misfortunes than Robert Bruce, although he at length rose to great honour.

After the deed was done, Bruce might be called desperate. He had committed an action which was sure to bring down upon him the vengeance of all Comyn's relations, the resentment of the King of England, and the displeasure of the Church, on account of having slain his enemy within consecrated ground. He determined, therefore, to bid them all defiance at once, and to assert his pretensions to the throne of Scotland. He drew his own followers together, summoned to meet him such barons as still entertained hopes of the freedom of the country, and was crowned King at the Abbey of Scone, the usual place where the kings of Scotland assumed their authority.

Everything relating to the ceremony was hastily performed. A small circlet of gold was hurriedly made, to represent the ancient crown of Scotland, which Edward had carried off to England. The Earl of Fife, descendant of the brave Macduff, whose duty it was to have placed the crown on the King's head, would not give his attendance. But the ceremonial was performed by his sister, Isabella, Countess of Buchan, though without the consent either of her brother or husband. A few barons, whose names ought to be dear to their country, joined Bruce in his attempt to vindicate the independence of Scotland.

Edward was dreadfully incensed when he heard that, after all the pains which he had taken, and all the blood which had been spilled, the Scots were making this new attempt to shake off his authority. Though now old, feeble, and sickly, he made a solemn vow, at a great festival, in presence of all his court, that he would take the most ample vengeance upon Robert the Bruce and his adherents; after which he would never again draw his sword upon a Christian, but would only fight against the unbelieving Saracens for the recovery of the Holy Land. He marched against Bruce accordingly, at the head of a powerful army.

The commencement of Bruce's undertaking was most disastrous. He was crowned on 29th March 1306. On the 18th May he was excommunicated by the Pope, on account of the murder of Comyn within consecrated ground, a sentence which excluded him from all the benefits of religion, and authorised any one to kill him. Finally, on the 19th June, the new King, was completely defeated near Methven by the English Earl of Pembroke. Robert's horse was killed under him in the action, and he was for a moment a prisoner. But he had fallen into the power of a Scottish knight, who, though he served in the English army, did not choose to be the instrument of putting Bruce into their hands, and allowed him to escape. The conquerors executed their prisoners with their usual cruelty. Among these were some gallant young men of the first Scottish families—Hay, ancestor of the Earls of Errol, Somerville, Fraser, and others, who were mercilessly put to death.

Bruce, with a few brave adherents, among whom was the young Lord of Douglas, who was afterwards called the Good Lord James, retired into the Highland mountains, where they were chased from one place of refuge to another, often in great danger, and suffering many hardships. The Bruce's wife, now Queen of Scotland, with several other ladies, accompanied her husband and his few followers during their wanderings. There was no other way of providing for them save by hunting and fishing. It was remarked that Douglas was the most active and successful in procuring for the unfortunate ladies such supplies as his dexterity in fishing or in killing deer could furnish them.

Driven from one place in the Highlands to another, starved out of some districts, and forced from others by the opposition of the inhabitants, Bruce attempted to force his way into Lorn; but he found enemies everywhere. The M'Dougals, a powerful family, then called Lords of Lorn, were friendly to the English, and putting their men in arms, attacked Bruce and his wandering companions as soon as they attempted to enter their territory. The chief of these M'Dougals, called John of Lorn, hated Bruce on account of his having slain the Red Comyn, to whom this M'Dougal was nearly related.[1] Bruce was again defeated by this chief, through force of numbers, at a place called Dalry; but he showed, amidst his misfortunes, the greatness of his strength and courage. He directed his men to retreat through a narrow pass, and placing himself last of the party, he fought with and slew such of the enemy as attempted to press hard on them. Three followers of M'Dougal, a father and two sons, called M'Androsser, all very strong men, when they saw Bruce thus protecting the retreat of his followers, made a vow that they would either kill this redoubted cham-

---

[1] According to Wyntown, M'Dougal married the third daughter of Comyn.

pion or make him prisoner. The whole three rushed on the King at once. Bruce was on horseback, in the strait pass we have described, betwixt a precipitous rock and a deep lake. He struck the first man who came up, and seized his horse's rein, such a blow with his sword, as cut off his hand and freed the bridle. The man bled to death. The other brother had grasped Bruce in the meantime by the leg, and was attempting to throw him from horseback. The King, setting spurs to his horse, made the animal suddenly spring forward, so that the Highlander fell under the horse's feet; and, as he was endeavouring to rise again Bruce cleft his head in two with his sword. The father, seeing his two sons thus slain, flew desperately at the King, and grasped him by the mantle so close to his body, that he could not have room to wield his long sword. But with the heavy pommel of that weapon, or, as others say, with an iron hammer which hung, at his saddle-bow, the King struck this third assailant so dreadful a blow that he dashed out his brains. Still, however, the Highlander kept his dying grasp on the King's mantle; so that, to be free of the dead body, Bruce was obliged to undo the brooch, or clasp, by which it was fastened, and leave that, and the mantle itself, behind him. The brooch, which fell thus into the possession of M'Dougal of Lorn, is still preserved in that ancient family, as a memorial that the celebrated Robert Bruce once narrowly escaped falling into the hands of their ancestor.[1] Robert greatly resented this attack upon him; and when he was in happier circumstances, did not fail to take his revenge on M'Dougal, or, as he is usually called, John of Lorn.

The King met with many such encounters amidst his dangerous and dismal wanderings; yet, though almost always defeated by the superior numbers of the English, and of such Scots as sided with them, he still kept up his own spirits and those of his followers. He was a better scholar than was usual in those days, when, except clergymen, few people received much education. But King Robert had been well

---

[1] "Barbour adds the following circumstance, highly characteristic of the sentiments of chivalry. MacNaughton, a Baron of Cowal, pointed out to the Lord of Lorn the deeds of valour which Bruce performed on this memorable retreat, with the highest expression of admiration. 'It seems to give thee pleasure,' said Lorn, 'that he makes such havoc among our friends.' 'Not so, by my faith,' replied MacNaughton; 'but be he friend or foe who achieves high deeds of chivalry, men should bear faithful witness to his valour; and never have I heard of one, who by his knightly feats has extricated himself from such dangers as have this day surrounded Bruce.'"—*Note to* Sir Walter Scott's *Lord of the Isles.*

instructed in the learning of the times; and we are told that he sometimes read aloud to his companions, to amuse them when they were
crossing the great Highland lakes in such wretched leaky boats as they
could find for that purpose. Loch Lomond, in particular, is said to have
witnessed such scenes. You may see by this how useful it is to possess
knowledge and accomplishments. If Bruce could not have read to his
associates, and diverted their thoughts from their dangers and sufferings, he might not perhaps have been able to keep up their spirits, or
secure their continued attachment.

At last dangers increased so much around the brave King Robert,
that he was obliged to separate himself from his Queen and her ladies;
for the winter was coming on, and it would be impossible for the
women to endure this wandering sort of life when the frost and snow
should set in. So Bruce left his Queen, with the Countess of Buchan
and others, in the only castle which remained to him, which was called
Kildrummie, and is situated near the head of the river Don in
Aberdeenshire. The King also left his youngest brother, Nigel Bruce, to
defend the castle against the English; and he himself, with his second
brother Edward, who was a very brave man, but still more rash and
passionate than Robert himself, went over to an island called Rachrin,
on the coast of Ireland, where Bruce and the few men that followed his
fortunes passed the winter of 1306. In the meantime ill luck seemed to
pursue all his friends in Scotland. The castle of Kildrummie was taken
by the English, and Nigel Bruce, a beautiful and brave youth, was cruelly put to death by the victors. The ladies who had attended on
Robert's Queen, as well as the Queen herself, and the Countess of
Buchan, were thrown into strict confinement, and treated with the
utmost severity.

The Countess of Buchan, as I before told you, had given Edward
great offence by being the person who placed the crown on the head of
Robert Bruce. She was imprisoned within the castle of Berwick, in a
cage made on purpose. Some Scottish authors have pretended that this
cage was hung over the walls with the poor countess, like a parrot's
cage out at a window. But this is their own ignorant idea. The cage of
the Lady Buchan was a strong wooden and iron piece of framework,
placed within an apartment, and resembling one of those places in
which wild beasts are confined. There were such cages in most old
prisons to which captives were consigned, who, either for mutiny, or
any other reason, were to be confined with peculiar rigour.

The news of the taking of Kildrummie, the captivity of his wife, and the execution of his brother, reached Bruce while he was residing in a miserable dwelling at Rachrin, and reduced him to the point of despair.

It was about this time that an incident took place, which, although it rests only on tradition in families of the name of Bruce, is rendered probable by the manners of the times. After receiving the last unpleasing intelligence from Scotland, Bruce was lying one morning on his wretched bed, and deliberating with himself whether he had not better resign all thoughts of again attempting to make good his right to the Scottish crown, and, dismissing his followers, transport himself and his brothers to the Holy Land, and spend the rest of his life in fighting against the Saracens; by which he thought, perhaps, he might deserve the forgiveness of Heaven for the great sin of stabbing Comyn in the church at Dumfries. But then, on the other hand, he thought it would be both criminal and cowardly to give up his attempts to restore freedom to Scotland, while there yet remained the least chance of his being successful in an undertaking which, rightly considered, was much more his duty than to drive the infidels out of Palestine, though the superstition of his age might think otherwise.

While he was divided betwixt these reflections, and doubtful of what he should do, Bruce was looking upward to the roof of the cabin in which he lay; and his eye was attracted by a spider, which, hanging at the end of a long thread of its own spinning, was endeavouring, as is the fashion of that creature, to swing itself from one beam in the roof to another, for the purpose of fixing the line on which it meant to stretch its web. The insect made the attempt again and again without success; and at length Bruce counted that it had tried to carry its point six times, and been as often unable to do so. It came into his head that he had himself fought just six battles against the English and their allies, and that the poor persevering spider was exactly in the same situation with himself, having made as many trials, and been as often disappointed in what it aimed at. "Now," thought Bruce, "as I have no means of knowing what is best to be done, I will be guided by the luck which shall attend this spider. If the insect shall make another effort to fix its thread, and shall be successful, I will venture a seventh time to try my fortune in Scotland; but if the spider shall fail, I will go to the wars in Palestine, and never return to my native country more."

While Bruce was forming this resolution, the spider made another exertion with all the force it could muster, and fairly succeeded in fastening its thread to the beam which it had so often in vain attempted to reach. Bruce, seeing the success of the spider, resolved to try his own fortune; and as he had never before gained a victory, so he never afterwards sustained any considerable or decisive check or defeat. I have often met with people of the name of Bruce, so completely persuaded of the truth of this story that they would not on any account kill a spider; because it was that insect which had shown the example of perseverance, and given a signal of good luck to their great namesake.

Having determined to renew his efforts to obtain possession of Scotland, notwithstanding the smallness of the means which he had for accomplishing so great a purpose, the Bruce removed himself and his followers from Rachrin to the island of Arran, which lies in the mouth of the Clyde. The King landed, and inquired of the first woman he met what armed men were in the island. She returned for answer, that there had arrived there very lately a body of armed strangers, who had defeated an English officer, the governor of the castle of Brathwick,[1] had killed him and most of his men, and were now amusing themselves with hunting about the island. The King, having caused himself to be guided to the woods which these strangers most frequented, there blew his horn repeatedly. Now, the chief of the strangers who had taken the castle was James Douglas, whom we have already mentioned as one of the best of Bruce's friends, and he was accompanied by some of the bravest of that patriotic band. When he heard Robert Bruce's horn, he knew the sound well, and cried out, that yonder was the King, he knew by his manner of blowing. So he and his companions hastened to meet King Robert, and there was great joy on both sides; whilst at the same time they could not help weeping when they considered their own forlorn condition, and the great loss that had taken place among their friends since they had last parted. But they were stout-hearted men, and looked forward to freeing their country, in spite of all that had yet happened.

The Bruce was now within sight of Scotland, and not distant from his own family possessions, where the people were most likely to be attached to him. He began immediately to form plans with Douglas, how they might best renew their enterprise against the English. The Douglas resolved to go disguised to his own country, and raise his followers, in order to begin their enterprise by taking revenge on an

---

[1] Or Brodick: now a seat of the Duke of Hamilton, Earl of Arran.

English nobleman called Lord Clifford, upon whom Edward had conferred his estates, and who had taken up his residence in the castle of Douglas.

Bruce, on his part, opened a communication with the opposite coast of Carrick, by means of one of his followers called Cuthbert. This person had directions, that if he should find the countrymen in Carrick disposed to take up arms against the English, he was to make a fire on a headland, or lofty cape, called Turnberry, on the coast of Ayrshire, opposite to the island of Arran. The appearance of a fire on this place was to be a signal for Bruce to put to sea with such men as he had, who were not more than three hundred in number, for the purpose of landing in Carrick and joining the insurgents.

Bruce and his men watched eagerly for the signal, but for some time in vain. At length a fire on Turnberry-head became visible, and the King and his followers merrily betook themselves to their ships and galleys, concluding their Carrick friends were all in arms, and ready to join with them. They landed on the beach at midnight, where they found their spy Cuthbert alone in waiting for them, with very bad news. Lord Percy, he said, was in the country, with two or three hundred Englishmen, and had terrified the people so much, both by threats and actions, that none of them dared to think of rebelling against King Edward.

"Traitor!" said Bruce, "why, then, did you make the signal?"

"Alas," replied Cuthbert, "the fire was not made by me, but by some other person, for what purpose I know not; but as soon as I saw it burning, I knew that you would come over, thinking it my signal, and therefore I came down to wait for you on the beach, to tell you how the matter stood."

King Robert's first idea was to return to Arran after this disappointment; but his brother Edward refused to go back. He was, as I have told you, a man daring even to rashness.

"I will not leave my native land," he said, "now that I am so unexpectedly restored to it. I will give freedom to Scotland, or leave my carcass on the surface of the land which gave me birth."

Bruce, also, after some hesitation, determined that since he had been thus brought to the mainland of Scotland, he would remain there, and take such adventure and fortune as Heaven should send him.

Accordingly he began to skirmish with the English so successfully as obliged the Lord Percy to quit Carrick. Bruce then dispersed his men

upon various adventures against the enemy, in which they were generally successful. But then, on the other hand, the King, being left with
small attendance, or sometimes almost alone, ran great risk of losing
his life by treachery, or by open violence. Several of these incidents are
very interesting. I will tell you some of them.

At one time a near relation of Bruce's, in whom he entirely confided, was induced by the bribes of the English to attempt to put him
to death. This villain, with his two sons, watched the King one morning, till he saw him separated from all his men, excepting a little boy,
who waited on him as a page. The father had a sword in his hand, one
of the sons had a sword and a spear, the other had a sword and a
battle-axe. Now, when the King saw them so well armed, when there
were no enemies near, he began to call to mind some hints which had
been given to him, that these men intended to murder him. He had no
weapons excepting his sword; but his page had a bow and arrow. He
took them both from the little boy, and bade him stand at a distance;
"for," said the King, "if I overcome these traitors, thou shalt have
enough of weapons; but if I am slain by them, you may make your
escape, and tell Douglas and my brother to revenge my death." The
boy was very sorry, for he loved his master; but he was obliged to do as
he was bidden.

In the meantime the traitors came forward upon Bruce, that they
might assault him at once. The King called out to them, and commanded them to come no nearer, upon peril of their lives; but the
father answered with flattering words, pretending great kindness, and
still continuing to approach his person. Then the King again called to
them to stand. "Traitors," said he, "ye have sold my life for English
gold; but you shall die if you come one foot nearer to me." With that
he bent the page's bow; and as the old conspirator continued to
advance, he let the arrow fly at him. Bruce was an excellent archer; he
aimed his arrow so well that it hit the father in the eye, and penetrated
from that into his brain, so that he fell down dead. Then the two sons
rushed on the King. One of them fetched a blow at him with an axe,
but missed his stroke and stumbled, so that the King with his great
sword cut him down before he could recover his feet. The remaining
traitor ran on Bruce with his spear; but the King, with a sweep of his
sword, cut the steel head off the villain's weapon, and then killed him
before he had time to draw his sword. Then the little page came running, very joyful of his master's victory; and the King wiped his bloody

sword, and looking upon the dead bodies, said, "These might have been reputed three gallant men, if they could have resisted the temptation of covetousness."

In the present day it is not necessary that generals or great officers should fight with their own hand, because it is only their duty to direct the movements and exertions of their followers. The artillery and the soldiers shoot at the enemy, and men seldom mingle together, and fight hand to hand. But in ancient times kings and great lords were obliged to put themselves into the very front of the battle, and fight like ordinary men, with the lance and other weapons. It was, therefore, of great consequence that they should be strong men, and dexterous in the use of their arms. Robert Bruce was so remarkably active and powerful that he came through a great many personal dangers, in which he must otherwise have been slain. I will tell you another of his adventures, which I think will amuse you.

After the death of these three traitors, Robert the Bruce continued to keep himself concealed in his own earldom of Carrick, and in the neighbouring country of Galloway, until he should have matters ready for a general attack upon the English. He was obliged, in the meantime, to keep very few men with him, both for the sake of secrecy, and from the difficulty of finding provisions. Now, many of the people of Galloway were unfriendly to Bruce. They lived under the government of one M'Dougal, related to the Lord of Lorn, who, as I before told you, had defeated Bruce at Dalry, and very nearly killed or made him prisoner. These Galloway men had heard that Bruce was in their country, having no more than sixty men with him; so they resolved to attack him by surprise, and for this purpose they got two hundred men together, and brought with them two or three bloodhounds. These animals were trained to chase a man by the scent of his footsteps, as foxhounds chase a fox, or as beagles and harriers chase a hare. Although the dog does not see the person whose trace he is put upon, he follows him over every step he has taken. At that time these bloodhounds or sleuthhounds (so called from *slot* or *sleut*, a word which signifies the scent left by an animal of chase) were used for the purpose of pursuing great criminals. The men of Galloway thought themselves secure, that if they missed taking Bruce, or killing him at the first onset, and if he should escape into the woods, they would find him out by means of these bloodhounds.

The good King Robert Bruce, who was always watchful and vigilant, had received some information of the intention of this party to come upon him suddenly and by night. Accordingly he quartered his little troop of sixty men on the side of a deep and swift-running river, that had very steep and rocky banks. There was but one ford by which this river could be crossed in that neighbourhood, and that ford was deep and narrow, so that two men could scarcely get through abreast; the ground on which they were to land on the side where the King was, was steep, and the path which led upwards from the water's edge to the top of the bank extremely narrow and difficult.

Bruce caused his men to lie down to take some sleep, at a place about half a mile distant from the river, while he himself, with two attendants, went down to watch the ford, through which the enemy must needs pass before they could come to the place where King Robert's men were lying. He stood for some time looking at the ford, and thinking how easily the enemy might be kept from passing there, providing it was bravely defended, when he heard at a distance the baying of a hound, which was always coming nearer and nearer. This was the bloodhound which was tracing the King's steps to the ford where he had crossed, and the two hundred Galloway men were along with the animal, and guided by it. Bruce at first thought of going back to awaken his men; but then he reflected that it might be only some shepherd's dog. "My men," he said, "are sorely tired; I will not disturb their sleep for the yelping of a cur, till I know something more of the matter." So he stood and listened; and by and by, as the cry of the hound came nearer, he began to hear a trampling of horses, and the voices of men, and the ringing and clattering of armour, and then he was sure the enemy were coming to the riverside. Then the King thought, "If I go back to give my men the alarm, these Galloway men will get through the ford without opposition; and that would be a pity, since it is a place so advantageous to make defence against them." So he looked again at the steep path and the deep river, and he thought that they gave him so much advantage that he himself could defend the passage with his own hand until his men came to assist him. His armour was so good and strong that he had no fear of arrows, and therefore the combat was not so very unequal as it must have otherwise been. He therefore sent his followers to waken his men, and remained alone by the bank of the river.

In the meanwhile, the noise and trampling of the horses increased; and the moon being bright, Bruce beheld the glancing arms of about two hundred men, who came down to the opposite bank of the river.

The men of Galloway, on their part, saw but one solitary figure, guarding the ford, and the foremost of them plunged into the river without minding him. But as they could only pass the ford one by one, the Bruce, who stood high above them on the bank where they were to land, killed the foremost man with a thrust of his long spear, and with a second thrust stabbed the horse, which fell down, kicking and plunging in his agonies, on the narrow path, and so prevented the others who were following from getting out of the river. Bruce had thus an opportunity of dealing his blows at pleasure among them, while they could not strike at him again. In the confusion, five or six of the enemy were slain, or, having been borne down the current, were drowned in the river. The rest were terrified, and drew back.

But when the Galloway men looked again, and saw they were opposed by only one man, they themselves being so many, they cried out that their honour would be lost for ever if they did not force their way; and encouraged each other with loud cries to plunge through and assault him. But by this time the King's soldiers came up to his assistance, and the Galloway men retreated, and gave up their enterprise.[1]

I will tell you another story of this brave Robert Bruce during his wanderings. His adventures are as curious and entertaining as those which men invent for story books, with this advantage, that they are all true.

About the time when the Bruce was yet at the head of but few men, Sir Aymer de Valence, who was Earl of Pembroke, together with John of Lorn, came into Galloway, each of them being at the head of a large body of men. John of Lorn had a bloodhound with him, which it was said had formerly belonged to Robert Bruce himself; and having been fed by the King with his own hands, it became attached to him, and would follow his footsteps anywhere, as dogs are well known to trace their master's steps, whether they be bloodhounds or not. By means of this hound, John of Lorn thought he should certainly find out Bruce, and take revenge on him for the death of his relation Comyn.

When these two armies advanced upon King Robert, he at first thought of fighting with the English earl; but becoming aware that John of Lorn was moving round with another large body to attack him

---

[1] "When the soldiers came up, they found the King wearied, but unwounded, and sitting on a bank, where he had cast off his helmet to wipe his brow, and cool himself in the night air."—Tytler.

in the rear, he resolved to avoid fighting at that time, lest he should be oppressed by numbers. For this purpose, the King divided the men he had with him into three bodies, and commanded them to retreat by three different ways, thinking the enemy would not know which party to pursue. He also appointed a place at which they were to assemble again. But when John of Lorn came to the place where the army of Bruce had been thus divided, the bloodhound took his course after one of these divisions, neglecting the other two, and then John of Lorn knew that the King must be in that party; so he also made no pursuit after the two other divisions of the Scots, but followed that which the dog pointed out, with all his men.

The King again saw that he was followed by a large body, and being determined to escape from them, if possible, he made all the people who were with him disperse themselves different ways, thinking thus that the enemy must needs lose trace of him. He kept only one man along with him, and that was his own foster-brother, or the son of his nurse. When John of Lorn came to the place where Bruce's companions had dispersed themselves, the bloodhound, after it had snuffed up and down for a little, quitted the footsteps of all the other fugitives, and ran barking upon the track of two men out of the whole number. Then John of Lorn knew that one of these two must needs be King Robert. Accordingly he commanded five of his men that were speedy of foot to follow hard, and either make him prisoner or slay him. The Highlanders started off accordingly, and ran so fast that they gained sight of Robert and his foster-brother. The King asked his companion what help he could give him, and his foster-brother answered he was ready to do his best. So these two turned on the five men of John of Lorn, and killed them all. It is to be supposed they were better armed than the others were, as well as stronger and more desperate.

But by this time Bruce was very much fatigued, and yet they dared not sit down to take any rest; for whenever they stopped for an instant, they heard the cry of the bloodhound behind them, and knew by that that their enemies were coming up fast after them. At length they came to a wood, through which ran a small river. Then Bruce said to his foster-brother, "Let us wade down this stream for a great way, instead of going straight across, and so this unhappy hound will lose the scent; for if we were once clear of him, I should not be afraid of getting away from the pursuers." Accordingly the King and his attendant walked a great way down the stream, taking care to keep their feet in the water, which could not retain any scent where they had stepped. Then they came ashore on the further side from the enemy, and went deep into the wood before they stopped to rest themselves. In the meanwhile, the hound led John of Lorn straight to the place where the King went into the water, but there the dog began to be puzzled, not knowing where to go next; for you are well aware that the running water could not retain the scent of a man's foot, like that which remains on turf. So John of Lorn seeing the dog was at fault, as it is called, that is, had lost the track of what he pursued, gave up the chase, and returned to join with Aymer de Valence.

But King Robert's adventures were not yet ended. His foster-brother and he had rested themselves in the wood, but they had got no food, and were become extremely hungry. They walked on, however, in hopes of coming to some habitation. At length, in the midst of the forest, they met with three men who looked like thieves or ruffians. They were well armed, and one of them bore a sheep on his back, which it seemed as if they had just stolen. They saluted the King civilly; and he, replying to their salutation, asked them where they were going. The men answered, they were seeking for Robert Bruce, for that they intended to join with him. The King answered, that if they would go with him, he would conduct them where they would find the Scottish King. Then the man who had spoken changed countenance, and Bruce, who looked sharply at him, began to suspect that the ruffian guessed who he was, and that he and his companions had some design against his person, in order to gain the reward which had been offered for his life.

So he said to them, "My good friends, as we are not well acquainted with each other, you must go before us, and we will follow near to you."

"You have no occasion to suspect any harm from us," answered the man.

"Neither do I suspect any," said Bruce; "but this is the way in which I choose to travel."

The men did as he commanded, and thus they travelled till they came together to a waste and ruinous cottage, where the men proposed to dress some part of the sheep, which their companion was carrying. The King was glad to hear of food; but he insisted that there should be two fires kindled, one for himself and his foster-brother at one end of the house, the other at the other end for their three companions. The men did as he desired. They broiled a quarter of mutton for themselves, and gave another to the King and his attendant.

They were obliged to eat it without bread or salt; but as they were very hungry, they were glad to get food in any shape, and partook of it very heartily.

Then so heavy a drowsiness fell on King Robert, that, for all the danger he was in, he could not resist an inclination to sleep. But first he desired his foster-brother to watch while he slept, for he had great suspicion of their new acquaintances. His foster-brother promised to keep awake, and did his best to keep his word. But the King had not been long asleep ere his foster-brother fell into a deep slumber also, for he had undergone as much fatigue as the King. When the three villains saw the King and his attendant asleep, they made signs to each other, and rising up at once, drew their swords with the purpose to kill them both. But the King slept but lightly, and for as little noise as the traitors made in rising, he was awakened by it, and starting up, drew his sword, and went to meet them. At the same moment he pushed his foster-brother with his foot, to awaken him, and he got on his feet; but ere he got his eyes cleared to see what was about to happen, one of the ruffians that were advancing to slay the King, killed him with a stroke of his sword. The King was now alone, one man against three, and in the greatest danger of his life; but his amazing strength, and the good armour which he wore, freed him once more from this great peril, and he killed the three men, one after another. He then left the cottage, very sorrowful for the death of his faithful foster-brother, and took his direction towards the place where he had appointed his men to assemble after their dispersion. It was now near night, and the place of meeting being a farm-house, he went boldly into it, where he found the mistress, an old true-hearted Scotswoman, sitting alone. Upon seeing a stranger enter, she asked him who and what he was. The King answered that he was a traveller, who was journeying through the country.

"All travellers," answered the good woman, "are welcome here, for the sake of one."

"And who is that one," said the King, "for whose sake you make all travellers welcome?"

"It is our rightful king, Robert the Bruce," answered the mistress, "who is the lawful lord of this country; and although he is now pursued and hunted after with hounds and horns, I hope to live to see him King over all Scotland."

"Since you love him so well, dame," said the King, "know that you see him before you. I am Robert the Bruce."

"You!" said the good woman, in great surprise; "and wherefore are you thus alone?—where are all your men?"

"I have none with me at this moment," answered Bruce, "and therefore I must travel alone."

"But that shall not be," said the brave old dame, "for I have two stout sons, gallant and trusty men who shall be your servants for life and death."

So she brought her two sons, and though she well knew the dangers to which she exposed them, she made them swear fidelity to the King; and they afterwards became high officers in his service.

Now, the loyal old woman was getting everything ready for the King's supper, when suddenly there was a great trampling of horses heard round the house. They thought it must be some of the English, or John of Lorn's men, and the good wife called upon her sons, to fight to the last for King Robert. But shortly after they heard the voice of the Good Lord James of Douglas, and of Edward Bruce, the King's brother, who had come with a hundred and fifty horsemen to this farm-house, according to the instructions that the King had left with them at parting.

Robert the Bruce was right joyful to meet his brother, and his faithful friend Lord James; and had no sooner found himself once more at the head of such a considerable body of followers than, forgetting hunger and weariness, he began to inquire where the enemy who had pursued them so long had taken up their abode for the night; "for," said he, "as they must suppose us totally scattered and fled, it is likely that they will think themselves quite secure, and disperse themselves into distant quarters, and keep careless watch."

"That is very true," answered James of Douglas, "for I passed a village where there are two hundred of them quartered, who had placed no sentinels; and if you have a mind to make haste, we may surprise them this very night, and do them more mischief than they have been able to do us during all this day's chase."

Then there was nothing but mount and ride; and as the Scots came by surprise on the body of English whom Douglas had mentioned, and rushed suddenly into the village where they were quartered, they easily dispersed and cut them to pieces; thus, as Douglas had said, doing their pursuers more injury than they themselves had received during the long and severe pursuit of the preceding day.

The consequence of these successes of King Robert was that soldiers came to join him on all sides, and that he obtained several victories both over Sir Aymer de Valence, Lord Clifford, and other English comman-ders; until at length the English were afraid to venture into the open country as formerly, unless when they could assemble themselves in con-siderable bodies. They thought it safer to lie still in the towns and castles which they had garrisoned, and wait till the King of England should once more come to their assistance with a powerful army.

IX

Douglas and Randolph

1307-1314

Wᴴᴇɴ King Edward the First heard that Scotland was again in arms against him, he marched down to the Borders, as I have already told you, with many threats of what he would do to avenge himself on Bruce and his party, whom he called rebels. But he was now old and feeble, and while he was making his preparations, he was taken very ill and after lingering a long time, at length died on the 6th July 1307, at a place in Cumberland called Burgh upon the Sands, in full sight of Scotland, and not three miles from its frontier. His hatred to that country was so inveterate, that his thoughts of revenge seemed to occupy his mind on his deathbed. He made his son promise never to make peace with Scotland until the nation was subdued. He gave also very singular directions concerning the disposal of his dead body. He ordered that it should be boiled in a cauldron till the flesh parted from the bones, and that then the bones should be wrapt up in a bull's hide, and carried at the head of the English army, as often as the Scots attempted to recover their freedom. He thought that he had inflicted such distresses on the Scots, and invaded and defeated them so often, that his very dead bones would terrify them. His son, Edward the Second, did not choose to execute this strange injunction, but caused his father to be buried in Westminster Abbey; where his tomb is still to be seen, bearing for an inscription, HERE LIES THE HAMMER OF THE SCOTTISH NATION.[1] And, indeed, it was true, that during his life he did them as much injury as a hammer does to the substances which it dashes to pieces.

Edward the Second was neither so brave nor so wise as his father: on the contrary, he was a weak prince, fond of idle amusements, and worthless favourites. It was lucky for Scotland that such was his disposition. He marched a little way into Scotland[2] with the large army which Edward the First had collected, but retired without fighting; which gave great encouragement to Bruce's party.

Several of the Scottish nobility now took arms in different parts of the country, declared for King Robert, and fought against the English troops and garrisons. The most distinguished of these was the Good Lord James of Douglas, whom we have often mentioned before. Some of his most memorable exploits respected his own castle of Douglas, in which, being an important fortress, and strongly situated, the English had placed a large garrison. James of Douglas saw, with great displeasure, his castle filled with English soldiers, and stored with great quantities of corn, and cattle, and wine, and ale, and other supplies which they were preparing, to enable them to assist the English army with provisions. So he resolved, if possible, to be revenged upon the captain of the garrison and his soldiers.

For this purpose, Douglas went in disguise to the house of one of his old servants, called Thomas Dickson, a strong, faithful, and bold man, and laid a scheme for taking the castle. A holiday was approaching, called Palm Sunday. Upon this day it was common, in the Roman Catholic times, that the people went to church in procession, with green boughs in their hands. Just as the English soldiers, who had marched down from the castle, got into church, one of Lord James's followers raised the cry of *Douglas, Douglas!* which was the shout with which that family always began battle. Thomas Dickson and some friends whom he had collected instantly drew their swords and killed the first Englishman whom they met. But as the signal had been given too soon, Dickson was borne down and slain. Douglas and his men presently after forced their way into the church. The English soldiers

---

[1] Edwardus longus Scotorum Malleus hic est.

[2] To Cumnock, on the frontiers of Ayrshire.

attempted to defend themselves; but, being taken by surprise and unprepared, they were, for the greater part, killed or made prisoners, and that so suddenly, and with so little noise, that their companions in the castle never heard of it. So that when Douglas and his men approached the castle gate, they found it open, and that part of the garrison which were left at home, busied cooking provisions for those that were at church. So Lord James got possession of his own castle without difficulty, and he and his men eat up all the good dinner which the English had made ready. But Douglas dared not stay there, lest the English should come in great force and besiege him; and therefore he resolved to destroy all the provisions which the English had stored up in the castle, and to render the place unavailing to them.

It must be owned he executed this purpose in a very cruel and shocking manner, for he was much enraged at the death of Thomas Dickson. He caused all the barrels containing flour, meal, wheat, and malt, to be knocked in pieces, and their contents mixed on the floor; then he staved the great hogsheads of wine and ale, and mixed the liquor with the stores; and, last of all, he killed his prisoners, and flung the dead bodies among this disgusting heap, which his men called, in derision of the English, the Douglas Larder. Then he flung dead horses into the well to destroy it—after which he set fire to the castle; and finally marched away, and took refuge with his followers in the hills and forests. "He loved better," he said, "to hear the lark sing than the mouse squeak." That is, he loved better to keep in the open field with his men, than to shut himself and them up in castles.

When Clifford, the English general, heard what had happened, he came to Douglas Castle with a great body of men, and rebuilt all the defences which Lord James had destroyed, and cleared out the well, and put a good soldier, named Thirlwall to command the garrison, and desired him to be on his guard, for he suspected that Lord James would again attack him. And, indeed, Douglas, who did not like to see the English in his father's castle, was resolved to take the first opportunity of destroying this garrison, as he had done the former. For this purpose he again had recourse to stratagem. He laid a part of his followers in ambush in the wood, and sent fourteen men, disguised like countrymen, driving cattle past the gates of the castle. As soon as Thirlwall saw this, he swore that he would plunder the Scots' drovers of their cattle, and came out with a considerable part of his garrison for that purpose. He had followed the cattle past the place where Douglas was lying concealed, when all of a sudden the Scotsmen threw off their carriers' cloaks, and appearing in armour, cried the cry of Douglas, and, turning back suddenly, ran to meet the pursuers; and before Thirlwall could make any defence, he heard the same war-cry behind him, and saw Douglas coming up with those Scots who had been lying in ambush. Thirlwall himself was killed, fighting bravely in the middle of his enemies, and only a very few of his men found their way back to the castle.

When Lord James had thus slain two English commanders or governors of his castle, and was known to have made a vow that he would be revenged on any one who should dare to take possession of his father's house, men became afraid; and the fortress was called, both in England and Scotland, the Perilous Castle of Douglas, because it proved so dangerous to any Englishman who was stationed there. Now, in those warlike times, Master Littlejohn, you must know that the ladies would not marry any man who was not very brave and valiant, so that a coward, let him be ever so rich or high-born, was held in universal contempt. And thus it became the fashion for the ladies to demand proofs of the courage of their lovers, and for those knights who desired to please the ladies, to try some extraordinary deed of arms, to show their bravery and deserve their favour.

At the time we speak of, there was a young lady in England whom many knights and noblemen asked in marriage, because she was extremely wealthy, and very beautiful. Once upon a holiday she made a great feast, to which she asked all her lovers, and numerous other gallant knights; and after the feast she arose and told them that she was much obliged to them for their good opinion of her, but as she desired to have for her husband a man of the most incontestable bravery, she had formed her resolution not to marry any one save one who should show his courage by defending the Perilous Castle of Douglas against the Scots for a year and a day. Now this made some silence among the gentlemen present; for although the lady was rich and beautiful, yet there was great danger in placing themselves within the reach of the Good Lord James of Douglas. At last a brave young knight started up and said, that for the love of that lady he was willing to keep the Perilous Castle for a year and a day, if the King pleased to give him leave. The King of England was satisfied, and well pleased to get a brave man to hold a place so dangerous. Sir John Wilton was the name of this gallant knight. He kept the castle very safely for some time; but Douglas at last, by a stratagem,[1] induced him to venture out with a part of the garrison, and then set upon them and slew them. Wilton himself was killed, and a letter from the lady was found in his pocket. Douglas was sorry for his unhappy end, and did not put to death any of the prisoners as he had formerly done, but dismissed them in safety to the next English garrison.

Other great lords, besides Douglas, were now exerting themselves to attack and destroy the English. Amongst those was Sir Thomas Randolph, whose mother was a sister of King Robert. He had joined with the Bruce when he first took up arms. Afterwards being made prisoner by the English, when the King was defeated at Methven, as I told you, Sir Thomas Randolph was obliged to adhere to Edward First to save his life. He remained so constant in this, that he was in company with Aymer de Valence and John of Lorn when they forced the Bruce to disperse his little band; and he followed the pursuit so close, that he made his uncle's standard-bearer prisoner, and took his banner. Afterwards, however, he was himself made prisoner, at a solitary house on Lynewater,[2] by the Good Lord James Douglas, who brought him captive to the King. Robert reproached his nephew for having deserted his cause; and Randolph, who was very hot-tempered, answered insolently, and was sent by King Robert to prison. Shortly after, the uncle and nephew were reconciled, and Sir Thomas Randolph, created Earl of Murray by the King, was ever afterwards one of Bruce's best supporters. There was a sort of rivalry between Douglas and him, which should do the boldest and most hazardous actions. I will just mention one or two circumstances, which will show you what awful dangers were to be encountered by these brave men in order to free Scotland from its enemies and invaders.

While Robert Bruce was gradually getting possession of the country, and driving out the English, Edinburgh, the principal town of Scotland, remained, with its strong castle, in possession of the invaders. Sir Thomas Randolph was extremely desirous to gain this important place; but, as you well know, the castle is situated on a very steep and lofty

---

[1] This stratagem was, in its contrivance and success, the same as his former one, save that in place of cattle-driving, Sir James made fourteen of his men take so many sacks, and fill them with grass, as if corn for the county market-town of Lanark, distant twelve miles from the Castle of Douglas.—See Introduction to "Castle Dangerous," *Waverley Novels.*

[2] The Lyne falls into the Tweed a little above Peebles.

rock, so that it is difficult or almost impossible even to get up to the foot of the walls, much more to climb over them.

So while Randolph was considering what was to be done, there came to him a Scottish gentleman named Francis, who had joined Bruce's standard, and asked to speak with him in private. He then told Randolph that in his youth he had lived in the castle of Edinburgh, and that his father had then been keeper of the fortress. It happened at that time that Francis was much in love with a lady who lived in a part of the town beneath the castle, which is called the Grassmarket. Now, as he could not get out of the castle by day to see his mistress, he had practised a way of clambering by night down the castle rock on the south side, and returning at his pleasure; when he came to the foot of the wall, he made use of a ladder to get over it, as it was not very high at that point, those who built it having trusted to the steepness of the crag; and, for the same reason, no watch was placed there. Francis had gone and come so frequently in this dangerous manner that, though it was now long ago, he told Randolph he knew the road so well, that he would undertake to guide a small party of men by night to the bottom of the wall; and as they might bring ladders with them, there would be no difficulty in scaling it. The great risk was, that of their being discovered by the watchmen while in the act of ascending the cliff, in which case every man of them must have perished.

Nevertheless, Randolph did not hesitate to attempt the adventure. He took with him only thirty men (you may be sure they were chosen for activity and courage), and came one dark night to the foot of the rock, which they began to ascend under the guidance of Francis, who went before them, upon his hands and feet, up one cliff, down another, and round another, where there was scarce room to support themselves. All the while, these thirty men were obliged to follow in a line, one after the other, by a path that was fitter for a cat than a man. The noise of a stone falling, or a word spoken from one to another, would have alarmed the watchmen. They were obliged, therefore, to move with the greatest precaution. When they were far up the crag, and near the foundation of the wall, they heard the guards going their rounds, to see that all was safe in and about the castle. Randolph and his party had nothing for it but to lie close and quiet each man under the crag, as he happened to be placed, and trust that the guards would pass by without noticing them. And while they were waiting in breathless alarm, they got a new cause of fright. One of the soldiers of the castle, willing to startle his comrades, suddenly threw a stone from the wall, and cried out, "Aha, I see you well!" The stone came thundering down over the heads of Randolph and his men, who naturally thought themselves discovered. If they had stirred, or made the slightest noise, they would have been entirely destroyed; for the soldiers above might have killed every man of them merely by rolling down stones. But being courageous and chosen men, they remained quiet, and the English soldiers, who thought their comrade was merely playing them a trick (as, indeed, he had no other meaning in what he did and said), passed on, without further examination.

Then Randolph and his men got up, and came in haste to the foot of the wall, which was not above twice a man's height in that place. They planted the ladders they had brought, and Francis mounted first to show them the way; Sir Andrew Grey, a brave knight, followed him, and Randolph himself was the third man who got over. Then the rest followed. When once they were within the walls, there was not so much to do, for the garrison were asleep and unarmed, excepting the watch, who were speedily destroyed. Thus was Edinburgh castle taken in March 1312–13.

It was not, however, only by the exertions of great and powerful barons, like Randolph and Douglas, that the freedom of Scotland was to be accomplished. The stout yeomanry, and the bold peasantry of the land, who were as desirous to enjoy their cottages in honourable independence as the nobles were to reclaim their castles and estates from the English, contributed their full share in the efforts which were made to deliver their country from the invaders. I will give you one instance among many.

There was a strong castle near Linlithgow, or Lithgow, as the word is more generally pronounced, where an English governor, with a powerful garrison, lay in readiness to support the English cause, and used to exercise much severity upon the Scots in the neighbourhood. There lived, at no great distance from this stronghold, a farmer, a bold and stout man, whose name was Binnock, or as it is now pronounced, Binning. This man saw with great joy the progress which the Scots were making in recovering their country from the English, and resolved to do something to help his countrymen, by getting possession, if it were possible, of the castle of Lithgow. But the place was very strong, situated by the side of a lake, defended not only by gates, which were usually kept shut against strangers, but also by a portcullis. A portcullis is a sort of door formed of cross-bars of iron, like a grate. It has not hinges like a door, but is drawn up by pulleys, and let down when any danger approaches. It may be let go in a moment, and then falls down into the doorway; and as it has great iron spikes at the bottom, it crushes all that it lights upon; thus in case of a sudden alarm, a portcullis may be let suddenly fall to defend the entrance, when it is not possible to shut the gates. Binnock knew this very well, but he resolved to be provided against this risk also when he attempted to surprise the castle. So he spoke with some bold courageous countrymen, and engaged them in his enterprise, which he accomplished thus.

Binnock had been accustomed to supply the garrison of Linlithgow with hay, and he had been ordered by the English governor to furnish some cart-loads, of which they were in want. He promised to bring it accordingly; but the night before he drove the hay to the castle, he stationed a party of his friends, as well armed as possible, near the entrance, where they could not be seen by the garrison, and gave them directions that they should come to his assistance as soon as they should hear his signal, which was to be,—"Call all, call all!" Then he loaded a great waggon with hay. But in the waggon he placed eight strong men, well armed, lying flat on their breasts, and covered over with hay, so that they could not be seen. He himself walked carelessly beside the waggon, and he chose the stoutest and bravest of his servants to be the driver, who carried at his belt a strong axe or hatchet. In this way Binnock approached the castle early in the morning; and the watchman, who only saw two men, Binnock being one of them, with a cart of hay, which they expected, opened the gates, and raised up the portcullis, to permit them to enter the castle. But as soon as the cart had got under the gateway, Binnock made a sign to his servant, who with his axe suddenly cut asunder the *saom*, that is the yoke which fastens the horses to the cart, and the horses finding themselves free, naturally started forward, the cart remaining behind under the arch of the gate. At the same moment, Binnock cried as loud as he could, "Call all, call all!" and drawing the sword which he had under his country habit, he killed the porter. The armed men then jumped up from under the hay where they lay concealed, and rushed on the English guard. The Englishmen tried to shut the gates, but they could not, because the cart of hay remained in the gateway, and prevented the folding-doors from being closed. The portcullis was also let fall, but the grating was caught on the cart, and so could not drop to the ground. The men who were in ambush near the gate hearing the signal agreed on, ran to assist those who had leaped out from amongst the hay; the castle was taken, and all the Englishmen killed or made prisoners. King Robert rewarded Binnock by bestowing on him an estate, which his posterity long afterwards enjoyed.

Perhaps you may be tired, my dear child, of such stories; yet I will tell you how the great and important castle of Roxburgh was taken from the English, and then we will pass to other subjects.

You must know Roxburgh was then a very large castle, situated near where two fine rivers, the Tweed and the Teviot, join each other. Being within five or six miles of England, the English were extremely desirous of retaining it, and the Scots equally eager to obtain possession of it. I will tell you how it was taken.

It was upon the night of what is called Shrovetide, a holiday which Roman Catholics paid great respect to, and solemnised with much gaiety and feasting. Most of the garrison of Roxburgh Castle were drinking and carousing, but still they had set watches on the battlements of the castle, in case of any sudden attack; for, as the Scots had succeeded in so many enterprises of the kind, and as Douglas was known to be in the neighbourhood, they conceived themselves obliged to keep a very strict guard.

An Englishwoman, the wife of one of the officers, was sitting on the battlements with her child in her arms; and looking out on the fields below, she saw some black objects, like a herd of cattle, straggling near the foot of the wall, and approaching the ditch or moat of the castle. She pointed them out to the sentinel, and asked him what they were.—"Pooh, pooh," said the soldier, "it is farmer such a one's cattle" (naming a man whose farm lay near to the castle); "the good man is keeping a jolly Shrovetide, and has forgot to shut up his bullocks in their yard; but if the Douglas come across them before morning, he is likely to rue his negligence." Now these creeping objects which they saw from the castle wall were no real cattle, but Douglas himself and his soldiers, who had put black cloaks above their armour, and were creeping about on hands and feet, in order, without being observed, to get so near to the foot of the castle wall as to be able to set ladders to it. The poor woman, who knew nothing of this, sat quietly on the wall, and began to sing to her child. You must know that the name of Douglas had become so terrible to the English that the women used to frighten their children with it, and say to them, when they

behaved ill, that they "would make the Black Douglas take them." And
this soldier's wife was singing to her child,

> "Hush ye, hush ye, little pet ye,
> Hush ye, hush ye, do not fret ye,
> The Black Douglas shall not get ye."

"You are not so sure of that," said a voice close beside her. She felt
at the same time a heavy hand, with an iron glove, laid on her shoulder, and when she looked round, she saw the very Black Douglas she
had been singing about, standing close beside her, a tall, swarthy,
strong man. At the same time, another Scotsman was seen ascending
the walls, near to the sentinel. The soldier gave the alarm, and rushed
at the Scotsman, whose name was Simon Ledehouse, with his lance;
but Simon parried the stroke, and closing with the sentinel, struck him
a deadly blow with his dagger. The rest of the Scots followed up to
assist Douglas and Ledehouse, and the castle was taken. Many of the
soldiers were put to death, but Douglas protected the woman and the
child. I daresay she made no more songs about the Black Douglas.

While Douglas, Randolph, and other true-hearted patriots, were
thus taking castles and strongholds from the English. King Robert, who
had now a considerable army under his command, marched through
the country, beating and dispersing such bodies of English as he met
on his way. He went to the north country, where he conquered the
great and powerful family of Comyn, who retained strong ill-will
against him for having slain their relation, the Red Comyn. They had
joined the English with all their forces; but now, as the Scots began to
get the upper hand, they were very much distressed. Bruce caused
more than thirty of them to be beheaded in one day, and the place
where they are buried is called "the Grave of the headless Comyns."

Neither did Bruce forget or forgive John M'Dougal of Lorn, who
defeated him at Dalry, and had very nearly made him prisoner, by the
hands of his vassals, the M'Androssers, and afterwards pursued him
with a bloodhound. When John of Lorn heard that Bruce was marching against him, he hoped to defend himself by taking possession of a
very strong pass on the side of one of the largest mountains in Scotland, Ben Cruachen. The ground was very strait, having lofty rocks
on the one hand, and on the other deep precipices, sinking down on
a great lake called Lochawe; so that John of Lorn thought himself
perfectly secure, as he could not be attacked except in front, and by a

very difficult path. But King Robert, when he saw how his enemies were posted, sent a party of light-armed archers, under command of Douglas, with directions to go, by a distant and difficult road, around the northern side of the hill, and thus to attack the men of Lorn in the rear as well as in front; that is, behind, as well as before. He had signals made when Douglas arrived at the place appointed. The King then advanced upon the Lorn men in front, when they raised a shout of defiance, and began to shoot arrows and roll stones down the path, with great confidence in the security of their own position. But when they were attacked by the Douglas and his archers in the rear, the soldiers of M'Dougal lost courage and fled. Many were slain among the rocks and precipices, and many were drowned in the lake, and the great river which runs out of it. John of Lorn only escaped by means of a boat, which he had in readiness upon the lake. Thus King Robert had full revenge upon him, and deprived him of a great part of his territory.

The English now possessed scarcely any place of importance in Scotland, excepting Stirling, which was besieged, or rather blockaded, by Edward Bruce, the King's brother. To blockade a town or castle is to quarter an army around it, so as to prevent those within from getting provisions. This was done by the Scots before Stirling, till Sir Philip Mowbray, who commanded the castle, finding that he was likely to be reduced to extremity for want of provisions, made an agreement with Edward Bruce that he would surrender the place, provided he were not relieved by the King of England before midsummer. Sir Edward agreed to these terms, and allowed Mowbray to go to London, to tell King Edward of the conditions he had made. But when King Robert heard what his brother had done, he thought it was too great a risk, since it obliged him to venture a battle with the full strength of Edward II., who had under him England, Ireland, Wales, and great part of France, and could within the time allowed assemble a much more powerful army than the Scots could, even if all Scotland were fully under the King's authority. Sir Edward answered his brother with his naturally audacious spirit, "Let Edward bring every man he has, we will fight them, were they more." The King admired his courage, though it was mingled with rashness. "Since it is so, brother," he said, "we will manfully abide battle, and assemble all who love us, and value the freedom of Scotland, to come with all the men they have, and help us to oppose King Edward, should be come with his army to rescue Stirling."

X

The Battle of Bannockburn

1314

KING Edward II., as we have already said, was not a wise and brave man like his father, but a foolish prince, who was influenced by unworthy favourites, and thought more of pleasure than of governing his kingdom. His father, Edward I., would have entered Scotland at the head of a large army before he had left Bruce time to reconquer so much of the country. But we have seen that, very fortunately for the Scots, that wise and skilful, though ambitious King, died when he was on the point of marching into Scotland. His son Edward had afterwards neglected the Scottish war, and thus lost the opportunity of defeating Bruce when his force was small. But now when Sir Philip Mowbray, the governor of Stirling, came to London to tell the King that Stirling, the last Scottish town of importance which remained in possession of the English, was to be surrendered if it were not relieved by force of arms before midsummer, then all the English nobles called out it would be a sin and shame to permit the fair conquest which Edward I. had made to be forfeited to the Scots for want of fighting. It was, therefore, resolved, that the King should go himself to Scotland, with as great forces as he could possibly muster.

King Edward the Second, therefore, assembled one of the greatest armies which a King of England ever commanded. There were troops brought from all his dominions. Many brave soldiers from the provinces which the King of England possessed in France,—many Irish, many Welsh,—and all the great English nobles and barons, with their followers, were assembled in one great army. The number was not less than one hundred thousand men.

King Robert the Bruce summoned all his nobles and barons to join him, when he heard of the great preparation which the King of England was making. They were not so numerous as the English by many thousand men. In fact, his whole army did not very much exceed thirty thousand, and they were much worse armed than the wealthy Englishmen; but then Robert, who was at their head, was one of the most expert generals of the time; and the officers he had under him were his brother Edward, his nephew Randolph, his faithful follower the Douglas, and other brave and experienced leaders, who commanded the same men that had been accustomed to fight and gain victories under every disadvantage of situation and numbers.

The King, on his part, studied how he might supply, by address and stratagem, what he wanted in numbers and strength. He knew the superiority of the English, both in their heavy-armed cavalry, which were much better mounted and armed than that of the Scots, and in their archers, who were better trained than any others in the world. Both these advantages he resolved to provide against. With this purpose, he led his army down into a plain near Stirling, called the Park, near which, and beneath it, the English army must needs pass through a boggy country, broken with watercourses, while the Scots occupied hard dry ground. He then caused all the ground upon the front of his line of battle, where cavalry were likely to act, to be dug full of holes, about as deep as a man's knee. They were filled with light brushwood, and the turf was laid on the top, so that it appeared a plain field, while in reality it was all full of these pits as a honeycomb is of holes. He also, it is said, caused steel spikes, called calthrops, to be scattered up and down in the plain, where the English cavalry were most likely to advance, trusting in that manner to lame and destroy their horses.

When the Scottish army was drawn up, the line stretched north and south. On the south, it was terminated by the banks of the brook called Bannockburn, which are so rocky that no troops could attack them there. On the left, the Scottish line extended near to the town of Stirling. Bruce reviewed his troops very carefully; all the useless servants, drivers of carts, and such like, of whom there were very many, he ordered to go behind a height, afterwards, in memory of the event, called the Gillies' Hill, that is, the Servants' hill. He then spoke to the soldiers, and expressed his determination to gain the victory, or to lose his life on the field of battle. He desired that all those who did not propose to fight to the last should leave the field before the battle began, and that none should remain except those who were determined to take the issue of victory or death, as God should send it.

When the main body of his army was thus placed in order, the King posted Randolph, with a body of horse, near to the church of St. Ninian's, commanding him to use the utmost diligence to prevent any succours from being thrown into Stirling Castle. He then despatched James of Douglas, and Sir Robert Keith, the Mareschal of the Scottish army, in order that they might survey, as nearly as they could, the English force, which was now approaching from Falkirk. They returned with information that the approach of that vast host was one of the most beautiful and terrible sights which could be seen,—that the whole country seemed covered with men-at-arms on horse and foot,— that the number of standards, banners, and pennons (all flags of different kinds), made so gallant a show that the bravest and most numerous host in Christendom might be alarmed to see King Edward moving against them.

It was upon the 23d of June (1314) the King of Scotland heard the news, that the English were approaching Stirling. He drew out his army, therefore, in the order which he had before resolved on. After a short time Bruce, who was looking out anxiously for the enemy, saw a body of English cavalry trying to get into Stirling from the eastward. This was the Lord Clifford, who, with a chosen body of eight hundred horse, had been detached to relieve the castle.

"See, Randolph," said the King to his nephew, "there is a rose fallen from your chaplet." By this he meant, that Randolph had lost some honour, by suffering the enemy to pass where he had been stationed to hinder them. Randolph made no reply, but rushed against Clifford with little more than half his number. The Scots were on foot. The English turned to charge them with their lances, and Randolph drew up his men in close order to receive the onset. He seemed to be in so much danger that Douglas asked leave to go and assist him. The King refused him permission.

"Let Randolph," he said, "redeem his own fault; I cannot break the order of battle for his sake." Still the danger appeared greater, and the

English horse seemed entirely to encompass the small handful of Scottish infantry. "So please you," said Douglas to the King, "my heart will not suffer me to stand idle and see Randolph perish—I must go to his assistance." He rode off accordingly; but long before they had reached the place of combat, they saw the English horses galloping off, many with empty saddles.

"Halt!" said Douglas to his men, "Randolph has gained the day; since we were not soon enough to help him in the battle, do not let us lessen his glory by approaching the field." Now, that was nobly done; especially as Douglas and Randolph were always contending which should rise highest in the good opinion of the King and the nation.

The van of the English army now came in sight, and a number of their bravest knights drew near to see what the Scots were doing. They saw King Robert dressed in his armour, and distinguished by a gold crown, which he wore over his helmet. He was not mounted on his great warhorse, because he did not expect to fight that evening. But he rode on a little pony up and down the ranks of his army, putting his men in order, and carried in his hand a sort of battle-axe made of steel. When the King saw the English horsemen draw near, he advanced a little before his own men, that he might look at them more nearly.

There was a knight among the English, called Sir Henry de Bohun, who thought this would be a good opportunity to gain great fame to himself, and put an end to the war, by killing King Robert. The King being poorly mounted, and having no lance, Bohun galloped on him suddenly and furiously, thinking, with his long spear, and his tall powerful horse, easily to bear him down to the ground. King Robert saw him, and permitted him to come very near, then suddenly turned his pony a little to one side, so that Sir Henry missed him with the lance-point, and was in the act of being carried past him by the career of his horse. But as he passed, King Robert rose up in his stirrups, and struck Sir Henry on the head with his battle-axe so terrible a blow, that it broke to pieces his iron helmet as if it had been a nut-shell, and hurled him from his saddle. He was dead before he reached the ground. This gallant action was blamed by the Scottish leaders, who thought Bruce ought not to have exposed himself to so much danger when the safety of the whole army depended on him. The King only kept looking at his weapon, which was injured by the force of the blow, and said, "I have broken my good battle-axe."

The next morning being the 24th June, at break of day the battle began in terrible earnest. The English as they advanced saw the Scots getting into line. The Abbot of Inchaffray walked through their ranks barefooted, and exhorted them to fight for their freedom. They kneeled down as he passed, and prayed to Heaven for victory. King Edward, who saw this, called out, "They kneel down—they are asking forgiveness." "Yes," said a celebrated English baron, called Ingelram. de Umphraville, "but they ask it from God, not from us—these men will conquer, or die upon the field."

The English King ordered his men to begin the battle. The archers then bent their bows, and began to shoot so closely together that the arrows fell like flakes of snow on a Christmas day. They killed many of the Scots, and might, as at Falkirk and other places, have decided the victory; but Bruce, as I told you before, was prepared for them. He had in readiness a body of men-at-arms, well mounted, who rode at full gallop among the archers, and as they had no weapons save their bows and arrows, which they could not use when they were attacked hand to hand, they were cut down in great numbers by the Scottish horsemen, and thrown into total confusion.

The fine English cavalry then advanced to support their archers, and to attack the Scottish line. But coming over the ground which was dug full of pits, the horses fell into these holes, and the riders lay tumbling about, without any means of defence, and unable to rise, from the weight of their armour. The Englishmen began to fall into general disorder; and the Scottish King, bringing up more of his forces, attacked and pressed them still more closely.

On a sudden, while the battle was obstinately maintained on both sides, an event happened which decided the victory. The servants and attendants on the Scottish camp had, as I told you, been sent behind the army to a place afterwards called the Gillies' Hill. But when they saw that their masters were likely to gain the day, they rushed from their place of concealment with such weapons as they could get, that they might have their share in the victory and in the spoil. The English, seeing them come suddenly over the hill, mistook this disorderly rabble for another army coming to sustain the Scots, and, losing all heart, began to shift every man for himself. Edward left the field as fast as he could ride. A valiant knight, Sir Giles de Argentine, much renowned in the wars of Palestine, attended the King till he got him out of the press of the combat. But he would retreat no farther. "It is not my custom," he said, "to fly." With that he took leave of the King, set spurs to his horse, and calling out his war-cry of Argentine! Argentine! he rushed into the thickest of the Scottish ranks, and was killed.

The young Earl of Gloucester was also slain, fighting valiantly. The Scots would have saved him, but as he had not put on his armorial bearings, they did not know him, and he was cut to pieces.

Edward first fled to Stirling Castle, and entreated admittance. But Sir Philip Mowbray, the governor, reminded the fugitive Sovereign that he was obliged to surrender the castle next day, so Edward was fain to fly through the Torwood, closely pursued by Douglas with a body of cavalry. An odd circumstance happened during the chase, which showed how loosely some of the Scottish barons of that day held their political opinions. As Douglas was riding furiously after Edward, he met a Scottish knight, Sir Laurence Abernethy, with twenty horse. Sir Laurence had hitherto owned the English interest, and was bringing this band of followers to serve King Edward's army. But learning from Douglas that the English King was entirely defeated, he changed sides on the spot, and was easily prevailed upon to join Douglas in pursuing the unfortunate Edward, with the very followers whom he had been leading to join his standard.

Douglas and Abernethy continued the chase, not giving King Edward time to alight from horseback even for an instant, and followed him as far as Dunbar, where the English still had a friend in the governor, Patrick, Earl of March. The earl received Edward in his forlorn condition, and furnished him with a fishing skiff, or small ship, in which he escaped to England, having entirely lost his fine army, and a great number of his bravest nobles.

The English never before or afterwards, whether in France or Scotland, lost so dreadful a battle as that of Bannockburn, nor did the Scots ever gain one of the same importance. Many of the best and bravest of the English nobility and gentry, as I have said, lay dead on the field; a great many more were made prisoners; and the whole of King Edward's immense army was dispersed or destroyed.[1]

---

[1] "Multitudes of the English were drowned when attempting to cross the river Forth. Many, in their flight, fell into the pits, which they seem to have avoided in their first attack, and were there suffocated or slain; others, who vainly endeavoured to pass the rugged banks of the stream called Bannockburn, were slain in that quarter; so that this little river was so completely heaped up with the dead bodies of men and horses, that

The English, after this great defeat, were no longer in a condition to support their pretensions to be masters of Scotland, or to continue, as they had done for nearly twenty years, to send armies into that country to overcome it. On the contrary, they became for a time scarce able to defend their own frontiers against King Robert and his soldiers.

There were several battles fought within England itself, in which the English had greatly the worst. One of these took place near Mitton, in Yorkshire. So many priests took part in the fight, that the Scots called it the Chapter of Mitton,[2]—a meeting of the clergymen belonging to a cathedral being called a Chapter. There was a great slaughter in and after the action. The Scots laid waste the country of England as far as the gates of York, and enjoyed a considerable superiority over their ancient enemies, who had so lately threatened to make them subjects of England.

Thus did Robert Bruce arise from the condition of an exile, hunted with bloodhounds like a stag or beast of prey, to the rank of an independent sovereign, universally acknowledged to be one of the wisest and bravest kings who then lived. The nation of Scotland was also raised once more from the situation of a distressed and conquered province to that of a free and independent state, governed by its own laws, and subject to its own princes; and although the country was,

---

men might pass dry over the mass as if it were a bridge. Thirty thousand of the English were left dead upon the field; and amongst these two hundred belted knights, and seven hundred esquires. A large body of Welsh fled from the field, under the command of Sir Maurice Berkclay, but the greater part of them were slain, or taken prisoners, before they reached England. Such, also, might have been the fate of the King of England himself, had Bruce been able to spare a sufficient body of cavalry to follow up the fight."—"The riches obtained by the plunder of the English, and the subsequent ransom for the multitude of the prisoners, must have been very great. Their exact amount cannot be easily estimated, but some idea of its greatness may be formed by the tone of deep lamentation assumed by the Monk of Malmesburg. 'O day of vengeance and of misfortune!' says he (p. 152)—'day of disgrace and perdition! unworthy to be included in the circle of the year, which tarnished the fame of England, and enriched the Scots with the plunder of the precious stuffs of our nation, to the extent of two hundred thousand pounds (*nearly three millions of our present money*). Alas! of how many noble barons, and accomplished knights, and high-spirited young soldiers,—of what a store of excellent arms, and golden vessels, and costly vestments, did one short and miserable day deprive us!'—The loss of the Scots in the battle was incredibly small, and proves how effectually the Scottish squares had repelled the English cavalry. Sir William Vipont, and Sir Walter Ross, the bosom friend of Edward Bruce, were the only persons of note who were slain."—Tytler.

[2] "20th September 1319. Three hundred ecclesiastics fell in this battle."—Hailes.

after the Bruce's death, often subjected to great loss and distress, both by the hostility of the English, and by the unhappy civil wars among the Scots themselves, yet they never afterwards lost the freedom for which Wallace had laid down his life, and which King Robert had recovered, not less by his wisdom than by his weapons. And therefore most just it is, that while the country of Scotland retains any recollection of its history, the memory of those brave warriors and faithful patriots should be remembered with honour and gratitude.

XI

The End of Robert Bruce

1315-1330

YOU will be naturally curious to hear what became of Edward, the brother of Robert Bruce, who was so courageous, and at the same time so rash. You must know that the Irish, at that time, had been almost fully conquered by the English; but becoming weary of them, the Irish chiefs, or at least a great many of them, invited Edward Bruce to come over, drive out the English, and become their king. He was willing enough to go, for he had always a high courageous spirit, and desired to obtain fame and dominion by fighting. Edward Bruce was as good a soldier as his brother, but not so prudent and cautious; for, except in the affair of killing the Red Comyn, which was a wicked and violent action, Robert Bruce, in his latter days, showed himself as wise as he was courageous. However, he was well contented that his brother Edward, who had always fought so bravely for him, should be raised up to be King of Ireland. Therefore King Robert not only gave him an army to assist in making the conquest, but passed over the sea to Ireland himself in person, with a considerable body of troops, to assist him. The Bruces gained several battles, and penetrated far into Ireland; but the English forces were too numerous, and so many of the Irish joined with them rather than with Edward Bruce, that King Robert and his brother were obliged to retreat before them.

The chief commander of the English was a great soldier, called Sir Edmund Butler, and he had assembled a much greater army than Edward Bruce and his brother King Robert had to oppose to him. The Scots were obliged to retreat every morning, that they might not be forced to battle by an army more numerous than their own.

I have often told you that King Robert the Bruce was a wise and a good prince. But a circumstance happened during this retreat which showed he was also a kind and humane man. It was one morning, when the English and their Irish auxiliaries were pressing hard upon Bruce, who had given his army orders to continue a hasty retreat; for to have risked a battle with a much more numerous army, and in the midst of a country which favoured his enemies, would have been extremely imprudent. On a sudden, just as King Robert was about to mount his horse, he heard a woman shrieking in despair. "What is the matter?" said the King; and he was informed by his attendants that a poor woman, a laundress, or washerwoman, mother of an infant who had just been born, was about to be left behind the army, as being too weak to travel. The mother was shrieking for fear of falling into the hands of the Irish, who were accounted very cruel, and there were no carriages nor means of sending the woman and her infant on in safety. They must needs be abandoned if the army retreated.

King Robert was silent for a moment when he heard this story, being divided betwixt the feelings of humanity, occasioned by the poor woman's distress, and the danger to which a halt would expose his army. At last he looked round on his officers, with eyes which kindled like fire. "Ah, gentlemen," he said, "never let it be said that a man who was born of a woman, and nursed by a woman's tenderness, should leave a mother and an infant to the mercy of barbarians! In the name of God, let the odds and the risk be what they will, I will fight Edmund Butler rather than leave these poor creatures behind me. Let the army, therefore, draw up in line of battle, instead of retreating."

The story had a singular conclusion; for the English general, seeing that Robert the Bruce halted and offered him battle, and knowing that the Scottish King was one of the best generals then living, conceived that he must have received some large supply of forces, and was afraid to attack him. And thus Bruce had an opportunity to send off the poor woman and her child, and then to retreat at his leisure, without suffering any inconvenience from the halt.

But Robert was obliged to leave the conquest of Ireland to his brother Edward, being recalled by pressing affairs to his own country. Edward, who was rash as he was brave, engaged, against the advice of his best officers, in battle with an English general, called Sir Piers de Bermingham. The Scots were surrounded on all sides, but continued to defend themselves valiantly, and Edward Bruce showed the example by fighting in the very front of the battle. At length a strong English champion, called John Maupas, engaged Edward hand to hand; and they fought till they killed each other. Maupas was found lying after the battle upon the body of Bruce, both were dead men.[1] After Edward Bruce's death, the Scots gave up further attempts to conquer Ireland.

Robert Bruce continued to reign gloriously for several years, and was so constantly victorious over the English, that the Scots seemed during his government to have acquired a complete superiority over their neighbours. But then we must remember that Edward II., who then reigned in England, was a foolish prince, and listened to bad counsels; so that it is no wonder that he was beaten by so wise and experienced a general as Robert Bruce, who had fought his way to the crown through so many disasters, and acquired in consequence so much renown that, as I have often said, he was generally accounted one of the best soldiers and wisest sovereigns of his time.

In the last year of Robert the Bruce's reign he became extremely sickly and infirm, chiefly owing to a disorder called the leprosy, which he had caught during the hardships and misfortunes of his youth, when he was so frequently obliged to hide himself in woods and morasses, without a roof to shelter him. He lived at a castle called Cardross, on the beautiful banks of the river Clyde, near to where it joins the sea; and his chief amusement was to go upon the river, and down to the sea in a ship, which he kept for his pleasure. He was no longer able to sit upon his war-horse, or to lead his army to the field.

---

[1] "The corpse of Edward Bruce was not treated with honours like those which the King of Scots bestowed on the brave English who fell at Bannockburn. His body was quartered, and distributed for a public spectacle over Ireland. Bermingham presented the head of Edward Bruce to the English King, and obtained the dignity of *Earl of Louth,* as a reward of his services."—Hailes.

While Bruce was in this feeble state, Edward II., King of England, died, and was succeeded by his son Edward III. He turned out afterwards to be one of the wisest and bravest kings whom England ever had; but when he first mounted the throne he was very young, and under the entire management of his mother, who governed by means of a wicked favourite called Mortimer.

The war between the English and the Scots still lasting at the time, Bruce sent his two great commanders, the Good Lord James Douglas, and Thomas Randolph, Earl of Murray, to lay waste the counties of Northumberland and Durham, and distress the English as much as they could.

Their soldiers were about twenty thousand in number, all lightly armed, and mounted on horses that were but small in height, but excessively active. The men themselves carried no provision, except a bag of oatmeal; and each had at his saddle a small plate of iron called a girdle, on which, when they pleased, they could bake the oatmeal into cakes. They killed the cattle of the English, as they travelled through the country, roasted the flesh on wooden spits, or boiled it in the skins of the animals themselves, putting in a little water with the beef, to prevent the fire from burning the hide to pieces. This was rough cookery. They made their shoes, or rather sandals, in as coarse a way; cutting them out of the raw hides of the cattle, and fitting them to their ankles, like what are now called short gaiters. As this sort of buskin had the hairy side of the hide outermost, the English called those who wore them *rough-footed* Scots, and sometimes, from the colour of the hide, *red-shanks.*

As such forces needed to carry nothing with them, either for provisions or ammunition, the Scots moved with amazing speed, from mountain to mountain, and from glen to glen, pillaging and destroying the country wherever they came. In the meanwhile, the young King of England pursued them with a much larger army; but as it was encumbered by the necessity of carrying provisions in great quantities, and by the slow motions of men in heavy armour, they could not come up with the Scots, although they saw every day the smoke of the houses and villages which they were burning. The King of England was extremely angry; for, though only a boy of sixteen years old, he longed to fight the Scots, and to chastise them for the mischief they were doing to his country; and at length he grew so impatient, that he offered a large reward to any one who would show him where the Scottish army were.

At length, after the English host had suffered severe hardships, from want of provisions, and fatiguing journeys through fords, and swamps, and morasses, a gentleman named Rokeby came into the camp, and claimed the reward which the King had offered. He told the King that he had been made prisoner by the Scots, and that they had said they should be as glad to meet the English King as he to see them. Accordingly, Rokeby guided the English army to the place where the Scots lay encamped.

But the English King was no nearer to the battle which he desired; for Douglas and Randolph, knowing the force and numbers of the English army, had taken up their camp on a steep hill, at the bottom of which ran a deep river, called the Wear, having a channel filled with large stones, so that there was no possibility for the English to attack the Scots without crossing the water, and then climbing up the steep hill in the very face of their enemy; a risk which was too great to be attempted.

Then the King sent a message of defiance to the Scottish generals, inviting them either to draw back their forces, and allow him freedom to cross the river, and time to place his army in order of battle on the other side, that they might fight fairly, or offering, if they liked it better, to permit them to cross over to his side without opposition, that they might join battle on a fair field. Randolph and Douglas did nothing but laugh at this message. They said, that when they fought, it should be at their own pleasure, and not because the King of England chose to ask for a battle. They reminded him, insultingly, how they had been in his country for many days, burning, taking spoil, and doing what they thought fit. If the King was displeased with this, they said, he must find his way across the river to fight them the best way he could.

The English King, determined not to quit sight of the Scots, encamped on the opposite side of the river to watch their motions, thinking that want of provisions would oblige them to quit their strong position on the mountains. But the Scots once more showed Edward their dexterity in marching, by leaving their encampment, and taking up another post, even stronger and more difficult to approach than the first which they had occupied. King Edward followed, and again encamped opposite to his dexterous and troublesome enemies, desirous to bring them to a battle, when he might hope to gain an easy victory, having more than double the number of the Scottish army, all troops of the very best quality.

While the armies lay thus opposed to each other, Douglas resolved to give the young King of England a lesson in the art of war. At the dead of night he left the Scottish camp with a small body of chosen horse, not above two hundred, well armed. He crossed the river in deep silence, and came to the English camp, which was but carelessly guarded. Seeing this, Douglas rode past the English sentinels as if he had been an officer of the English army, saying,—"Ha, Saint George! You keep bad watch here."—In those days, you must know, the English used to swear by Saint George, as the Scots did by Saint Andrew. Presently after, Douglas heard an English soldier, who lay stretched by the fire, say to his comrade,—"I cannot tell what is to happen to us in this place; but, for my part, I have a great fear of the Black Douglas playing us some trick."

"You shall have cause to say so," said Douglas to himself

When he had thus got into the midst of the English camp without being discovered, he drew his sword and cut asunder the ropes of a tent, calling out his usual war-cry,—"Douglas, Douglas! English thieves, you are all dead men." His followers immediately began to cut down and overturn the tents, cutting and stabbing the English soldiers as they endeavoured to get to arms.

Douglas forced his way to the pavilion of the King himself, and very nearly carried that young prince prisoner out of the middle of his great army. Edward's chaplain, however, and many of his household, stood to arms bravely in his defence, while the young King escaped by creeping away beneath the canvas of his tent. The chaplain and several of the King's officers were slain; but the whole camp was now alarmed and in arms, so that Douglas was obliged to retreat, which he did by bursting through the English at the side of the camp opposite to that by which he had entered. Being separated from his men in the confusion, he was in great danger of being slain by an Englishman who encountered him with a huge club. This man he killed, but with considerable difficulty; and then blowing his horn to collect his soldiers, who soon gathered around him, he returned to the Scottish camp, having sustained very little loss.

Edward, much mortified at the insult which he had received, became still more desirous of chastising those audacious adversaries; and one of them at least was not unwilling to afford him an opportunity of revenge. This was Thomas Randolph, Earl of Murray. He asked Douglas when he returned to the Scottish camp, "What he had done?"—"We have drawn some blood."—"Ah," said the earl, "had we gone all together to the night attack, we should have discomfited them."—"It might well have been so," said Douglas, "but the risk would have been too great."—"Then will we fight them in open battle," said Randolph, "for if we remain here, we shall in time be famished for want of provisions."—"Not so," replied Douglas; "we will deal with this great army of the English as the fox did with the fisherman in the fable."—"And how was that?" said the Earl of Murray.—Hereupon the Douglas told him this story:—

"A fisherman," he said, "had made a hut by a riverside, that he might follow his occupation of fishing. Now, one night he had gone out to look after his nets, leaving a small fire in his hut; and when he came back, behold there was a fox in the cabin, taking the liberty to eat one of the finest salmon he had taken. 'Ho, Mr. Robber!' said the fisherman, drawing his sword, and standing in the doorway to prevent the fox's escape, 'you shall presently die the death.' The poor fox looked for some hole to get out at, but saw none; whereupon he pulled down with his teeth a mantle, which was lying on the bed, and dragged it across the fire. The fisherman ran to snatch his mantle from the fire—the fox flew out at the door with the salmon;—and so," said Douglas, "shall we escape the great English army by subtilty, and without risking battle with so large a force."

Randolph agreed to act by Douglas's counsel, and the Scottish army kindled great fires through their encampment, and made a noise and shouting, and blowing of horns, as if they meant to remain all night there, as before. But in the meantime Douglas had caused a road to be made through two miles of a great morass which lay in their rear. This was done by cutting down to the bottom of the bog, and filling the trench with faggots of wood. Without this contrivance it would have been impossible that the army could have crossed; and through this passage, which the English never suspected, Douglas and Randolph, and all their men, moved at the dead of night. They did not leave so much as an errand-boy behind, and so bent their march towards Scotland, leaving the English disappointed and affronted. Great was their wonder in the morning when they saw the Scottish camp empty, and found no living men in it, but two or three English prisoners tied to trees, whom they had left with an insulting message to the King of England, saying, "If he were displeased with what they had done, he might come and revenge himself in Scotland."

The place where the Scots fixed this famous encampment, was in the forest of Weardale, in the bishopric of Durham; and the road which they cut for the purpose of their retreat, is still called the *Shorn Moss*.

After this a peace was concluded with Robert Bruce, on terms highly honourable to Scotland; for the English King renounced all pretensions to the sovereignty of the country, and, moreover, gave his sister, a princess called Joanna, to be wife to Robert Bruce's son, called David. This treaty was very advantageous for the Scots. It was called the treaty of Northampton, because it was concluded at that town in the year 1328.

Good King Robert did not long survive this joyful event. He was not aged more than fifty-four years, but, as I said before, his bad health was caused by the hardships which he sustained during his youth, and at length he became very ill. Finding that he could not recover, he assembled around his bedside the nobles and counsellors in whom he most trusted. He told them, that now, being on his deathbed, he sorely repented all his misdeeds, and particularly, that he had, in his passion, killed Comyn with his own hand, in the church and before the altar. He said that if he had lived, he had intended to go to Jerusalem, to make war upon the Saracens who held the Holy Land, as some expiation for the evil deeds he had done. But since he was about to die, he requested of his dearest friend and bravest warrior, and that was the Good Lord James Douglas, that he should carry his heart to the Holy Land.

To make you understand the meaning of this request, I must tell you, that at this time a people called Saracens, who believed in the false prophet Mahomet, had obtained by conquest possession of Jerusalem, and the other cities and places which are mentioned in the Holy Scripture; and the Christians of Europe, who went thither as pilgrims to worship at these places, where so many miracles had been wrought, were insulted by these heathen Saracens. Hence many armies of Christians went from their own countries out of every kingdom of Europe, to fight against these Saracens; and believed that they were doing a great service to religion, and that what sins they had committed would be pardoned by God Almighty, because they had taken a part in this which they called a holy warfare. You may remember that Bruce thought of going upon this expedition when he was in despair of recovering the crown of Scotland; and now he desired his heart to be carried to Jerusalem after his death, and requested Lord James of

Douglas to take the charge of it. Douglas wept bitterly as he accepted this office,—the last mark of the Bruce's confidence and friendship.

The King soon afterwards expired [at Cardross]; and his heart was taken out from his body and embalmed, that is, prepared with spices and perfumes, that it might remain a long time fresh and uncorrupted. Then the Douglas caused a case of silver to be made, into which he put the Bruce's heart, and wore it around his neck, by a string of silk and gold. And he set forward for the Holy Land, with a gallant train of the bravest men in Scotland, who, to show their value and sorrow for their brave King Robert, resolved to attend his heart to the city of Jerusalem. It had been much better for Scotland if the Douglas and his companions had stayed at home to defend their own country, which was shortly afterwards in great want of their assistance.

Neither did Douglas ever get to the end of his journey. In going to Palestine he landed in Spain, where the Saracen King, or Sultan of Grenada, called Osmyn, was invading the realms of Alphonso, the Spanish King of Castile. King Alphonso received Douglas with great honour and distinction, and people came from all parts to see the great soldier, whose fame was well known through every part of the Christian world. King Alphonso easily persuaded the Scottish earl, that he would do good service to the Christian cause, by assisting him to drive back the Saracens of Grenada, before proceeding on his voyage to Jerusalem. Lord Douglas and his followers went accordingly to a great battle against Osmyn, and had little difficulty in defeating the Saracens who were opposed to them. But being ignorant of the mode of fighting among the cavalry of the East, the Scots pursued the chase too far, and the Moors, when they saw them scattered and separated from each other, turned suddenly back, with a loud cry of *Allah illah Allah,* which is their shout of battle, and surrounded such of the Scottish knights and squires as had advanced too hastily, and were dispersed from each other.

In this new skirmish, Douglas saw Sir William St. Clair of Roslyn fighting desperately, surrounded by many Moors, who were hewing at him with their sabres. "Yonder worthy knight will be slain," Douglas said, "unless he have instant help." With that he galloped to his rescue, but presently was himself also surrounded by many Moors. When he found the enemy press so thick round him, as to leave him no chance of escaping, the Earl took from his neck the Bruce's heart, and speaking to it, as he would have done to the King had he been alive,—"Pass first in fight," he said, "as thou were wont to do, and Douglas will follow thee, or die." He then threw the King's heart among the enemy, and rushing forward to the place where it fell, was there slain. His body was found lying above the silver case, as if it had been his last object to defend the Bruce's heart.

This Good Lord James of Douglas was one of the best and wisest soldiers that ever drew a sword. He was said to have fought in seventy battles, being beaten in thirteen, and victorious in fifty-seven. The English accused him of being cruel; and it is said that he had such a hatred of the English archers, that when he made one of them prisoner, he would not dismiss him until he was either blinded of his right eye, or had the first finger of his right hand struck off. The Douglas's Larder also seems a very cruel story; but the hatred at that time betwixt the two countries was at a high pitch, and Lord James was much irritated at the death of his faithful servant Thomas Dickson; on ordinary occasions he was mild and gentle to his prisoners. The Scottish historians describe the good Lord James as one who was never dejected by bad fortune, or unduly elated by that which was good. They say he was modest and gentle in time of peace, but had a very different countenance upon the day of battle. He was tall, strong, and well made, of a swarthy complexion, with dark hair, from which he was called the Black Douglas. He lisped a little in his speech, but in a manner which became him very much. Notwithstanding the many battles in which he had fought, his face had escaped without a wound. A brave Spanish knight at the court of King Alphonso, whose face was scarred by the marks of Moorish sabres, expressed wonder that Douglas's countenance should be unmarked with wounds. Douglas replied modestly, he thanked God, who had always enabled his hands to guard and protect his face.

Many of Douglas's followers were slain in the battle in which he himself fell. The rest resolved not to proceed on their journey to Palestine, but to return to Scotland. Since the time of the Good Lord James, the Douglases have carried upon their shields a bloody heart, with a crown upon it, in memory of this expedition. I formerly, when speaking of William the Lion, explained to you, that in ancient times men painted such emblems on their shields that they might be known by them in battle, for their helmet hid their face; and that now, as men no longer wear armour in battle, the devices, as they are called, belonging to particular families, are engraved upon their seals, or upon their silver plate, or painted upon their carriages.

Thus, for example, there was one of the brave knights who was in the company of Douglas, and was appointed to take charge of the Bruce's heart homewards again, who was called Sir Simon Lockhard of Lee. He took afterwards for his device, and painted on his shield, a man's heart, with a padlock upon it, in memory of Bruce's heart, which was padlocked in the silver case. For this reason, men changed Sir Simon's name from Lockhard to Lockheart, and all who are descended from Sir Simon are called Lockhart to this day. Did you ever hear of such a name, Master Hugh Littlejohn?

Well, such of the Scottish knights as remained alive returned to their own country. They brought back the heart of the Bruce, and the bones of the Good Lord James. These last were interred in the church of St. Bride, where Thomas Dickson and Douglas held so terrible a Palm Sunday. The Bruce's heart was buried below the high altar in Melrose Abbey. As for his body, it was laid in the sepulchre in the midst of the church of Dunfermline, under a marble stone. But the church becoming afterwards ruinous, and the roof falling down with age, the monument was broken to pieces, and nobody could tell where it stood. But a little while before Master Hugh Littlejohn was born, which I take to be six or seven years ago, when they were repairing the church at Dunfermline, and removing the rubbish, lo! they found fragments of the marble tomb of Robert Bruce. Then they began to dig farther, thinking to discover the body of this celebrated monarch; and at length they came to the skeleton of a tall man, and they knew it must be that of King Robert, both as he was known to have been buried in a winding-sheet of cloth of gold, of which many fragments were found about this skeleton, and also because the breastbone appeared to have been sawed through, in order to take out the heart. So orders were sent from the King's Court of Exchequer to guard the bones carefully, until a new tomb should be prepared, into which they were laid with profound respect. A great many gentlemen and ladies attended, and almost all the common people in the neighbourhood; and as the church could not hold half the numbers, the people were allowed to pass through it, one after another, that each one, the poorest as well as the richest, might see all that remained of the great King Robert Bruce, who restored the Scottish monarchy. Many people shed tears; for there was the wasted skull, which once was the head that thought so wisely and boldly for his country's deliverance; and there was the dry bone, which had once been the sturdy arm that killed Sir Henry de Bohun, between the two armies, at a single blow, on the evening before the battle of Bannockburn.

It is more than five hundred years since the body of Bruce was first laid into the tomb; and how many many millions of men have died since that time, whose bones could not be recognised, nor their names known, any more than those of inferior animals! It was a great thing to see that the wisdom, courage, and patriotism of a King, could preserve him for such a long time in the memory of the people over whom he once reigned. But then, my dear child, you must remember, that it is only desirable to be remembered for praiseworthy and patriotic actions, such as those of Robert Bruce. It would be better for a prince to be forgotten like the meanest peasant, than to be recollected for actions of tyranny or oppression.

XII

Feudal Scotland

1330

I FEAR my dear Hugh, that this will be rather a dull Chapter, and somewhat difficult to be understood; but if you do not quite comprehend
it at the first reading, you may perhaps do so upon a second trial, and I
will strive to be as plain and distinct as I can.

As Scotland was never so great nor so powerful as during the reign
of Robert Bruce, it is a fit time to tell you the sort of laws by which the
people were governed, and the society which then subsisted.

And first, you must observe, that there are two kinds of government; one called *despotic* or *absolute,* in which the king can do whatever he pleases with his subjects—seize upon their property, or deprive
them of their lives at pleasure. This is the case of almost all the kingdoms of the East, where the kings, emperors, sultans, or whatever
other name they bear, may do whatever they like to their subjects,
without being controlled by any one. It is very unfortunate for the
people who live under such a government, whose subjects can be considered as no better than slaves, neither life nor property being safe.
Some kings, it is true, are good men, and use the power which is put
into their hands only to do good to the people. But then others are
thoughtless; and cunning and wicked persons contrive to get their
confidence, by flattery and other base means, and lead them to do

injustice, even when perhaps they themselves do not think of it. And, besides, there are bad kings, who, if they have the uncontrolled power of taking the money and the goods of their subjects, of throwing them into prison, or putting them to death at their pleasure, are apt to indulge their cruelty and their greediness at the expense of the people, and are called by the hateful name of Tyrants.

Those states are therefore a thousand times more happy which have what is called a free government; that is, where the king himself is subject to the laws, and cannot rule otherwise than by means of them. In such governments the king is controlled and directed by the laws, and can neither put a man to death unless he has been found guilty of some crime for which the law condemns him to die, nor force him to pay any money beyond what the laws give the sovereign a right to collect for the general expenses of the state. Almost all the nations of modern Europe have been originally free governments; but, in several of them, the kings have acquired a great deal too much power, although not to such an unbounded degree as we find in the Eastern countries. But few countries, like that of Great Britain, have had the good fortune to retain a free constitution, which protects and preserves those who live under it from all oppression, or arbitrary power. We owe this blessing to our brave ancestors, who were at all times ready to defend these privileges with their lives; and we are, on our part, bound to hand them down, in as ample form as we receive them, to the posterity who shall come after us.

In Scotland, and through most countries of Europe, the principles of freedom were protected by the Feudal System, which was now universally introduced. You recollect that the king, according to that system, bestowed large estates upon the nobles and great barons, who were called vassals for the fiefs, or possessions, which they thus received from the king, and were obliged to follow him when he summoned them to battle, and to attend upon his Great Council, in which all matters concerning the affairs of the kingdom were considered, and resolved upon. It was in this great council, now called a Parliament, that the laws of the kingdom were resolved upon, or altered, at the pleasure, not of the king alone, nor of the council alone, but as both the king and council should agree together. I must now tell you particularly how this great council was composed, and who had the privilege of sitting there.

At first, there is no doubt that every vassal who held lands directly of the crown had this privilege; and a baron, or royal vassal, not only had the right, but was obliged, to attend the great council of the kingdom. Accordingly, all the great nobility usually came on the king's summons; but then it was very inconvenient and expensive for men of smaller estates to be making long journeys to the Parliament, and remaining, perhaps, for many days, or weeks, absent from their own families, and their own business. Besides, if all the royal vassals, or free-holders, as they began to be called, had chosen to attend, the number of the assembly would have been far too great for any purpose of delib-eration—it would not have been possible to find a room large enough to hold such a meeting, nor could any one have spoken so as to have made himself understood by such an immense multitude. From this it happened that, instead of attending all of them in their own persons, the lesser barons (as the smaller freeholders were called, to distinguish them from the great nobles) assembled in their different districts, or shires, as the divisions of the country are termed, and there made choice of one or two of the wisest and most experienced of their number to attend the Parliament, or great council, in the name, and to take care of the interest, of the whole body. Thus the crown vassals who attended upon and composed the Parliament, or the National Council of Scotland, came to consist of two different bodies; namely, the peers, or great nobility, whom the king especially summoned, and such of the lesser barons as were sent to represent the crown vassals in the different shires or counties of Scotland. But besides these two dif-ferent classes, the great council also contained the representatives of the clergy, and of the boroughs, or considerable towns.

In the times of the Roman Catholic religion, the churchmen exer-cised very great power and authority in every kingdom of Europe, and omitted no opportunity by which their importance could be magni-fied. It is therefore not wonderful that the chief men of the clergy, such as the bishops, and those abbots of the great abbeys who were called mitred abbots, from their being entitled to wear mitres, like bishops, should have obtained seats in Parliament. They were admitted there for the purpose of looking after the affairs of the church, and ranked along with the peers or nobles having titles.

It remains to mention the boroughs. You must know, that in order to increase the commerce and industry of the country, and also to estab-lish some balance against the immense power of the great lords, the kings of Scotland, from an early period, had been in the use of granting considerable privileges to many of the towns in their dominions, which, in consequence of the charters which they obtained from the crown, were termed royal boroughs. The citizens of these boroughs had the privilege of electing their own magistrates, and had considerable revenues, some from lands conferred on them by the king, others from tolls and taxes upon commodities brought into the town. These revenues were laid out by the magistrates (usually called the provost and bailies), for the use of the town. The same magistrates, in those warlike days, led out the burghers, or townsmen, to battle, either in defence of the town's lands and privileges, which were often attacked by the great lords and barons in their neighbourhood, or for the purpose of fighting against the English. The burghers were all well trained to arms, and were obliged to attend the king's army, or host, whenever they were summoned to do so. They were also bound to defend the town itself, which had in most cases walls and gates. This was called keeping watch and ward. Besides other privileges, the boroughs had the very important right of sending representatives or commissioners, who sat in Parliament, to look after the interests of the towns which they represented, as well as to assist in the general affairs of the nation.

You may here remark that, so far as we have gone, the Scottish Parliament entirely resembled the English in the nature of its constitution. But there was this very material difference in the mode of transacting business, that in England, the peers, or great nobility, with the bishops and great abbots, sat, deliberated, and voted, in a body by themselves, which was called the House of Lords, or of Peers, and the representatives of the counties, or shires, together with those of the boroughs, occupied a different place of meeting, and were called the Lower House, or House of Commons. In Scotland, on the contrary, the nobles, prelates, representatives for the shires, and delegates for the boroughs, all sat in the same apartment, and debated and voted as members of the same assembly. Since the union of the kingdoms of England and Scotland, the Parliament, which represents both countries, sits and votes in two distinct bodies, called the two Houses of Parliament, and there are many advantages attending that form of conducting the national business.

You now have some idea of the nature of the Parliament, or grand council of the nation, and of the various classes of persons who had a right to sit there. I am next to tell you, that they were summoned together and dismissed by the king's orders; and that all business belonging to the nation was transacted by their advice and opinion. Whatever measures they proposed passed into laws, on receiving the consent of the king, which was intimated by touching with the sceptre the bills that were passed by the Parliament. Thus you see that the laws by which the country was governed were, in a great measure, of the people's own making, being agreed to by their representatives in Parliament. When, in particular, it was necessary to raise money for any public purpose, there was a necessity for obtaining the consent of Parliament, both as to the amount of the sum, and the manner in which it was to be collected; so that the king could not raise any money from his subjects, without the approbation of his grand council.

It may be said, in general, of the Scottish laws, that they were as wisely adapted for the purpose of government as those of any state in Europe, at that early period; nay, more, that they exhibit the strongest marks of foresight and sagacity. But it was the great misfortune of Scotland, that the good laws which the kings and Parliaments agreed upon were not carried steadily into execution; but, on the contrary, were broken through and neglected, just as if they had not existed at all. I will endeavour to explain some of the causes of this negligence.

The principal evil was the great power of the nobility, which was such as to place them almost beyond the control of the king's authority. The chief noblemen had obtained the right of administering justice each upon his own estate; and therefore the whole power of detecting, trying, and punishing crimes, rested in the first place with those great men. Now, most of those great lords were much more interested in maintaining their own authority, and extending their own power, within the provinces which they occupied, than in promoting general good order and tranquillity throughout the country at large. They were almost constantly engaged in quarrels with each other, and often with the king himself. Sometimes they fought amongst themselves, sometimes they united together against the sovereign. On all occasions they were disposed for war, rather than peace, and therefore took little care to punish the criminals who offended against public order. Instead of bringing to trial the persons who committed murder, robbery, and other violent actions, they often protected them, and enlisted them in their own immediate service; and frequently, from revenge or ambition, were actually the private encouragers of the mischief which these men perpetrated.

The judges named by the king, and acting under his authority, had a right indeed to apprehend and to punish such offenders against the public peace when they could get hold of them; but then it was very difficult to seize upon the persons accused of such acts of violence, when the powerful lords in whose territory they lived were disposed to assist them in concealing themselves, or making their escape. And even when the king's courts were able to seize such culprits, there was a law which permitted the lord on whose territory the crime had been committed, to demand that the accused person should be delivered up to him, to be tried in his own court. A nobleman or baron making such a demand was, indeed, obliged to give security that he would execute justice on the persons within a certain reasonable time. But such was the weakness of the royal government, and such the great power of the nobility, and the barons of high rank, that if they once got the person accused into their own hand, they might easily contrive either to let him escape, or to have him acquitted after a mock trial. Thus it was always difficult, and often impossible, to put in execution the good laws which were made in the Scottish Parliament, on account of the great power possessed by the nobles, who, in order to preserve and extend their own authority, threw all manner of interruption in the way of public justice.

Each of these nobles within the country which was subject to him, more resembled a king himself than a subject of the monarch of Scotland: and, in one or two instances, we shall see that some of them became so powerful as to threaten to dispossess the king of his throne and dominions. The very smallest of them often made war on each other without the king's consent, and thus there was a universal scene of disorder and bloodshed through the whole country. These disorders seemed to be rendered perpetual, by a custom which was called by the name of *deadly feud*. When two men of different families quarrelled, and the one injured or slew the other, the relatives of the deceased, or wronged person, knowing that the laws could afford them no redress, set about obtaining revenge, by putting to death some relation of the individual who had done the injury, without regarding how innocent the subject of their vengeance might have been of the original cause of offence. Then the others, in their turn, endeavoured to execute a similar revenge upon some one of the family who had first received the injury; and thus the quarrel was carried on from father to son, and often lasted betwixt families that were neighbours and ought to have been good friends, for several generations, during which time they were said to be at *deadly feud* with each other.

From the want of due exercise of the laws, and from the revengeful disposition which led to such long and fatal quarrels, the greatest distresses ensued to the country. When, for example, the kings of Scotland

assembled their armies, in order to fight against the English, who were
then the public enemy, they could bring together indeed a number of
brave nobles, with their followers, but there always was great difficulty,
and sometimes an absolute impossibility, of making them act together;
each chief being jealous of his own authority, and many of them
engaged in personal quarrels, either of their own making, or such as
existed in consequence of this fatal and cruel custom of *deadly feud,*
which, having been originally perhaps some quarrel of little importance, had become inveterate by the cruelties and crimes which had
been committed on both sides, and was handed down from father to
son. It is true, that under a wise and vigorous prince, like Robert the
Bruce, those powerful barons were overawed by his wisdom and
authority; but we shall see too often, that when kings and generals of
inferior capacity were at their head, their quarrels amongst themselves
often subjected them to defeat and to disgrace. And this accounts for a
fact which we shall often have occasion to notice, that when the Scots
engaged in great battles with large armies, in which, of course, many of
those proud independent nobles were assembled, they were frequently
defeated by the English: whereas, when they fought in smaller bodies
with the same enemy, they were much more often victorious over
them; because at such times the Scots were agreed among themselves,
and obeyed the commands of one leader, without pretending to dispute his authority.

These causes of private crimes and public defeat subsisted even in
the midland counties of Scotland, such as the three Lothians, Fifeshire,
and other provinces, where the king generally resided, and where he
necessarily possessed most power to maintain his own authority, and
enforce the execution of the laws. But there were two great divisions of
the country, the Highlands namely, and the Borders, which were so
much wilder and more barbarous than the others, that they might be
said to be altogether without law; and although they were nominally
subjected to the King of Scotland, yet when he desired to execute any
justice in either of those great districts, he could not do so otherwise
than by marching there in person, at the head of a strong body of
forces, and seizing upon the offenders, and putting them to death with
little or no form of trial. Such a rough course of justice, perhaps, made
these disorderly countries quiet for a short time, but it rendered them
still more averse to the royal government in their hearts, and disposed
on the slightest occasion to break out, either into disorders amongst

themselves, or into open rebellion. I must give you some more particular account of these wild and uncivilised districts of Scotland, and of the particular sort of people who were their inhabitants, that you may know what I mean when I speak of Highlanders and Borderers.

The Highlands of Scotland, so called from the rocky and mountainous character of the country, consist of a very large proportion of the northern parts of that kingdom. It was into these pathless wildernesses that the Romans drove the ancient inhabitants of Great Britain; and it was from these that they afterwards sallied to invade and distress that part of Britain which the Romans had conquered, and in some degree civilized. The inhabitants of the Highlands spoke, and still speak, a language totally different from the Lowland Scots. That last language does not greatly differ from English, and the inhabitants of both countries easily understand each other, though neither of them comprehend the Gaelic, which is the language of the Highlanders. The dress of these mountaineers was also different from that of the Lowlanders. They wore a plaid, or mantle of frieze, or of a striped stuff called tartan, one end of which being wrapt round the waist, formed a short petticoat, which descended to the knee, while the rest was folded round them like a sort of cloak. They had buskins made of raw hide; and those who could get a bonnet, had that covering for their heads, though many never wore one during their whole lives, but had only their own shaggy hair tied back by a leathern strap. They went always armed, carrying bows and arrows, large swords, which they wielded with both hands, called claymores, pole-axes, and daggers for close fight. For defence, they had a round wooden shield, or target, stuck full of nails; and their great men had shirts of mail, not unlike to the flannel shirts now worn, only composed of links of iron instead of threads of worsted; but the common men were so far from desiring armour, that they sometimes threw their plaids away, and fought in their shirts, which they wore very long and large, after the Irish fashion.

This part of the Scottish nation was divided into clans, that is, tribes. The persons composing each of these clans believed themselves all to be descended, at some distant period, from the same common ancestor, whose name they usually bore. Thus, one tribe was called MacDonald, which signifies the sons of Donald; another MacGregor, or the sons of Gregor; MacNeil, the sons of Neil, and so on. Every one of these tribes had its own separate chief, or commander, whom they supposed to be the immediate representative of the great father of the tribe from whom they were all descended. To this chief they paid the most unlimited obedience, and willingly followed his commands in peace or war; not caring although, in doing so, they transgressed the laws of the king, or went into rebellion against the king himself. Each tribe lived in a valley, or district of the mountains, separated from the others; and they often made war upon, and fought desperately with each other. But with Lowlanders they were always at war. They differed from them in language, in dress, and in manners; and they believed that the richer grounds of the low country had formerly belonged to their ancestors, and therefore they made incursions upon it, and plundered it without mercy. The Lowlanders, on the other hand, equal in courage and superior in discipline, gave many severe checks to the Highlanders; and thus there was almost constant war or discord between them, though natives of the same country.

Some of the most powerful of the Highland chiefs set themselves up as independent sovereigns. Such were the famous Lords of the Isles, called MacDonald, to whom the island, called the Hebrides, lying on the north-west of Scotland, might be said to belong in property. These petty sovereigns made alliances with the English in their own name. They took the part of Robert the Bruce in the wars, and joined him with their forces. We shall find, that after his time, they gave great disturbance to Scotland. The Lords of Lorn, MacDougals by name, were also extremely powerful; and you have seen that they were able to give battle to Bruce, and to defeat him, and place him in the greatest jeopardy. He revenged himself afterwards by driving John of Lorn out of the country, and by giving great part of his possessions to his own nephew, Sir Colin Campbell, who became the first of the great family of Argyll, which afterwards enjoyed such power in the Highlands.

Upon the whole, you can easily understand that these Highland clans, living among such high and inaccessible mountains, and paying obedience to no one save their own chiefs, should have been very instrumental in disturbing the tranquillity of the kingdom of Scotland. They had many virtues, being a kind, brave, and hospitable people, and remarkable for their fidelity to their chiefs; but they were restless, revengeful, fond of plunder, and delighting rather in war than in peace, in disorder than in repose.

The Border counties were in a state little more favourable to a quiet or peaceful government. In some respects the inhabitants of the counties of Scotland lying opposite to England, greatly resembled the

Highlanders, and particularly in their being, like them, divided into clans, and having chiefs, whom they obeyed in preference to the king, or the officers whom he placed among them. How clanship came to prevail in the Highlands and Borders, and not in the provinces which separated them from each other, it is not easy to conjecture, but the fact was so. The Borders are not, indeed, so mountainous and inaccessible a country as the Highlands but they also are full of hills, especially on the more western part of the frontier, and were in early times covered with forests, and divided by small rivers and morasses into dales and valleys, where the different clans lived, making war sometimes on the English, sometimes on each other, and sometimes on the more civilised country which lay behind them.

But though the Borderers resembled the Highlanders in their mode of government and habits of plundering, and, as it may be truly added, in their disobedience to the general government of Scotland, yet they differed in many particulars. The Highlanders fought always on foot, the Borderers were all horsemen. The Borderers spoke the same language with the Lowlanders, wore the same sort of dress, and carried the same arms. Being accustomed to fight against the English, they were also much better disciplined than the Highlanders. But in point of obedience to the Scottish government, they were not much different from the clans of the north.

Military officers, called Wardens, were appointed along the Borders, to keep these unruly people in order; but as these wardens were generally themselves chiefs of clans, they did not do much to mend the evil. Robert the Bruce committed great part of the charge of the Borders to the good Lord James of Douglas, who fulfilled his trust with great fidelity. But the power which the family of Douglas thus acquired, proved afterwards, in the hands of his successors, very dangerous to the crown of Scotland.

Thus you see how much the poor country of Scotland was torn to pieces, by the quarrels of the nobles, the weakness of the laws, the disorders of the Highlands, and the restless incursions of the Borderers. If Robert the Bruce had lived, and preserved his health, he would have done much to bring the country to a more orderly state. But Providence had decreed that in the time of his son and successor, Scotland was to fall back into a state almost as miserable as that from which this great prince rescued it.

XIII

The Battles of Dupplin and Halidon Hill

1329-1333

ROBERT BRUCE, the greatest king who ever wore the Scottish crown, being dead, as you have been told, the kingdom descended to his son David, who was called David the Second, to distinguish him from the first king of that name, who reigned about a hundred years before. This David the Second was only four years old at his father's death, and although we have seen children who thought themselves very wise at that age, yet it is not usual to give them the management of kingdoms. So Randolph, Earl of Murray, of whom you have heard so much, became what is called Regent of the kingdom of Scotland; that is, he exercised the royal authority until the King should be old enough to take the charge upon himself. This wise provision had been made by Bruce, with consent of the Parliament of Scotland, and was very acceptable to the kingdom.

The Regent was very strict in administering justice. If a husbandman had the plough-irons stolen from his plough when he left them in the field, Randolph caused the sheriff of the county to pay the value; because it was the duty of that magistrate to protect property left in the open fields. A fellow tried to cheat under colour of this law: he hid his own plough-irons, and pretending that they had been stolen, claimed the price from the sheriff, and was paid accordingly the estimated value, which was two shillings. But the fraud being discovered, the Regent caused the man to be hanged.

Upon one occasion, a criminal who had slain a priest, and afterwards fled to Rome, and done penance there, was brought before the Regent. The culprit confessed the murder, but pleaded that he had obtained the Pope's pardon. "The Pope," said Randolph, "might pardon you for killing a priest, but his remission cannot avail you for murdering a subject of the King of Scotland;" and accordingly he caused the culprit to be executed. This was asserting a degree of independence of the Pope's authority, which was very unusual among the princes and governors of that time.

While the Regent was sitting in judgment at Wigtown in Galloway, a man stepped forward to complain, that at the very time he was speaking, a company of his enemies were lying in ambush in a neighbouring forest to put him to death. Randolph sent a party of his attendants to seize the men, and bring them before him. "Is it you," said he, "who lie in wait to kill the King's liege subjects?—To the gallows with them instantly."

Randolph was to be praised for his justice, but not for his severity. He appears to have taken a positive pleasure in putting criminals to death, which marked the ferocity of the times and the turn of his own disposition. Having sent his coroner before him to Ellandonan Castle in the Highlands to execute certain thieves and robbers, that officer caused their heads to be hung round the walls of the castle, to the number of fifty. When Randolph came down the lake in a barge, and saw the castle adorned with these grim and bloody heads, he said, "He loved better to look upon them than on any garland of roses he had ever seen."

The efforts of the Regent to preserve the establishment of justice and order were soon interrupted, and he was called upon to take measures for the defence of the country; for Robert Bruce was no sooner in his grave than the enemies of his family began to plot the means of destroying the government which he had established. The principal person concerned in these machinations was Edward Baliol, the son of that John Baliol, who was formerly created King of Scotland by Edward I., and afterwards dethroned by him, and committed to prison, when Edward desired to seize upon the country for himself. After being long detained in prison, John Baliol was at length suffered to go to France, where he died in obscurity. But his son, Edward Baliol, seeing, as he thought, a favourable opportunity, resolved to renew the claim of his father to the Scottish throne. He came over to England with this purpose, and although Edward III., then King of England, remembering the late successes of the Scots, did not think it prudent to enter into a war with them, yet Baliol found a large party of powerful English barons well disposed to aid his enterprise. Their cause of resentment was as follows:—

When Scotland was freed from the dominion of England all the Englishmen to whom Edward the First, or his successors, had given lands within that kingdom, were of course deprived of them. But there was another class of English proprietors in Scotland, who claimed estates to which they succeeded, not by the grant of the English prince, but by inheritance from Scottish families, to whom they were related, and their pretensions were admitted by Robert Bruce himself, at the treaty of peace made at Northampton, in 1328, in which it was agreed that these English lords should receive back their Scottish inheritances. Notwithstanding this agreement, Bruce, who did not desire to see Englishmen enjoy land in Scotland, under what pretext soever, refused, or delayed at least, to fulfil this part of the treaty. Hence, upon the death of that monarch, the disinherited lords resolved to levy forces, and unite themselves with Edward Baliol, to recover their estates, and determined to invade Scotland for that purpose. But their united forces did not amount to more than four hundred men-at-arms, and about four thousand archers and soldiers of every description. This was a small army with which to invade a nation which had defended itself so well against the whole English forces; but Scotland was justly supposed to be much weakened by the death of her valiant king.

A great misfortune befell the country, in the unexpected death of the Regent Randolph, whose experience and valour might have done so much for the protection of Scotland. He had assembled an army, and was busied with preparations for defence against the enterprise of Baliol and the disinherited lords, when, wasted by a painful and consuming disorder, he died at Musselburgh, July 1332. The regret of the Scottish nation for the Regent's death was so great, that it has occasioned their historians to allege that he was poisoned by the English; but for this there seems no foundation.

Donald, Earl of Mar, nephew to Robert Bruce, was appointed by the Scottish Parliament to be Regent in the room of the Earl of Murray;

but he was without experience as a soldier, and of far inferior talents as a man.

Meantime, the King of England, still affecting to maintain peace with Scotland, prohibited the disinherited lords from invading that country from the English frontier. But he did not object to their equipping a small fleet in an obscure English seaport, for the purpose of accomplishing the same object by sea. They landed in Fife, with Baliol at their head, and defeated the Earl of Fife, who marched hastily to oppose them. They then advanced northward towards Dupplin, near which the Earl of Mar lay encamped with a large army, whilst another, under the Earl of March, was advancing from the southern counties of Scotland to attack the disinherited lords in the flank and in the rear.

It seemed as if that small handful of men must have been inevitably destroyed by the numbers collected to oppose them, but Edward Baliol took the bold resolution of attacking the Regent's army by night, and in their camp. With this purpose he crossed the Earn, which river divided the two hostile armies. The Earl of Mar had neither placed sentries, nor observed any other of the usual precautions against surprise, and the English came upon his army while the men were asleep and totally unprepared. They made a great slaughter amongst the Scots, whose numbers only served to increase the confusion. The Regent was himself slain, with the Earls of Carrick, of Murray, of Menteith, and many other men of eminence. Many thousands of the Scots were slain with the sword, smothered in the fight, or drowned in the river. The English were themselves surprised at gaining, with such inferior numbers, so great and decided a victory.

I said that the Earl of March was advancing with the southland forces to assist the Regent. But upon learning Mar's defeat and death, March acted with so little activity or spirit, that he was not unjustly suspected of being favourably inclined to Baliol's cause. That victorious general now assumed the crown of Scotland, which was placed upon his head at Scone; a great part of Scotland surrendered to his authority, and it seemed as if the fatal battle of Dupplin, fought 12th August 1332, had destroyed all the advantages which had been gained by that of Bannockburn.

Edward Baliol made an unworthy use of his success. He hastened again to acknowledge the King of England as his liege lord and superior, although every claim to such supremacy had been renounced, and the independence of Scotland explicitly acknowledged by the treaty of

Northampton. He also surrendered to the King of England the strong town and castle of Berwick, and engaged to become his follower in all his wars at his own charges. Edward III. engaged on his part to maintain Baliol in possession of the crown of Scotland. Thus was the kingdom reduced pretty much to the same state of dependence and subjection to England, as when the grandfather of Edward placed the father of Baliol on the throne, in the year 1292, about forty years before.

But the success of Baliol was rather apparent than real. The Scottish patriots were in possession of many of the strongholds of the country, and the person of the young King David was secured in Dumbarton Castle, one of the strongest fortresses in Scotland, or perhaps in the world.

At no period of her history was Scotland devoid of brave men, able and willing to defend her rights. When the scandalous treaty, by which Baliol had surrendered the independence of his country to Edward, came to be known in Scotland, the successors of Bruce's companions were naturally among the first to assert the cause of freedom. John Randolph, second son of the Regent, had formed a secret union with Archibald Douglas, a younger brother of the Good Lord James, and they proceeded to imitate the actions of their relatives. They suddenly assembled a considerable force, and attacking Baliol, who was feasting near Annan, they cut his guards in pieces, killed his brother, and chased him out of Scotland in such haste, that he escaped on horseback without time to clothe himself, or even to saddle his horse.

Archibald Douglas, who afterwards became Earl of Douglas was a brave man like his brother, but not so good a general, nor so fortunate in his undertakings.

There was another Douglas, called Sir William, a natural son of the Good Lord James, who made a great figure at this period. Although illegitimate by birth, he had acquired a large fortune by marrying the heiress of the Grahames of Dalkeith, and possessed the strong castle of that name, with the still more important one called the Hermitage, a large and massive fortress situated in the wild country of Liddesdale, within three or four miles of the English Border. This Sir William Douglas, called usually the Knight of Liddesdale, was a very brave man and a valiant soldier, but he was fierce, cruel, and treacherous; so that he did not keep up the reputation of his father the Good Lord James, as a man of loyalty and honour, although he resembled him in military talents.

Besides these champions, all of whom declared against Baliol, there was Sir Andrew Murray of Bothwell, who had married Christian, sister of Robert Bruce, and aunt of the young King David. He had so high a reputation, that the Scottish Parliament appointed him Regent in room of the Earl of Mar, slain at Dupplin.

Edward III. of England now formally declared war against Scotland, proposing to support the cause of Baliol, to take possession of Berwick, which that pretended king had yielded up to him, and to chastise the Scots for what he called their rebellion. He placed himself at the head of a great army, and marched towards the frontier.

In the meantime, the war had begun in a manner most unfavourable for Scotland. Sir Andrew Murray, and the Knight of Liddesdale, were both made prisoners in separate skirmishes with the English, and their loss at the time was of the worst consequence to Scotland.

Archibald Douglas, the brother, as I have just said, of the Good Lord James, was hastily appointed Regent in the room of Sir Andrew Murray, and advanced with a large army to relieve the town of Berwick, then closely besieged by Edward III. with all his host. The garrison made a determined defence, and the Regent endeavoured to relieve them by giving battle to the English, in which he showed more courage than military conduct.

The Scottish army were drawn up on the side of an eminence called Halidon Hill, within two miles of Berwick. King Edward moved with his whole host to attack them. The battle, like that of Falkirk and many others, was decided by that formidable force, the archers of England. They were posted in a marshy ground, from which they discharged their arrows in the most tremendous and irresistible volleys against the Scots, who, drawn up on the slope of the hill, were fully exposed to this destructive discharge, without having the means of answering it.

I have told you before that these English archers were the best ever known in war. They were accustomed to the use of the bow from the time they were children of seven years old, when they were made to practice with a little bow suited to their size and strength, which was every year exchanged for one larger and stronger, till they were able to draw that of a full-grown man. Besides being thus familiarised with the weapon, the archers of England were taught to draw the bowstring to their right ear, while other European nations only drew it to their breast. If you try the difference of the posture, you will find that a much longer arrow can be drawn to the ear than to the breast, because the right hand has more room.

While the Scots suffered under these practised and skilful archers, whose arrows fell like hail amongst them, throwing their ranks into disorder, and piercing the finest armour as if it had been pasteboard, they made desperate attempts to descend the hill, and come to close combat.[1] The Earl of Ross advanced to the charge, and had he been seconded by a sufficient body of the Scottish cavalry, he might have changed the fate of the day; but as this was not the case, the Earls of Ross, Sutherland, and Menteith, were overpowered and slain, while their followers were dispersed by the English cavalry, who advanced to protect the archers. The defeat of the Scots was then complete. A number of their best and bravest nobility were slain, and amongst them Archibald Douglas, the Regent; very many were made prisoners. Berwick surrendered in consequence of the defeat, and Scotland seemed again to be completely conquered by the English.

Edward once more overran the kingdom, seized and garrisoned castles, extorted from Edward Baliol, the nominal king, the complete cession of great part of the southern districts, named governors of the castles and sheriffs of the counties, and exercised complete authority, as over a conquered country. Baliol, on his part, assumed once more the rule of the northern and western part of Scotland, which he was permitted to retain under the vassalage of the English monarch. It was the opinion of most people that the Scottish wars were ended, and that there no longer remained a man of that nation who had influence to raise an army, or skill to conduct one.

---

[1] "The fatal hail-shower,
   The storm of England's wrath—sure, swift, resistless,
   Which no mail-coat can brook.—Brave English hearts,
   How close they shoot together! as one eye
   Had aimed five thousand shafts—as if one hand
   Had loosed five thousand bow-strings!"
See "*Halidon Hill,*" Sir Walter Scott's *Poetical Works*

XIV

The Regency of
Andrew Murray

1333 - 1338

THE English, a more powerful and richer nation, better able to furnish forth and maintain large armies, often gained great victories over the Scots; but, in return, the Scots had a determined love of independence, and hatred of foreign tyranny, which induced them always to maintain their resistance under the most unfavourable circumstances, and to repair, by slow, stubborn, and continued exertions, the losses which they sustained.

Throughout the whole country of Scotland only four castles and a small tower acknowledged the sovereignty of David Bruce after the battle of Halidon; and it is wonderful to see how, by their efforts, the patriots soon afterwards changed for the better that unfavourable and seemingly desperate state of things. In the several skirmishes and battles which were fought all over the kingdom, the Scots, knowing the country, and having the goodwill of the inhabitants, were generally successful, as also in surprising castles and forts, cutting off convoys of provisions which were going to the English, and destroying scattered parties of the enemy; so that, by a long and incessant course of fighting, the patriots gradually regained what they lost in great battles. I will tell you one or two of the incidents which befell during this bloody war.

Lochleven Castle, situated on an island upon a large lake, was one of the four which held out in name of David the Bruce, and would not submit to Edward Baliol. The governor was a loyal Scotsman, called Alan Vipont, assisted by Jaques or James Lamby. The castle was besieged by Sir John Stirling, follower of John Baliol, with an army of English. As the besiegers dared not approach the island with boats, Stirling fell on a singular device to oblige the garrison to surrender. There is a small river, called the Leven, which runs out of the eastern extremity of the lake or loch. Across this stream the besiegers reared a very strong and lofty mound or barrier, so as to prevent the waters of the Leven from leaving the lake. They expected that the waters of the lake would rise in consequence of being thus confined, and that they would overflow the island, and oblige Vipont to surrender. But Vipont, sending out at dead of night a small boat with four men, they made a breach in the mound; and the whole body of water, breaking forth with incredible fury, swept away the tents, baggage, and troops of the besiegers, and nearly destroyed their army. The remains of the English mound are shown to this day, though some doubt has been expressed as to the truth of the incident. It is certain the English were obliged to raise the siege with loss.

While these wars were proceeding with increased fury, the Knight of Liddesdale and Sir Andrew Murray of Bothwell returned to Scotland, having been freed from their imprisonment by paying a large ransom; the Earl of March also embraced the party of David Bruce. An equally brave champion was Sir Alexander Ramsay of Dalwolsy, who, placing himself at the head of a gallant troop of young Scotsmen, chose for his residence the large caves which are still to be seen in the glen of Roslin, from which he used to sally forth, and fight with Englishmen and their adherents. From this place of refuge he sometimes made excursions as far as Northumberland, and drove spoil from that country. No young Scottish soldier was thought entitled to make pretension to any renown in arms, unless he had served in Ramsay's band.

A considerable battle was fought in the north of Scotland, which turned to the advantage of the young King. Kildrummie Castle was one of the four which held out for David Bruce. It was defended by King David's aunt, a venerable matron, Christian Bruce, the wife of Sir Andrew Murray, and the sister of the brave King Robert; for in those warlike days women commanded castles, and sometimes fought in battle. This castle, which was one of the last places of refuge for the patriots, was besieged by David Hastings, the Earl of Athole, one of the disinherited lords, who, having changed sides more than once during the war, had at length turned entirely to the English party. Sir Andrew Murray of Bothwell, who had resumed his office of Regent, resolved to assemble the strongest force which the patriots could muster, and calling together the Knight of Liddesdale, Ramsay, and the Earl of March, he moved against the Earl of Athole, to compel him to raise the siege of Kildrummie, and relieve its heroic defender. All these great nobles were unable to raise above one thousand men, while Athole had three times that number under his command.

But as the Scots approached the territory of Kildrummie, they were joined by one John Craig. This gentleman belonged to the royalists of Scotland, but having been made prisoner by the Earl of Athole, he had agreed to pay a large ransom, and the morrow was the time appointed for producing the money. He was, therefore, anxious to accomplish the defeat or death of Athole before the money was paid to him, and thus to save his ransom. With this purpose he conducted the Scotsmen through the forest of Braemar, where they were joined by the natives of that territory, and thus came suddenly on the Earl of Athole, who lay encamped in the forest. Athole started up in surprise when he saw his enemies appear so unexpectedly; but he was a stout-hearted man, though fickle in his political attachments. He looked at a great rock which lay beside him, and swore an oath that he would not fly that day until that rock should show him the example. A small brook divided the two parties. The Knight of Liddesdale, who led the van of the Scots, advanced a little way down the bank on his side, then taking his spear by the middle, and keeping his own men back with it, he bade them halt, which occasioned some murmurs. The Earl of Athole, seeing this pause, exclaimed, "These men are half discomfited;" and rushed to charge them, followed by his men in some disorder. When they had passed the brook, and were ascending the bank on the other side, "Now is our time," said the Knight of Liddesdale, and charged down hill with levelled lances, bearing Athole's followers backwards into the ford. The earl himself, disdaining quarter, was slain under a great oak-tree. This was the battle of Kilblene, fought on St. Andrew's Day, 1335.

Among the warlike exploits of this period, we must not forget the defence of the castle of Dunbar by the celebrated Countess of March. Her lord, as we have seen, had embraced the side of David Bruce, and had taken the field with the Regent. The countess, who from her

complexion was termed Black Agnes, by which name she is still famil-
iarly remembered, was a high-spirited and courageous woman, the
daughter of that Thomas Randolph, Earl of Murray, whom I have so
often mentioned, and the heiress of his valour and patriotism. The
castle of Dunbar itself was very strong, being built upon a chain of
rocks stretching into the sea, and having only one passage to the mainland, which was well fortified. It was besieged by Montague, Earl of
Salisbury, who employed to destroy its walls great military engines,
constructed to throw huge stones, with which machines fortifications
were attacked before the use of cannon.

Black Agnes set all his attempts at defiance, and showed herself
with her maids on the walls of the castle, wiping the places where the
huge stones fell with a clean towel, as if they could do no ill to her
castle, save raising a little dust, which a napkin could wipe away.

The Earl of Salisbury then commanded his engineers to bring forward to the assault an engine of another kind, being a sort of wooden
shed, or house, rolled forward on wheels, with a roof of peculiar
strength, which, from resembling the ridge of a hog's back, occasioned
the machine to be called a sow. This, according to the old mode of warfare, was thrust close up to the walls of a besieged castle or city, and
served to protect from the arrows and stones of the besieged a party of
soldiers placed within the sow, who, being thus defended, were in the
meanwhile employed in undermining the wall, or breaking an entrance
through it with pickaxes and mining tools. When the Countess of
March saw this engine advanced to the walls of the castle, she called out
to the Earl of Salibury in derision and making a kind of rhyme,—

> "Beware, Montagow,
> For farrow shall thy sow,"

At the same time she made a signal, and a huge fragment of rock,
which hung prepared for the purpose, was dropped down from the
wall upon the sow, whose roof was thus dashed to pieces. As the English soldiers, who had been within it, were running as fast as they
could to get out of the way of the arrows and stones which were discharged on them from the wall, Black Agnes called out, "Behold the
litter of English pigs!"

The Earl of Salisbury could jest also on such serious occasions.
One day he rode near the walls with a knight dressed in armour of

proof, having three folds of mail over an acton, or leathern jacket; notwithstanding which, one William Spens shot an arrow from the battlements of the castle with such force, that it penetrated all these defences, and reached the heart of the wearer. "That is one of my lady's love-tokens," said the earl, as he saw the knight fall dead from his horse. "Black Agnes's love-shafts pierce to the heart."

Upon another occasion the Countess of March had wellnigh made the Earl of Salisbury her prisoner. She caused one of her people enter into treaty with the besiegers, pretending to betray the castle. Trusting to this agreement, the earl came at midnight before the gate, which he found open, and the portcullis drawn up. As Salisbury was about to enter, one John Copland, a squire of Northumberland, pressed on before him, and as soon as he passed the threshold, the portcullis was dropped, and thus the Scots missed their principal prey, and made prisoner only a person of inferior condition.

At length the castle of Dunbar was relieved by Alexander Ramsay of Dalwolsy, who brought the countess supplies by sea both of men and provisions. The Earl of Salisbury, learning this, despaired of success, and raised the siege, which had lasted nineteen weeks. The minstrels made songs in praise of the perseverance and courage of Black Agnes. The following lines are nearly the sense of what is preserved:

> "She kept a stir in tower and trench,
> That brawling boisterous Scottish wench:
> Came I early, came I late,
> I found Agnes at the gate."

The brave Sir Andrew Murray of Bothwell, the Regent of Scotland, died in 1338, while the war was raging on all sides. He was a good patriot, and a great loss to his country, to which he had rendered the highest services. There is a story told of him, which shows how composed he could be in circumstances of great danger. He was in the Highlands with a small body of followers, when the King of England came upon him with an army of twenty thousand. The Regent learned the news, but, being then about to hear mass, did not permit his devotions to be interrupted. When mass was ended, the people around him pressed him to order a retreat; "There is no haste," said Murray composedly. At length his horse was brought out, he was about to mount, and all expected that the retreat was to commence. But the Regent observed that a strap of his armour had given way, and this interposed new delays. He sent for a particular coffer, out of which he took a piece of skin, and cut and formed with his own hand, and with much deliberation, the strap which he wanted. By this time the English were drawing very near, and as they were so many in number, some of the Scottish knights afterwards told the historian who relates the incident, that no space of time ever seemed so long to them as that which Sir Andrew employed in cutting that thong of leather. Now, if this had been done in a mere vaunting or bragging manner, it would have been the behaviour of a vainglorious fool. But Sir Andrew Murray had already fixed upon the mode of retiring, and he knew that every symptom of coolness and deliberation which he might show would render his men steady and composed in their turn, from beholding the confidence of their leader. He at length gave the word, and putting himself at the head of his followers, made a most masterly retreat, during which the English, notwithstanding their numbers, were unable to obtain any advantage over him, so well did the Regent avail himself of the nature of the ground.

You may well imagine, my dear child, that during those long and terrible wars which were waged, when castles were defended and taken, prisoners made, many battles fought, and numbers of men wounded and slain, the state of the country of Scotland was most miserable. There was no finding refuge or protection in the law, at a time when everything was decided by the strongest arm and the longest sword. There was no use in raising crops, when the man who sowed them was not, in all probability, permitted to reap the grain. There was little religious devotion where so much violence prevailed; and the hearts of the people became so much inclined to acts of blood and fury that all laws of humanity and charity were transgressed without scruple. People were found starved to death in the woods with their families, while the country was so depopulated and void of cultivation that the wild-deer came out of the remote forests, and approached near to cities and the dwellings of men. Whole families were reduced to eat grass, and others, it is said, found a more horrible aliment in the flesh of their fellow-creatures. One wretch used to set traps for human beings as if for wild beasts, and subsisted on their flesh. This cannibal was called Christian of the Cleek, from the cleek or hook which he used in his horrid traps.

In the middle of all these horrors, the English and Scottish knights and nobles, when there was any truce between the countries, supplied the place of the wars in which they were commonly engaged, with tournaments and games of chivalry. These were meetings not for the express purpose of fighting, but for that of trying which was the best man-at-arms. But instead of wrestling, leaping, or running races on foot or horse, the fashion then was that the gentlemen tilted together, that is, rode against each other in armour with their long lances, and tried which could bear the other out of the saddle, and throw him to the ground. Sometimes they fought on foot with swords and axes; and although all was meant in courtesy and fair play, yet lives were often lost in this idle manner as much as if the contest had been carried on with the purpose of armed battle and deadly hatred. In later days they fought with swords purposely blunted on the edge, and with lances which had no steel point; but in the times we speak of at present, they used in tilts and tournaments the same weapons which they employed in war.

A very noted entertainment of this kind was given to both Scottish and English champions by Henry of Lancaster, then called Earl of Derby, and afterwards King Henry IV. of England. He invited the Knight of Liddesdale, the good Sir Alexander Ramsay, and about twenty other distinguished Scottish knights, to a tilting match, which was to take place near Berwick. After receiving and entertaining his Scottish guests nobly, the Earl of Derby began to inquire of Ramsay in what manner of armour the knights should tilt together.

"With shields of plate," said Ramsay, "such as men use in tournaments."

This may be supposed a peculiarly weighty and strong kind of armour, intended merely for this species of encounter.

"Nay," said the Earl of Derby, "we shall gain little praise if we tilt in such safety; let us rather use the lighter armour which we wear in battle."

"Content are we," answered Sir Alexander Ramsay, "to fight in our silk doublets, if such be your lordship's pleasure."

The Knight of Liddesdale was wounded on the wrist by the splinter of a spear, and was obliged to desist from the exercise. A Scottish knight, called Sir Patrick Grahame, tilted with a warlike English baron named Talbot, whose life was saved by his wearing two breastplates. The Scottish lance pierced through both, and sunk an inch into the breast. Had he been only armed as according to agreement, Talbot had been a dead man. Another English knight challenged the Grahame at supper-time to run three courses with him the next day.

"Dost thou ask to tilt with me?" said the Grahame; "rise early in the morning, confess your sins, and make your peace with God, for you shall sup in paradise." Accordingly, on the ensuing morning, Grahame ran him through the body with his lance, and he died on the spot. Another English knight was also slain, and one of the Scots mortally wounded. William Ramsay was borne through the helmet with a lance, the splinter of the broken spear remaining in his skull, and nailing his helmet to his head. As he was expected to die on the spot, a priest was sent for, who heard him confess his sins without the helmet being removed.

"Ah, it is a goodly sight," quoth the good Earl of Derby, much edified by this spectacle, "to see a knight make his shrift" (that is, confession of his sins) "in his helmet. God send me such an ending!"

But when the shrift was over, Sir Alexander Ramsay, to whom the wounded knight was brother, or kinsman, made him lie down at full length, and, with surgery as rough as their pastime, held his friend's head down with his foot, while, by main strength, he pulled the fragment of the spear out of the helmet, and out of the wound. Then William Ramsay started up, and said, "That he should do well enough."

"Lo! what stout hearts men may bear!" said the Earl of Derby, as much admiring the surgical treatment as he had done the religious. Whether the patient lived or died, does not appear.

In fixing the prizes, it was settled that the English knights should decide which of the Scots had done best, and the Scots should, in like manner, judge the valour of the English. Much equity was shown in the decision on both sides, and the Earl of Derby was munificent in distribution of gifts and prizes. This may serve to show you the amusements of this stirring period, of which war and danger were the sport as well as the serious occupation.

XV

David II.

1339-1370

NOTWITHSTANDING the valiant defence maintained by the Scots, their country was reduced to a most disastrous state, by the continued wars of Edward III., who was a wise and warlike king as ever lived. Could he have turned against Scotland the whole power of his kingdom, he might probably have effected the complete conquest, which had been so long attempted in vain. But while the wars in Scotland were at the hottest, Edward became also engaged in hostilities with France, having laid claim to the crown of that kingdom. Thus Edward was obliged to slacken his efforts in Scotland, and the patriots began to gain ground decisively in the dreadful contest which was so obstinately maintained on both sides.

The Scots sent an embassy to obtain money and assistance from the French; and they received supplies of both, which enabled them to recover their castles and towns from the English.

Edinburgh Castle was taken from the invaders by a stratagem. The Knight of Liddesdale, with two hundred chosen men, embarked at Dundee, in a merchant vessel commanded by one William Curry. The shipmaster, on their arrival at Leith, went with a party of his sailors to the castle, carrying barrels of wine and hampers of provisions, which he pretended it was his desire to sell to the English governor and his garrison. But getting entrance at the gate under this pretext, they raised the war-shout of Douglas, and the Knight of Liddesdale rushed in with his soldiers, and secured the castle. Perth, and other important places, were also retaken by the Scots, and Edward Baliol retired out of the country, in despair of making good his pretensions to the crown.

The nobles of Scotland, finding the affairs of the kingdom more prosperous, now came to the resolution of bringing back from France, where he had resided for safety, their young king, David II., and his consort, Queen Joanna. They arrived in 1341.

David II. was still a youth, neither did he possess at any period of life the wisdom and talents of his father, the great King Robert. The nobles of Scotland had become each a petty prince on his own estates; they made war on each other as they had done upon the English, and the poor king possessed no power of restraining them. A most melancholy instance of this discord took place, shortly after David's return from France.

I have told you how Sir Alexander Ramsay and the Knight of Liddesdale assisted each other in fighting against the English. They were great friends and companions-in-arms. But Ramsay, having taken by storm the strong castle of Roxburgh, the King bestowed on him the office of sheriff of that county, which was before enjoyed by the Knight of Liddesdale. As this was placing another person in his room, the Knight of Liddesdale altogether forgot his old friendship for Ramsay, and resolved to put him to death. He came suddenly upon him with a strong party of men, while he was administering justice at Hawick. Ramsay having no suspicion of injury from the hand of his old comrade, and having few men with him, was easily overpowered, and being wounded, was hurried away to the lonely castle of the Hermitage, which stands in the middle of the morasses of Liddesdale. Here he was thrown into a dungeon, where he had no other sustenance than some grain which fell down from a granary above; and after lingering seventeen days in that dreadful condition, the brave Sir Alexander Ramsay died. This was in 1342. Nearly four hundred and fifty years afterwards, that is, about forty years ago, a mason, digging amongst the ruins of Hermitage Castle,[1] broke into a

---

[1] "Some years ago a mason, employed in building a dike in the neighbourhood, had the curiosity to penetrate into a vault in the east end of the castle. Having made an opening, he descended by a ladder; and in a vault about eight feet square he found several human bones, with a saddle, a bridle, and sword; he brought out the bridle and sword. The bit was of an uncommon size; the curb of it is in the possession of Walter

dungeon, where lay a quantity of chaff, some human bones, and a bridle bit, which were supposed to mark the vault as the place of Ramsay's death. The bridle bit was given to grandpapa, who presented it to the present gallant Earl of Dalhousie, a brave soldier, like his ancestor Sir Alexander Ramsay, from whom he is lineally descended.

The King was much displeased at the commission of so great a crime, on the person of so faithful a subject. He made some attempts to avenge the murder, but the Knight of Liddesdale was too powerful to be punished, and the King was obliged to receive him again into friendship and confidence. But God in his own good time revenged this cruel deed. About five years after the crime was committed, the Knight of Liddesdale was taken prisoner by the English at the battle of Neville's Cross, near Durham, and is suspected of having obtained his liberty by entering into a treacherous league with the English monarch. He had no time to carry his treason, however, into effect; for, shortly after his liberation, he was slain whilst hunting in Ettrick Forest, by his near relation and godson, William, Lord Douglas. The place where he fell was called from his name, William-hope. It is a pity that the Knight of Liddesdale committed that great crime of murdering Ramsay, and entered into the treasonable treaty with the King of England. In other respects, he was ranked so high in public esteem, that he was called the Flower of Chivalry; and an old writer has said of him, "He was terrible in arms, modest and gentle in peace, the scourge of England, and the buckler and wall of Scotland; one whom good success never made presumptuous, and whom evil fortune never discouraged."

We return to the state of Scotland at the time when the young King was restored. Battles and skirmishes were fought on all sides; but the Scots having gained back the whole of their own country, the war became less inveterate; and although no settled peace took place, yet truces, to endure for a certain number of months and years, were agreed upon from time to time; and the English historians allege that the Scottish nation were always ready to break them when a tempting opportunity occurred.

Such a truce was in existence about 1346, when, Edward the Third being absent in France, and in the act of besieging Calais, David was

---

Scott, Esq., advocate. In the dungeon he found a great quantity of the husks of oats. Report says, the granary of the castle was immediately above this vault, and that Sir Alexander Ramsay subsisted for some time on what fell down into the vault."—*Statistical Account of Scotland.*

induced, by the pressing and urgent counsels of the French King, to renew the war, and profit by the King's absence from England. The young King of Scotland raised, accordingly, a large army, and entering England on the west frontier, he marched eastward towards Durham, harassing and wasting the country with great severity; the Scots boasting that, now the King and his nobles were absent, there were none in England to oppose them, save priests and base mechanics.

But they were greatly deceived. The lords of the northern counties of England, together with the Archbishop of York, assembled a gallant army. They defeated the vanguard of the Scots, and came upon the main body by surprise. The English army, in which there were many ecclesiastics, bore, as their standard, a crucifix, displayed amid the banners of the nobility. The Scots had taken post among some enclosures, which greatly embarrassed their movements, and their ranks remaining stationary were, as on former occasions, destroyed by the English arrows. Here Sir John Grahame offered his services to disperse the bowmen, if he were entrusted with a body of cavalry. But although this was the movement which decided the battle of Bannockburn, Grahame could not obtain the means of attempting it. In the meantime the Scottish army fell fast into disorder. The King himself fought bravely in the midst of his nobles and was twice wounded with arrows. At length he was captured by John Copland, a Northumberland gentleman; the same who was made prisoner at Dunbar. He did not secure his royal captive without resistance; for in the struggle the King dashed out two of Copland's teeth with his dagger. The left wing of the Scottish army continued fighting long after the rest were routed, and at length made a safe retreat. It was commanded by the Steward of Scotland and the Earl of March. Very many of the Scottish nobility were slain; very many made prisoners. The King himself was led in triumph through the streets of London, and committed to the Tower a close prisoner. This battle was fought at Neville's Cross, near Durham, on 17th October 1346.

Thus was another great victory gained by the English over the Scots. It was followed by further advantages, which gave the victors for a time possession of the country from the Scottish Border as far as the verge of Lothian. But the Scots, as usual, were no sooner compelled to momentary submission, than they began to consider the means of shaking off the yoke.

William Douglas, son to that Douglas who was killed at Halidon Hill, near Berwick, now displayed his share of that courage and conduct which seemed the birthright of that extraordinary family. He recovered his own territories of Douglasdale, drove the English out of Ettrick Forest, and assisted the inhabitants of Teviotdale in regaining their independence.

On this occasion, indeed, the invasion of the English was not attended with the same extensively bad effects as on former victories obtained by them. The title of Baliol was not again set up, and that nominal sovereign surrendered to the English monarch all his right and interest in the kingdom of Scotland, in testimony of which he presented him a handful of earth belonging to the country, and a crown of gold. Edward, in reward of this surrender of the Scottish crown, fixed a large annual income upon Baliol, who retired from public affairs, and lived ever afterwards in such obscurity, that historians do not even record the period of his death. Nothing which he afterwards did bore the same marks of courage and talent, as the enterprise in which he commanded the disinherited barons, and obtained the great victory at the battle of Dupplin. It seems therefore likely that he had upon that occasion some assistance which he did not afterwards enjoy.

Edward III. was not more fortunate in making war on Scotland in his own name than when he used the pretext of supporting Baliol. He marched into East Lothian in spring 1355, and committed such ravages that the period was long marked by the name of the *Burned Candlemas,* because so many towns and villages were burned. But the Scots had removed every species of provisions which could be of use to the invaders, and avoided a general battle, while they engaged in a number of skirmishes. In this manner Edward was compelled to retreat out of Scotland, after sustaining much loss.

After the failure of this effort, Edward seems to have despaired of the conquest of Scotland, and entered into terms for a truce, and for setting the King at liberty.

Thus David II. at length obtained his freedom from the English, after he had been detained in prison eleven years. The Scots agreed to pay a ransom of one hundred thousand merks, a heavy charge on a country always poor, and exhausted by the late wars. The people were so delighted to see the King once more that they followed him everywhere; and (which shows the rudeness of the times) rushed even into his private chamber, till, incensed at their troublesome and intrusive loyalty, the King snatched a mace from an officer, and broke with his own royal hand the head of the liegeman who was nearest to him.

After this rebuke, saith the historian, he was permitted to be private in his apartment.

The latter years of this King's life have nothing very remarkable excepting that, after the death of Joanna of England, his first wife, he made an imprudent marriage with one Margaret Logie, a woman of great beauty, but of obscure family; he was afterwards divorced or separated from her. He had no children by either of his wives. David the Second died at the age of forty-seven years, in the castle of Edinburgh, 22d February 1370–71. He had reigned forty-two years, of which eleven were spent in captivity.

XVI

Accession of the Stewarts

1370-1390

As David the Second died childless, the male line of his father, the great Robert Bruce, was at an end. But the attachment of the Scottish nation naturally turned to the family of that heroic prince, and they resolved to confer the crown on a grandson of his by the mother's side. Marjory, the daughter of Robert Bruce, had married Walter, the Lord High Steward of Scotland, and the sixth of his family who had enjoyed that high dignity, in consequence of possessing which the family had acquired the surname of Stewart. This Walter Stewart, with his wife Marjory, were ancestors of that long line of Stewarts who afterwards ruled Scotland, and came at length to be kings of England also. The last king of the Stewart family lost his kingdoms at the great national Revolution in 1688, and his son and grandsons died in exile. The female line have possession of the crown at this moment in the person of the present sovereign. When, therefore, you hear of the line of Stewart, you will know that the descendants of Walter Stewart and Marjory Bruce are the family meant by that term. It is said that the Stewarts were descended from Fleance, the son of Banquo, whose posterity the witches declared were to be kings of Scotland, and who was murdered by Macbeth. But this seems a very doubtful tradition.

Walter, the Steward of Scotland, who married Bruce's daughter, was a gallant man, and fought bravely at Bannockburn, where he had a high command. But he died young, and much regretted. Robert Stewart, his son by Marjory Bruce, grandson, of course, of King Robert, was the person now called to the throne. He was a good and kind-tempered prince. When young he had been a brave soldier; but he was now fifty-five years old, and subject to a violent inflammation in his eyes, which rendered them as red as blood. From these causes he lived a good deal retired, and was not active enough to be at the head of a fierce and unmanageable nation like the Scots.

Robert Stewart's ascent to the throne was not unopposed, for it was claimed by a formidable competitor. This was William, Earl of Douglas. That family, in which so many great men had arisen, was now come to a great pitch of power and prosperity, and possessed almost a sovereign authority in the southern parts of Scotland. The Earl of Douglas was on the present occasion induced to depart from his claim, upon his son being married to Euphemia, the daughter of Robert II. Stewart therefore was crowned without further opposition. But the extreme power of the Douglases, which raised them almost to a level with the crown, was afterwards the occasion of great national commotion and distress.

There were not many things of moment in the history of Robert II. But the wars with England were less frequent, and the Scots had learned a better way of conducting them. The following instances may be selected.

In 1385 the French finding themselves hard pressed by the English, in their own country, resolved to send an army into Scotland, to assist that nation in making war upon the English, and thus find work for the latter people at home. They sent, therefore, one thousand men-at-arms,—knights, and squires, that is, in full armour; and as each of these had four or five soldiers under him, the whole force was very considerable. They sent also twelve hundred suits of complete armour to the Scots, with a large sum of money, to assist them to make war. This great force was commanded by John de Vienne, High Admiral of France, a brave and distinguished general.

In the meantime, the King of England, Richard II., summoned together, on his side, a larger army perhaps than any King of England had ever before commanded, and moved toward the Scottish Border. The Scots also assembled large forces and the French Admiral expected there would be a great pitched battle. He said to the Scottish nobles, "You have always said, that if you had some hundreds of French men-at-arms to help you, you would give battle to the English. Now, here we are to give you aid—Let us give battle."

The Scottish nobles answered, that they would not run so great a hazard, as risk the fate of the country in one battle and one of them, probably Douglas, conveyed John de Vienne to a narrow pass, where, unseen themselves, they might see the army of England march through. The Scot made the admiral remark at the great multitude of archers, the number and high discipline of the English men-at-arms, and then asked the Frenchman, as a soldier, whether he could advise the Scots to oppose these clouds of archers with a few ill-trained High-land bowmen, or encounter with their small trotting nags, the onset of the brilliant chivalry of England.

The Admiral de Vienne could not but own that the risk was too unequal. "But yet, if you do not fight," he said, "what do you mean to do? If you do not oppose this great force, the English will destroy your country."

"Let them do their worst," said Douglas, smiling; "they will find but little to destroy. Our people are all retired into woods, hills, and morasses, and have driven off their cattle, which is their only property, along with them. The English will find nothing either to take away or to eat. The houses of the gentlemen are small towers, with thick walls, which even fire will not destroy; as for the common people, they dwell in mere huts, and if the English choose to burn them, a few trees from the wood is all that is necessary to build them up again."

"But what will you do with your army if you do not fight?" said the Frenchman; "and how will your people endure the distress, and famine, and plunder, which must be the consequences of the invasion?"

"You shall see that our army will not lie idle," said Douglas; "and as for our Scottish people, they will endure pillage, and they will endure famine, and every other extremity of war; but they will not endure an English master."

The event showed the truth of what Douglas had said. The great army of England entered Scotland on the eastern side of the frontier, and marched on, much embarrassed and distressed for want of provisions, laying waste the villages and what property they found, but finding very little to destroy, and nothing to subsist upon. On the contrary, no sooner did the Scottish nobles learn that the English were fairly engaged in Scotland, than, with a numerous army, consisting chiefly of light cavalry, like that led by Douglas and Randolph in 1327, they burst into the western counties of England, where they gained more spoil, and did more damage, in the course of a day or two's march, than the English could have done in Scotland had they burned the whole country from the Border to Aberdeen.

The English were quickly called back to the defence of their own country, and though there had been no battle, yet from bad roads, want of forage, scantiness of provisions, and similar causes, they had sustained a heavy loss of men and horses; while the Scottish army, on the contrary, had kept good cheer in a country so much richer than their own, and were grown wealthy by plunder. This wise scheme of defence had been recommended to his posterity by the Bruce as the only effectual mode of defending the Scottish frontier.

As to the French auxiliaries, they quarrelled very much with the reception they met with. They complained that the nation which they came to assist treated them with no kindness or good-will, and that they withheld from them forage, provisions, and other supplies. The Scots replied, on the other hand, that their allies were an expense to them, without being of any use; that their wants were many, and could not be supplied in so poor a country as Scotland; and finally, that they insulted the inhabitants, and pillaged the country wherever they durst. Nor would the Scots permit the French to leave Scotland till they gave security that they would pay the expenses of their own maintenance. The French knights, who had hoped to acquire both wealth and fame, returned in very bad humour from a kingdom where the people were so wild and uncivilised, and the country so mountainous and poor; where the patches of cultivated land bore no proportion to the extended wastes, and the wild animals were much more numerous than those which were trained for the use of man.

It was from prudence, not from want of courage, that the Scots avoided great battles with the English. They readily engaged in smaller actions, when they fought with the utmost valour on both sides, till, as an old historian expresses it, sword and lance could endure no longer, and then they would part from each other, saying, "Good day; and thanks for the sport you have shown." A very remarkable instance of such a desperate battle occurred in the year 1388.

The Scottish nobles had determined upon an invasion of England on a large scale, and had assembled a great army for that purpose; but learning that the people of Northumberland were raising an army on the eastern frontier, they resolved to limit their incursion to that which might be achieved by the Earl of Douglas, with a chosen band of four or five thousand men. With this force he penetrated into the mountainous frontier of England, where an assault was least expected, and issuing forth near Newcastle, fell upon the flat and rich country around, slaying, plundering, burning, and loading his army with spoil.

Percy, Earl of Northumberland, an English noble of great power, and with whom the Douglas had frequently had encounters, sent his two sons, Sir Henry and Sir Ralph Percy, to stop the progress of this invasion. Both were gallant knights; but the first, who, from his impetuosity, was called Hotspur, was one of the most distinguished warriors in England, as Douglas was in Scotland. The brothers threw themselves hastily into Newcastle, to defend that important town; and as Douglas, in an insulting manner, drew up his followers before the walls, they came out to skirmish with the Scots. Douglas and Henry Percy encountered personally; and it so chanced that Douglas in the struggle got possession of Hotspur's spear, to the end of which was attached a small ornament of silk, embroidered with pearls, on which was represented a lion, the cognisance, as it is called, of the Percies. Douglas shook this trophy aloft, and declared that he would carry it into Scotland, and plant it on his castle of Dalkeith.

"That," said Percy, "shalt thou never do. I will regain my lance ere thou canst get back into Scotland."

"Then," said Douglas, "come to seek it, and thou shalt find it before my tent."

The Scottish army, having completed the purpose of their expedition, began their retreat up the vale of the little river Reed, which afforded a tolerable road running north-westward towards their own frontier. They encamped at Otterburn, about twenty miles from the Scottish border, on the 19th August 1388.

In the middle of the night the alarm arose in the Scottish camp that the English host were coming upon them, and the moonlight showed the approach of Sir Henry Percy, with a body of men superior in number to that of Douglas. He had already crossed the Reed water, and was advancing towards the left flank of the Scottish army. Douglas, not choosing to receive the assault in that position, drew his men out of the camp, and with a degree of military skill which could scarce have been expected when his forces were of such an undisciplined character, he altogether changed the position of the army, and presented his troops with their front to the advancing English.

Hotspur, in the meantime, marched his squadrons through the deserted camp, where there were none left but a few servants and stragglers of the army. The interruptions which the English troops met with threw them a little into disorder, when the moon arising showed them the Scottish army, which they had supposed to be retreating, drawn up in complete order, and prepared to fight. The battle commenced with the greatest fury; for Percy and Douglas were the two most distinguished soldiers of their time, and each army trusted in the courage and talents of their commanders, whose names were shouted on either side. The Scots, who were outnumbered, were at length about to give way, when Douglas, their leader, caused his banner to advance, attended by his best men. He himself shouting his war-cry of "Douglas!" rushed forward, clearing his way with the blows of his battle-axe, and breaking into the very thickest of the enemy. He fell, at length, under three mortal wounds. Had his death been observed by the enemy, the event would probably have decided the battle against the Scots; but the English only knew that some brave man-at-arms had fallen. Meantime the other Scottish nobles pressed forward and found their general dying among several of his faithful esquires and pages, who lay slain around. A stout priest, called William of North Lerwick, the chaplain of Douglas, was protecting the body of his wounded patron with a long lance.

"How fares it, cousin?" said Sinclair, the first Scottish knight who came up to the expiring leader.

"Indifferently," answered Douglas; "but blessed be God, my ancestors have died in fields of battle, not on down-beds. I sink fast; but let them still cry my war-cry, and conceal my death from my followers. There was a tradition in our family that a dead Douglas should win a field, and I trust it will be this day accomplished."

The nobles did as he had enjoined; they concealed the Earl's body, and again rushed on to the battle, shouting "Douglas! Douglas!" louder than before. The English were weakened by the loss of the brave brothers, Henry and Ralph Percy, both of whom were made prisoners, fighting most gallantly, and almost no man of note amongst the English escaped death or captivity. Hence a Scottish poet has said of the name of Douglas,

> "Hosts have been known at that dread sound to yield,
> And, Douglas dead, his name hath won the field."

Sir Henry Percy became the prisoner of Sir Hugh Montgomery, who obliged him for ransom to build a castle for him at Penoon in Ayrshire. The battle of Otterburn was disastrous to the leaders on both sides—Percy being made captive, and Douglas slain on the field. It bas been the subject of many songs and poems, and the great historian Froissart says, that one other action only excepted, it was the best fought battle of that warlike time.

Robert II. died at his castle of Dundonald in Kyle, after a short illness, in the seventy-fifth year of his age, on the 19th April 1390. His reign of nineteen years did not approach in glory to that of his maternal grandfather, Robert Bruce; but it was far more fortunate than that of David II. The claims of Baliol to the crown were not revived; and though the English made more than one incursion into Scotland, they were never able to retain long possession of the country.

XVII

Robert III.

1390-1406

THE eldest son of Robert II. was originally called John. But it was a popular remark that the kings named John, both of France and England, had been unfortunate, and the Scottish people were very partial to the name of Robert, from its having been borne by the great Bruce. John Stewart, therefore, on ascending the Scottish throne, changed his name to that of Robert III. We shall see, however, that this poor king remained as unfortunate as if his name had still been John.

The disturbances of the Highlands were one of the plagues of his reign. You must recollect that that extensive range of mountains was inhabited by a race of men different in language and manners from the Lowlanders, and divided into families called Clans. The English termed them the Wild Scots, and the French the Scottish Savages; and, in good truth, very wild and savage they seem to have been. The losses which the Low Country had sustained by the English wars had weakened the districts next to the Highlands so much, that they became unable to repress the incursions of the mountaineers, who descended from their hills, took spoil, burned and destroyed, as if in the country of an enemy.

In 1392 a large body of these Highlanders broke down from the Grampian Mountains. The chiefs were called Clan-Donnochy, or sons of Duncan, answering to the clan now called Robertson. A party of the Ogilvies and Lindsays, under Sir Walter Ogilvy, Sheriff of Angus, marched hastily against them, and charged them with their lances. But notwithstanding the advantage of their being mounted and completely sheathed in armour, the Highlanders defended themselves with such obstinacy as to slay the sheriff and sixty of his followers, and repulse the Lowland gentlemen. To give some idea of their ferocity, it is told that Sir David Lindsay, having in the first encounter run his lance through the body of one of the Highlanders, bore him down and pinned him to the earth. In this condition, and in his dying agonies, the Highlander writhed himself upwards on the spear, and exerted his last strength in fetching a sweeping blow at the armed knight with his two-handed sword. The stroke, made with all the last energies of a dying man, cut through Lindsay's stirrup and steel-boot, and though it did not sever his leg from his body, yet wounded him so severely as to oblige him to quit the field.

It happened, fortunately perhaps for the Lowlands, that the wild Highlanders were as much addicted to quarrel with each other as with their Lowland neighbours. Two clans, or rather two leagues or confederacies, composed each of several separate clans,[1] fell into such deadly feud with each other as filled the whole neighbourhood with slaughter and discord.

When this feud or quarrel could be no otherwise ended, it was resolved that the difference should be decided by a combat of thirty men of the Clan Chattan, against the same number of the Clan Kay; that the battle should take place on the North Inch of Perth, a beautiful and level meadow, in part surrounded by the river Tay; and that it should be fought in presence of the King and his nobles. Now, there was a cruel policy in this arrangement; for it was to be supposed that all the best and leading men of each clan would desire to be among the thirty which were to fight for their honour, and it was no less to be expected that the battle would be very bloody and desperate. Thus, the probable event would be, that both clans, having lost very many of their best and bravest men, would be more easily managed in future. Such was probably the view of the King and his counsellors in

---

[1] See *"The Fair Maid of Perth,"* *Wavery Novels*

permitting this desperate conflict, which, however, was much in the spirit of the times.

The parties on each side were drawn out, armed with sword and target, axe and dagger, and stood looking on each other with fierce and ravage aspects, when, just as the signal for fight was expected, the commander of the Clan Chattan perceived that one of his men, whose heart had failed him, had deserted his standard. There was no time to seek another man from the clan, so the chieftain, as his only resource, was obliged to offer a reward to any one who would fight in the room of the fugitive. Perhaps you think it might be difficult to get a man, who, for a small hire, would undergo the perils of a battle which was likely to be so obstinate and deadly. But in that fighting age men valued their lives lightly. One Henry Wynd, a citizen of Perth, and a saddler by trade, a little bandy-legged man, but of great strength and activity, and well accustomed to use the broadsword, offered himself, for half a French crown, to serve on the part of the Clan Chattan in the battle of that day.

The signal was then given by sound of the royal trumpets, and of the great war-bagpipes of the Highlanders and the two parties fell on each other with the utmost fury; their natural ferocity of temper being excited by feudal hatred against the hostile clan, zeal for the honour of their own, and a consciousness that they were fighting in presence of the King and nobles of Scotland. As they fought with the two-handed sword and axe, the wounds they inflicted on each other were of a ghastly size and character. Heads were cloven asunder, limbs were lopped from the trunk. The meadow was soon drenched with blood, and covered with dead and wounded men.

In the midst of the deadly conflict, the chieftain of the Clan Chattan observed that Henry Wynd, after he had slain one of the Clan Kay, drew aside, and did not seem willing to fight more.

"How is this," said he, "art thou afraid?"

"Not I," answered Henry; "but I have done enough of work for half-a-crown."

"Forward and fight," said the Highland chief; "he that doth not grudge his day's work, I will not stint him in his wages."

Thus encouraged, Henry Wynd again plunged into the conflict, and, by his excellence as a swordsman, contributed a great deal to the victory, which at length fell to the Clan Chattan. Ten of the victors, with Henry Wynd, whom the Highlanders called the *Gow Chrom* (that is, the crooked or bandy-legged smith, for he was both a smith and a saddler, war-saddles being then made of steel), were left alive, but they were all wounded. Only one of the Clan Kay survived, and he was unhurt. But this single individual dared not oppose himself to eleven men, though all more or less injured, but, throwing himself into the Tay, swam to the other side, and went off to carry to the Highlands the news of his clan's defeat. It is said, he was so ill received by his kinsmen that he put himself to death.

Some part of the above story is matter of tradition, but the general fact is certain. Henry Wynd was rewarded to the Highland chieftain's best abilities; but it was remarked that, when the battle was over, he was not able to tell the name of the clan he had fought for, replying, when asked on which side he had been, that he was fighting for his own hand. Hence the proverb, "Every man for his own hand," as Henry Wynd fought.

In the meantime troubles, to which we have formerly alluded, broke out in the family of Robert III. The King had been lamed in early youth by the kick of a horse, which had prevented his engaging in war. He was by disposition peaceful, religious, and just, but not firm of mind, and easily imposed on by those about him, and particularly by his brother the Duke of Albany, a man of an enterprising character, but crafty, ambitious, and cruel.

This prince, the next heir to the crown, if the King's children could be displaced, continued to sow strife and animosity betwixt his father and the Duke of Rothsay, the eldest son of Robert III., and heir to his kingdom. Rothsay was young, gay, and irregular, his father old, and strict in his principles; occasions of quarrel easily arose betwixt them, and Albany represented the conduct of the son to the father in the worst light.

The King and Queen seem to have been of opinion that the marriage of the prince might put an end to his idle and licentious course of life. But Albany, whom they consulted, conducted this important affair in a manner disgraceful to the royal family. He proceeded upon the principle, that the prince should marry the daughter of such Scottish noble as was willing to pay the largest sum of money for the honour of connecting himself with the royal house. The powerful George, Earl of March, was at first the largest offerer. But although the prince was contracted to the daughter of that nobleman accordingly, yet the match was broken off by Albany, when a still larger sum was offered by the

Earl of Douglas. His predecessor Earl James, killed at Otterburn, had married the King's sister, and Earl Archibald was now desirous that his own daughter should be even more nearly connected with royalty, by wedding the heir of the throne. They were married accordingly, but in an evil hour.

The prince continued to give offence by the levity of his conduct; Albany continued to pour his complaints into the King's ear, and Douglas became also the enemy of his royal son-in-law.

The history of this reign being imperfect, we do not distinctly know what charges were brought against the Duke of Rothsay, or how far they were true or false. But it seems certain that he was delivered up by his father to the power of his uncle of Albany, and that of his father-in-law, the Earl of Douglas, who treated him with the utmost cruelty.

A villain named Ramorgny, with the assistance of Sir William Lindsay, was furnished with a warrant for apprehending and confining the person of the heir-apparent of Scotland. Armed with this authority, they seized upon him as he was journeying in Fife, without any suspicion—placed him upon an ordinary work-horse, and conducted him to the strong tower, or castle, of Falkland, belonging to Albany. It was a heavy fall of rain, but the poor prince was allowed no other shelter than a peasant's cloak. When in that gloomy fortress, he was thrown into a dungeon, and for fifteen days suffered to remain without food, under the charge of two ruffians named Wright and Selkirk, whose task it was to watch the agony of their victim till it terminated in death. It is said that one woman, touched with his lamentations, contrived to bring him from time to time thin barley cakes, concealed in her veil, which she passed through the bars of his prison; and that another woman supplied him with milk from her own bosom. Both were discovered, and what scanty resources their charity could afford were intercepted; and the unhappy prince died in the month of March 1402 of famine,—the most severe and lingering mode among the many by which life may be ended.[1]

---

[1] "When nature at last sunk, his body was found in a state too dreadful to be described, which showed that, in the extremities of hunger, he had pawed and torn his own flesh. It was then carried to the monastery of Lindores, and there privately buried, while a report was circulated that the prince had been taken ill and died of a dysentery."—Tytler.

There is no evidence that the old King, infirm and simple-minded as he was, suspected the foul play which his son had received; but the vengeance of God seemed to menace the country in which such a tragedy had been acted. The Earl of March, incensed at the breach of the contract betwixt his daughter and the prince, deserted the Scottish cause, and embraced that of England. He fled to Northumberland, and from thence made repeated incursions upon the Scottish frontier.

The Earl of Douglas, placing himself at the head of ten thousand men, made an incursion into England, with banner displayed, and took great spoil. But, in returning, he was waylaid by the celebrated Hotspur, who, with George of March and others, had assembled a numerous army. Douglas, with the same infatuation as had been displayed at so many other battles, took his ground on an eminence called Homildon, where his numerous ranks were exposed to the English arrows, the Scots suffering great loss, for which they were unable to repay the enemy. While they were thus sustaining a dreadfully unequal combat, a bold Scottish knight, named Sir John Swinton, called with a loud voice, "Why do we remain here on this hillside, to be shot like stags with arrows, when we might rush down upon the English, and dispute the combat hand to hand? Let those who will descend with me, that we may gain victory, or fall like men." There was a young nobleman in the host, called the Lord of Gordon. The person living whom he most detested was this same Sir John Swinton, because in some private quarrel he had slain Gordon's father. But when he heard him give such resolute and brave advice in that dreadful extremity, he required to be made a knight at Swinton's hand; "For," said he, "from the hand of no wiser leader, or braver man, can I ask that honour." Swinton granted his desire, and having hastily performed the ceremony by striking the young man on the neck with the flat of his sword, and bidding him arise a knight, he and Gordon rushed down side by side with their followers, and made considerable slaughter amongst the English. But not being supported by other chiefs, they were overpowered and cut to pieces. The Scots lost the battle, sustaining a total defeat; and Douglas, wounded, and having lost an eye, fell into the hands of the English as a prisoner.

A singular train of events followed, which belong rather to English than Scottish history, but which it is proper you should know.

The Earl of Northumberland, father to Hotspur, associated with other discontented nobles, had determined to rebel against Henry IV., then King of England. To strengthen their forces, they gave Douglas his liberty, and engaged him to assist them in the civil war which was impending. Douglas came accordingly with a band of his countrymen, and joined Henry Percy, called Hotspur. They marched together into England, and fought a memorable battle with the royal forces near Shrewsbury. As Henry IV. was personally present in the battle, Douglas resolved to seek him out, and end the contest by killing or making him prisoner. The King had, however, several other champions in the field, armed and mounted exactly like himself. Of these, Douglas killed no less than three, as they appeared one after another; so that when at length he encountered the real king, he called out, with amazement, "Where the devil do all these kings come from?" The Scottish earl attacked Henry himself with the same fury with which he had assaulted those who represented him, overthrew the royal banner, slaying a valiant knight, Sir Thomas Blunt, to whose care it had been committed, and was about to kill the King. But numbers, and especially the brave Prince of Wales, his son, came to the King of England's assistance; and before Douglas could fight his way forward to Henry, Hotspur was killed by an arrow-shot, and his party were obliged to fly. Douglas at length condescended to fly also, but his horse stumbling in ascending a hill, he was again wounded and taken.

We return to poor King Robert III., who was now exhausted by age, infirmities, and family calamity. He had still a remaining son, called James, about eleven years old, and he was probably afraid to entrust him to the keeping of Albany, as his death would have rendered that ambitious prince next heir to the throne. He resolved, therefore, to send the young prince to France, under pretence that he would receive a better education there than Scotland could afford him. An English vessel captured that on board of which the prince was sailing to France, and James was sent to London. When Henry heard that the Prince of Scotland was in his power, he resolved to detain him a prisoner. This was very unjust, for the countries of England and Scotland were at peace together at the time. The King sent him to prison, however, saying, that "The prince would be as well educated at his court as at that of France, for that he understood French well." This was said in mockery, but Henry kept his word in this point; and though the Scottish prince was confined unjustly, he received an excellent education at the expense of the English monarch.

This new misfortune, which placed the only remaining son of the poor old King in the hands of the English, seems to have broken the heart of Robert III., who died about a year afterwards, overwhelmed with calamities and infirmity.[1]

---

[1] "This last blow," says Sir Walter Scott elsewhere, "completely broke the heart of the unhappy King Robert III. Vengeance followed, though with a slow pace, the treachery and cruelty of his brother. Robert of Albany's own gray hairs went, indeed, in peace to the grave and he transferred the regency, which he had so foully acquired, to his son Murdoch. But nineteen years after the death of the old King, James I. returned to Scotland, and Duke Murdoch of Albany, with his sons, was brought to the scaffold, in expiation of his father's guilt and his own." *Fair Maid of Perth.* On the character of King Robert III., the second of the ill-fated family of Stewart who filled the throne of Scotland, Sir Walter remarks: "He had many virtues, and was not without talent, but it was his great misfortune that, like others of his devoted line, his merits were not of a kind suited to the part he was called upon to perform in life. The King of so fierce a people as the Scots then were, ought to have been warlike, prompt, and active, liberal in rewarding services, strict in punishing crimes; one whose conduct should make him feared as well as beloved. The qualities of Robert the Third were the reverse of all these. In youth he had indeed seen battles; but, without incurring disgrace, he had never manifested the chivalrous love of war and peril, or the eager desire to distinguish himself by dangerous achievements, which that age expected from all who were of noble birth, and had claims to authority. Besides, his military career was very short. Amidst the tumult of a tournament, the young Earl of Carrick, such was then his title, received a kick from a horse; in consequence of which, he was lame for the rest of his life. As Robert had never testified much predilection for violent exertion, he did not probably much regret the incapacities which exempted him from these active scenes."—*Ibid.*

XVIII

The Regencies of Albany

1406-1424

ALBANY, the brother of Robert III., was now Regent of the kingdom, of which he had long actually possessed the supreme government. He was, it may be supposed, in no great hurry to obtain the release of his nephew Prince James, whose return to Scotland must have ended his own power. He was, as we have seen, a wicked, cruel, and ambitious man; yet he was regular in administering justice, and took great care not to lay any taxes on the people. Even in his time, it would seem that the extent of writings used for the transference of property had become a subject of complaint. When upon this subject, Albany used often to praise the simplicity and brevity of an ancient charter by King Athelstane, a Saxon monarch. It had been granted to the ancient Northumbrian family called Roddam of Roddam, and had fallen into the hands of the Scots on some of their plundering parties.

Jedburgh Castle, which the English had kept ever since the battle of Durham, had been taken by the Teviotdale Borderers, and it was proposed that it should be pulled down, in order that it might not again afford the enemy a stronghold on the frontiers. This was a common policy with the Scots, who considered their desert woods and mountains as better points of defence than walled castles, which the English understood how to attack or defend much better than they did.

To defray the expense of maintaining the men engaged in demolishing this large and strong fortress, it was proposed to lay a small tax of two pennies on each hearth in Scotland. But the Regent determined to pay it out of his own and the King's revenue, resolved, as he said, that he would not begin his regency by a measure which must afflict the poor.

In other respects, Albany was an unworthy character. He was not even brave, which was a failing uncommon in his age and family; and though he engaged in several wars with England, he did not gain either honour or success in any of them.

One of the most remarkable events during his government was the battle of Harlaw. This was fought by a prince, called Donald of the Isles, who possessed all the islands on the west side of Scotland. He was also the proprietor of great estates on the mainland, and aspired to the rank and used the style of an independent sovereign.

This Donald, in the year 1411, laid claim to the earldom of Ross, then vacant, which the Regent had determined to bestow on a member of his own family. Donald of the Isles raised ten thousand men, all Highlanders like himself, and invading the north of Scotland, came as far as a place called Harlaw, about ten miles from Aberdeen. Here he was encountered by the Earl of Mar, at the head of an inferior army, but composed of Lowland gentlemen, better armed and disciplined than the followers of Donald. A most desperate battle ensued, in which both parties suffered great loss. On that of Donald, the chiefs of the clans called MacIntosh and MacLean were both slain, with about a thousand men. Mar lost nearly five hundred brave gentlemen, amongst them Ogilvy, Scrymgeour, Irvine of Drum, and other men of rank. The Provost of Aberdeen, who had brought to the Earl of Mar's host a detachment of the inhabitants of that city, was slain, fighting bravely. This loss was so much regretted by the citizens, that a resolution was adopted, that no Provost should in future go out in his official capacity beyond the limits of the immediate territory of the town. This rule is still observed.

But though the Lowlanders suffered severely, the Highlanders had the worst, and were obliged to retreat after the battle. This was fortunate for Scotland, since otherwise the Highlanders, at that time a wild and barbarous people, would have overrun, and perhaps actually conquered, a great part of the civilised country. The battle of Harlaw was long remembered, owing to the bravery with which the field was disputed, and the numbers which fell on both sides.

The Regent Albany, after having ruled Scotland for about thirty-four years, including the time under his father and brother, died at the castle of Stirling in the thirteenth year of his sole regency, aged upwards of eighty years, on the 3d September 1419. He was succeeded in his high office by his son Murdac, Duke of Albany, a man who had neither the vices nor the virtues of his father. Duke Robert was active, crafty, suspicious, and, in one sense at least, wise. The son was indulgent, indolent, and at the same time simple and easy to be imposed upon. Many quarrels and feuds broke out in the country, and even in his own family, which had been suppressed by the strong hand of his father. Little memorable took place in the regency of Murdac, but it was remarkable for the great renown which the Scots won in the wars of France.

I have told you that a body of French knights came to Scotland to assist the Scots against the English; and you must now know how the Scots repaid the obligation, by sending over a body of men to assist Charles, King of France, then in great danger of being completely conquered by Henry V. of England, who seemed on the point of expelling him from the kingdom, and possessing himself of the crown of France. A small army of about six or seven thousand chosen Scots had gone to France, under the command of John Stewart, Earl of Buchan, the second son of the Regent Robert, Duke of Albany. He had under him Lindsay, Swinton, and other men of consequence and fame. They gained an important victory over the English, then under command of the Duke of Clarence, brother to Henry V. This prince, hearing that there was a body of Scots encamped at a town called Baugé, and enraged that this northern people should not only defend their own country from the English, but also come over to give them trouble in France, made a hasty march to surprise them. He left behind him those celebrated archers, who had usually afforded the English means of conquest over the enemy, because he relied upon the rapidity of his motions, and understood the Scots were observing indifferent discipline, and not keeping a vigilant watch. He arrived at Baugé, followed only by the knights and men-at-arms on horseback. Having forced the passage of a bridge, Clarence was pressing forward at the head of his cavalry, distinguished by the richness of his armour, and by a splendid golden coronet which he wore over his helmet. At this moment the Scottish knights charged the enemy. Sir John Swinton galloped against the Duke of Clarence, and unhorsed him with his lance, and the Earl of Buchan dashed out his brains with a battle-axe or mace. A great many English knights and nobles were slain at this encounter. The French King, to reward the valour of the Scots, created the Earl of Buchan Constable of France (one of the highest offices in the kingdom), and Count of Aubigny.

The Scots, incited by the renown and wealth which their countrymen had acquired, came over to France in greater numbers, and the Earl of Douglas himself was tempted to bring over a little army, in which the best and noblest of the gentlemen of the south of Scotland of course enrolled themselves. They who did not go themselves, sent their sons and brothers. Sir Alexander Home of Home had intended to take this course; and his brother, David Home of Wedderburn, was equipped for the expedition. The chief himself came down to the vessel to see Douglas and his brother embark. But when the earl saw his old companion-in-arms about to take leave of him, he said, "Ah! Sir Alexander, who would have thought that thou and I should ever have parted!"

"Neither will we part now, my lord," said Sir Alexander; and suddenly changing his purpose, he sent back his brother David to take care of his castle, family, and estate, and going to France with his old friend, died with him at the battle of Verneuil.

The Earl of Douglas, whose military fame was so great, received high honours from the King of France, and was created Duke of Touraine. The earl was used to ridicule the Duke of Bedford, who then acted as Regent for Henry VI. in France, and gave him the nickname of *John with the leaden sword.* Upon the 17th August 1424, Douglas received a message from the Duke of Bedford, that he intended to come and dine and drink wine with him. Douglas well understood the nature of the visit, and sent back word, that he should be welcome. The Scots and French prepared for battle, while their chiefs consulted together, and unfortunately differed in opinion. The Earl of Douglas, who considered their situation as favourable, recommended that they should receive the attack of the English, instead of advancing to meet them. The French Count de Narbonne, however, insisted that they should march forward to the attack; and putting the French in motion, declared he would move to the fight whether the Scots did so or not. Douglas was thus compelled to advance likewise, but it was in disorder. The English archers in the meantime showered their arrows on the French; their men-at-arms charged; and a total route of the allied army was the consequence. Douglas and Buchan stood their ground, fought desperately, and died nobly. Rome, Lindsay, Swinton, and far the greater part of that brave Scottish band of auxiliaries, were killed on the spot.

The great Earl of Douglas, thus slain at Verneuil, was distinguished from the rest of his family by the name of *Tineman*, that is *Loseman*, as he was defeated in the great battles of Homildon, Shrewsbury, and finally in that of Verneuil, where he lost his life. His contemporary and rival, George, Earl of March, though not so celebrated a warrior, was as remarkable for being fortunate for whether he fought on the Scottish or English side, his party was always victorious. The slender remains of the Scottish forces were adopted by Charles of France as a life-guard; a body which was kept up by his successors for a great many years.

We return now to Scotland, where the Regent Murdac of Albany was so far from being able to guide the affairs of the state, that he could not control his own sons. There were two of them, haughty, licentious young men, who respected neither the authority of God nor man, and that of their father least of all. Their misbehaviour was so great, that Murdac began to think of putting an end to their bad conduct and his own government at the same time, by obtaining the deliverance of the King from English captivity. A singular piece of insolence, on the part of his eldest son, is said to have determined him to this measure.

At this time the amusement of hawking (that is, of taking birds of game by means of trained hawks) was a pastime greatly esteemed by the nobility. The Regent Murdac had one falcon of peculiar excellence, which he valued. His eldest son, Walter Stewart, had often asked this bird of his father, and been as often denied. At length one day when the Regent had the hawk sitting upon his wrist, in the way that falconers carry such birds, Walter renewed his importunity about the falcon; and when his father again refused it, he snatched it from his wrist, and wrung its neck round. His father, greatly offended at so gross an insult, said, in his anger, "Since thou wilt give me neither reverence nor obedience, I will fetch home one whom we must all obey." From that moment, be began to bargain with the English in good earnest that they should restore James, now King of Scotland, to his own dominions.

The English Government were not unwilling to deliver up James, the rather that he had fallen in love with Joanna, the Earl of Somerset's daughter, nearly related to the royal family of England. They considered that this alliance would incline the young prince to peace with England; and that the education which he had received, and the friendships which he had formed in that country, would incline him to be a good and peaceable neighbour. The Scots agreed to pay a considerable ransom; and upon these terms James, the first of that name, was set at liberty and returned to become king in Scotland, after eighteen years' captivity. He and his queen were crowned at Scone, 21st May 1424.

XIX

James I.

1424-1437

THIS King James, the first monarch of the name, was also the first of his unfortunate family who showed a high degree of talent. Robert II. and Robert III., his father and grandfather, were both rather amiable as individuals than respected for their endowments as monarchs. But James had received an excellent education, of which his talents had enabled him to make the best use. He was also prudent and just, consulted the interests of his people, and endeavoured, as far as he could, to repress those evils, which had grown up through the partial government of Robert, Duke of Albany, the rule of the feeble and slothful Duke Murdac, and the vicious and violent conduct of his sons.

The first vengeance of the laws fell upon Murdac, who, with his two sons, was tried, and condemned at Stirling for abuse of the King's authority, committed while Murdac was Regent. They were beheaded at the little eminence at Stirling, which is still shown on the Castle Hill. The Regent, from that elevated spot, might have a distant view of the magnificent castle of Doune, which he had built for his residence; and the sons had ample reason to regret their contempt of their father's authority, and to judge the truth of his words, when he said he would bring in one who would rule them all.

James afterwards turned his cares to the Highlands, which were in a state of terrible confusion. He marched into those disturbed districts with a strong army, and seized upon more than forty of the chiefs, by whom these broils and quarrels were countenanced, put many of them to death, and obliged others to find security that they would be quiet in future. Alaster MacDonald, Lord of the Isles, after more than a year's captivity, and his mother retained in vain as a hostage for his fidelity, endeavoured to oppose the royal authority; but the measures taken against him by James reduced his power so much, that he was at last obliged to submit to the King's mercy. For this purpose the humbled chief came to Edinburgh secretly, and suddenly appeared in the Cathedral Church, where the King was employed in his devotions upon Easterday. He appeared without bonnet, armour, or ornaments, with his legs and arms bare, and his body only covered with plaid. In this condition he delivered himself up to the King's pleasure; and holding a naked sword in his hand by the point, he offered the hilt to the King in token of unreserved submission. James forgave him his repeated offences, at the intercession of the Queen and nobles present, but he detained him a prisoner in the strong castle of Tantallon, in East Lothian. Yet, after this submission of their principal chief, the West Highlanders and people of the Isles again revolted, under the command of Donald Balloch, the kinsman of Alaster, who landed on the mainland with a considerable force, and defeated the Earls of Mar and of Caithness with great slaughter; but when he heard that James was coming against him, Donald thought it best to retreat to Ireland. James put to death many of his followers. Donald himself was afterwards killed in Ireland, and his head sent to the King.

There is another story, which will show the cruelty and ferocity of these Highland robbers. Another MacDonald, head of a band in Rossshire, had plundered a poor widow woman of two of her cows, and who, in her anger, exclaimed repeatedly that she would never wear shoes again till she had carried her complaint to the King for redress, should she travel to Edinburgh to seek him. "It is false," answered the barbarian; "I will have you shod myself before you reach the court." Accordingly, he caused a smith to nail shoes to the poor woman's naked feet, as if they had been those of a horse; after which he thrust her forth, wounded and bleeding, on the highway. The widow, however, being a woman of high spirit, was determined to keep her word; and as soon as her wounds permitted her to travel, she did actually go on foot to Edinburgh, and, throwing herself before James, acquainted him with the cruelty which had been exercised on her, and in evidence showed her feet, still seamed and scarred. James heard her with that mixture of pity, kindness, and uncontrollable indignation which marked his character, and, in great resentment, caused MacDonald, and twelve of his principal followers, to be seized, and to have their feet shod with iron shoes, in the same manner as had been done to the widow. In this condition they were exhibited to the public for three days, and then executed.

Thus James I. restored a considerable degree of tranquillity to the country, which he found in such a distracted state. He made wise laws for regulating the commerce of the nation, both at home and with other states, and strict regulations for the administration of justice betwixt those who had complaints against one another.

But his greatest labour, and that which he found most difficult to accomplish, was to diminish the power of the great nobles, who ruled like so many kings, each on his own territory and estate, and made war on the King, or upon one another, whenever it was their pleasure to do so. These disorders he endeavoured to check, and had several of these great persons brought to trial, and, upon their being found guilty, deprived them of their estates. The nobles complained that this was done out of spite against them, and that they were treated with hardship and injustice; and thus discontents were entertained against this good Prince. Another cause of offence was, that to maintain justice, and support the authority of the throne, it was found necessary that some taxes for this purpose should be raised from the subjects; and the Scottish people being poor, and totally unaccustomed to pay any such contributions, they imputed this odious measure to the King's avarice. And thus, though King James was so well-intentioned a King, and certainly the ablest who had reigned in Scotland since the days of Robert Bruce, yet both the high and the low murmured against him, which encouraged some wicked men amongst the nobility to conspire his death.

The chief person in the plot was one Sir Robert Graham, uncle to the Earl of Stratherne. He was bold and ambitious, and highly offended with the King on account of an imprisonment which he had sustained by the royal command. He drew into the plot the Earl of Athole, an old man of little talent, by promising to make his son, Sir Robert Stewart, King of Scotland, in place of James. Others were engaged in the conspiracy from different motives. To many of their attendants they pretended they only wished to carry away a lady out of the court. To prepare his scheme, Graham retreated into the remote Highlands, and from thence sent a defiance, renouncing his allegiance to the King, and threatening to put his sovereign to death with his own hand. A price was set upon his head, payable to any one who should deliver him up to justice; but he lay concealed in the wild mountains to prosecute his revenge against James.

The Christmas preceding his murder was appointed by the King for holding a feast at Perth. In his way to that town he was met by a Highland woman, calling herself a prophetess. She stood by the side of the ferry by which he was about to travel to the north, and cried with a loud voice,—"My Lord the King, if you pass this water, you will never return again alive." The King was struck with this for a moment, because he had read in a book that a king should be slain that year in Scotland; for it often happens, that when a remarkable deed is in agitation, rumours of it get abroad, and are repeated under pretence of prophecies; but which are, in truth, only conjectures of that which seems likely to happen. There was a knight in the court, on whom the King had conferred the name of the King of Love, to whom the King said in jest, "There is a prophecy that a king shall be killed in Scotland this year; now, Sir Alexander, that must concern either you or me, since we two are the only kings in Scotland." Other circumstances occurred, which might have prevented the good King's murder, but none of them were attended to. The King, while at Perth, took up his residence in an abbey of Black Friars, there being no castle or palace in the town convenient for his residence; and this made the execution of the conspiracy more easy, as his guards, and the officers of his household, were quartered among the citizens.

The day had been spent by the King in sport and feasting, and by the conspirators in preparing for their enterprise. They had destroyed the locks of the doors of the apartment, so that the keys could not be turned; and they had taken away the bars with which the gates were secured, and had provided planks by way of bridges, on which to cross the ditch which surrounded the monastery. At length, on the 20th February 1437, all was prepared for carrying their treasonable purpose into execution, and Graham came from his hiding-place in the neighbouring mountains, with a party of nigh three hundred men, and entered the gardens of the convent.

The King was in his night-gown and slippers. He had passed the evening gaily with the nobles and ladies of his court, in reading romances, and in singing and music, or playing at chess and tables. The Earl of Athole, and his son Sir Robert Stewart, who expected to succeed James on the throne, were among the last courtiers who retired. At this time James remained standing before the fire, and conversing gaily with the queen and her ladies before he went to rest. The Highland woman before mentioned again demanded permission to speak with the King, but was refused, on account of the untimeliness of the hour. All now were ordered to withdraw.

At this moment there was a noise and clashing heard, as of men in armour, and the torches in the garden cast up great flashes of light against the windows. The King then recollected his deadly enemy, Sir Robert Graham, and guessed that he was coming to murder him. He called to the ladies who were left in the chamber to keep the door as well as they could, in order to give him time to escape. He first tried to get out at the windows, but they were fast barred, and defied his strength. By help of the tongs, which were in the chimney, he raised, however, a plank of the flooring of the apartment, and let himself down into a narrow vault beneath, used as a common sewer. This vault had formerly had an opening into the court of the convent, by which he might have made his escape. But all things turned against the unfortunate James; for, only three days before, he had caused the opening to be built up, because when he played at ball in court-yard, the ball used to roll into the vault through that hole.

While the King was in this place of concealment, the conspirators were seeking him from chamber to chamber throughout the convent, and, at length, came to the room where the ladies were. The Queen and her women endeavoured, as well as they might, to keep the door shut and one of them, Catherine Douglas, boldly thrust her own arm across the door, instead of the bar, which had been taken away, as I told you. But the brave lady's arm was soon broken, and the traitors rushed into the room with swords and daggers drawn, hurting and throwing down such of the women as opposed them. The poor Queen stood half undressed, shrieking aloud; and one of the brutal assassins attacked, wounded, and would have slain her, had it not been for a son of Sir Robert Graham, who said to him, "What would you do to the Queen? She is but a woman—Let us seek the King."

They accordingly commenced a minute search, but without any success; so they left the apartment, and sought elsewhere about the monastery. In the meanwhile the King turned impatient, and desired the ladies to bring sheets and draw him up out of the inconvenient lurking place. In the attempt Elizabeth Douglas fell down beside the King, and at this unlucky moment the conspirators returned. One of them now recollected that there was such a vault, and that they had not searched it. And when they tore up the plank, and saw the King and the lady beneath in the vault, one of them called, with savage merriment to his followers, "Sirs, I have found the bride for whom we have sought and carolled all night." Then, first one and then another of the villains, brethren of the name of Hall, descended into the vault, with daggers drawn, to despatch the unfortunate King, who was standing there in his shirt, without weapons of any kind. But James, who was an active and strong man, threw them both down beneath his feet, and struggled to wrest the dagger from one or other of them, in which attempt his hands were severely cut and mangled. The murderers also were so vigorously handled, that the marks of the King's gripe were visible on their throats for weeks afterwards. Then Sir Robert Graham himself sprung down on the King, who finding no further defence possible, asked him for mercy, and for leisure to confess his sins to a priest. But Graham replied fiercely, "Thou never hadst mercy on those of thine own blood, nor on any one else, therefore thou shalt find no mercy here; and as for a confessor, thou shalt have none but this sword." So speaking he thrust the sword through the King's body. And yet it is said, that when he saw his prince lying bleeding under his feet, he was desirous, to have left the enterprise unfinished; but the other conspirators called on Graham to kill the King, otherwise he should himself die by their hands; upon which Graham, with the two men who had descended into the vault before him, fell on the unhappy prince with their daggers, and slew him by many stabs. There were sixteen wounds in his breast alone.

By this time, but too late, news of this outrage had reached the town, and the household servants of the King, with the people inhabiting the town of Perth, were hastening to the rescue, with torches and weapons. The traitors accordingly caught the alarm, and retreated into the Highlands, losing in their flight only one or two, taken or slain by the pursuers. When they spoke about their enterprise among themselves, they greatly regretted that they had not killed the Queen along with her husband, fearing that she would be active and inexorable in her vengeance.

Indeed their apprehensions were justified by the event, for Queen Joanna made so strict search after the villainous assassins, that in the course of a month most of them were thrown into prison, and being tried and condemned, they were put to death with new and hideous tortures. The flesh of Robert Stewart, and of a private chamberlain of the King, was torn from their bodies with pincers; while, even in the midst of these horrible agonies, they confessed the justice of their sentence. The Earl of Athole was beheaded, denying at his death that he had consented to the conspiracy, though he admitted that his son had told him of it; to which he had replied, by enjoining him to have no concern in so great a crime. Sir Robert Graham, who was the person with whom the cruel scheme had origin, spoke in defence of it to the last. He had a right to slay the King, he said, for he had renounced his allegiance, and declared war against him; and he expressed his belief, that his memory would be honoured for putting to death so cruel a tyrant. He was tortured in the most dreadful manner before his final execution, and, whilst he was yet living, his son was slain before his eyes.

Notwithstanding the greatness of their crime, it was barbarous cruelty to torture these wretched murderers in the manner we have mentioned, and the historian says justly, that it was a cruel deed cruelly revenged. But the people were much incensed against them; for, although they had murmured against King James while he lived, yet the dismal manner of his death, and the general feeling that his intentions towards his people were kind and just, caused him to be much regretted. He had also many popular qualities. His face was handsome, and his person strong and active. His mind was well cultivated with ornamental and elegant accomplishments, as well as stored with useful information. He understood music and poetry, and wrote verses, both serious and comic. Two of his compositions are still preserved, and read with interest and entertainment by those who understand the ancient language in which they are written. One of these is called "The King's Quhair," that is, the King's Book. It is a love poem, composed when he was a prisoner in England, and addressed to the Princess Joanna of Somerset, whom he afterwards married. The other is a comic poem, called "Christ's Kirk on the Green," in which the author gives an account of a merrymaking of the country people, held for the purpose of sport, where they danced, revelled, drank, and finally quarrelled and fought. There is much humour shown in this piece, though one would think the subject a strange one for a king to write upon. He particularly ridicules the Scots for want of acquaintance with archery. One man breaks his bow, another shoots his arrow wide of the mark, a third hits the man's body at whom he took aim, but with so little effect that he cannot pierce his leathern doublet. There is a meaning in this raillery. James I., seeing the advantage which the English possessed by their archery, was desirous to introduce that exercise more generally into Scotland, and ordered regular meetings to be held for this purpose. Perhaps he might hope to enforce these orders, by employing a little wholesome raillery on the awkwardness of the Scottish bowmen.

On the whole, James I. was much and deservedly lamented. The murderer Graham was so far from being remembered with honour, as he had expected, for the assassination which he had committed, that his memory was execrated in a popular rhyme then generally current:—

> "Robert Graham,
> That slew our king,
> God give him shame!"

XX

James II.

1437-1449

WHEN James I. was murdered, his son and heir, James II., was only six years old; so that Scotland was once more plunged into all the discord and confusions of a regency, which were sure to reach their height in a country where even the undisputed sway of a sovereign of mature age was not held in due respect, and was often disturbed by treason and rebellion.

The affairs of the kingdom, during the minority of James II., were chiefly managed by two statesmen, who seem to have been men of considerable personal talent, but very little principle or integrity. Sir Alexander Livingston was guardian of the King's person; Sir William Crichton was Chancellor of the kingdom. They debated betwixt themselves the degree of authority attached to their respective offices, and at once engaged in quarrels with each other, and with one who was more powerful than either of them—the great Earl of Douglas.

That mighty house was now at the highest pitch of its greatness. The Earl possessed Galloway, Annandale, and other extensive properties in the south of Scotland, where almost all the inferior nobility and gentry acknowledged him as their patron and lord. Thus the Douglases had at their disposal that part of Scotland which, from its constant wars with England, was most disciplined and accustomed to arms. They possessed the duchy of Touraine and lordship of Longueville in France, and they were connected by intermarriage with the Scottish royal family.

The Douglases were not only powerful from the extent of lands and territories, but also from the possession of great military talents, which seemed to pass from father to son, and occasioned a proverb, still remembered in Scotland—

> "So many, so good, as of the Douglases have been,
> Of one sirname in Scotland never yet were seen."

Unfortunately their power, courage, and military skill, were attended with arrogance and ambition, and the Douglases seemed to have claimed to themselves the rank and authority of sovereign princes, independent of the laws of the country, and of the allegiance due to the monarch. It was a common thing for them to ride with a retinue of a thousand horse; and as Archibald, the Earl of Douglas of the time, rendered but an imperfect allegiance even to the severe rule of James I., it might be imagined that his power could not be easily restrained by such men as Crichton and Livingston—great, indeed, through the high offices which they held, but otherwise of a degree far inferior to that of Douglas.

But when this powerful nobleman died, in 1439, and was succeeded by his son William, a youth of only sixteen years old, the wily Crichton began to spy an occasion to crush the Douglases as he hoped, for ever, by the destruction of the youthful earl and his brother, and for abating, by this cruel and unmerited punishment, the power and pride of this great family. Crichton proposed to Livingston to join him in this meditated treachery; and, though enemies to each other, the guardian of the King and the Chancellor of the kingdom united in the vile project of cutting off two boys, whose age alone showed their innocence of the guilt charged upon them. For this purpose flattery and fair words were used to induce the young Earl, and his brother David, with some of their nearest friends, to come to court, where it was pretended that they would be suitable companions and intimates for the young King. An old adherent of the family greatly dissuaded the Earl from accepting this invitation, and exhorted him, if he went to Edinburgh in person, to leave at least his brother David behind him. But the unhappy youth, thinking that no treachery was intended, could not be diverted from the fatal journey.

The Chancellor Crichton received the Earl of Douglas and his brother on their journey, at his own castle of Crichton, and with the utmost appearance of hospitality and kindness. After remaining a day or two at this place, the two brothers were inveigled to Edinburgh Castle, and introduced to the young King, who, not knowing the further purpose of his guardians, received them with affability, and seemed delighted with the prospect of enjoying their society.

On a sudden the scene began to change. At an entertainment which was served up to the Earl and his brother, the head of a black bull was placed on the table. The Douglases knew this, according to a custom which prevailed in Scotland, to be the sign of death, and leaped from the table in great dismay. But they were seized by armed men who entered the apartment. They underwent a mock trial, in which all the insolences of their ancestors were charged against them, and were condemned to immediate execution. The young King wept, and implored Livingston and Crichton to show mercy to the young noblemen, but in vain. These cruel men only reproved him for weeping at the death of those whom they called his enemies. The brothers were led out to the court of the castle, and beheaded without delay. Malcolm Fleming of Cumbernauld, a faithful adherent of their house, shared the same fate.

This barbarous proceeding was as unwise as it was unjust. It did not reduce the power of the Douglases, but only raised general detestation against those who managed the affairs of James II. A fat, quiet, peaceable person, called James the Gross, indolent from habit of body and temper of mind, next became Earl of Douglas, which was probably the reason that no public commotion immediately attended on the murder of the hapless brothers. But this corpulent dignitary lived only two years, and was in his turn succeeded by his son William, who was as active and turbulent as any of his ambitious predecessors, and engaged in various civil broils, for the purpose of revenging the death of his kinsmen.

James the Second, in the meanwhile, came to man's estate, and entered on the management of public affairs. He was a handsome man, but his countenance was marked on one side with a broad red spot, which gained him the surname of James with the Fiery Face. They might have called him James with the fiery temper, in like manner; for, with many good qualities, he had a hot and impetuous disposition, of which we shall presently see a remarkable instance.

William, who had succeeded to the earldom of Douglas, was enormously wealthy and powerful. The family had gradually added to their original patrimony the lordship of Galloway, the lordship of Bothwell, the dukedom of Touraine, and lordship of Longueville, in France, the lordship of Annandale, and the earldom of Wigtown. So that, in personal wealth and power, the Earl of Douglas not only approached to, but greatly exceeded the King himself. The Douglases, however, though ambitious and unruly subjects in time of peace, were always gallant defenders of the liberties of Scotland during the time of war; and if they were sometimes formidable to their own sovereigns, they were not less so to their English enemies.

In 1448 war broke out betwixt England and Scotland, and the incursions on both sides became severe and destructive. The English, under young Percy, destroyed Dumfries, and in return, the Scots, led by Lord Balveny, the youngest brother of Douglas, burnt the town of Alnwick. The Lord Percy of Northumberland, with the Earl of Huntingdon, advanced into Scotland with an army, said by the French historians to amount to fifteen thousand men. The Earl of Douglas, to whom the King had intrusted the defence of the frontiers, met him with a much inferior force, defeated the invaders, and made their leaders prisoners.

Incensed at this defeat, the English assembled an army of fifty thousand men, under the command of the Earl of Northumberland, who had under him a celebrated general, called Sir Magnus Redmain,[1] long governor of the town of Berwick; Sir John Pennington, ancestor of the family of Muncaster, and other leaders of high reputation. The task of encountering this mighty host fell upon Hugh, Earl of Ormond, brother also of the Earl of Douglas, who assembled an army of thirty thousand men, and marched to meet the invaders.

The English had entered the Scottish border, and advanced beyond the small river Sark, when the armies came in presence of each other. The English began the battle, as usual, with a fatal discharge of arrows. But William Wallace of Craigie, well worthy of the heroic name

---

[1] "He was remarkable by his long and red beard and was therefore called by the English 'Magnus Red-beard,' and by the Scots in derision, 'Magnus with the red mane,' as though his beard had been a horse-mane."—Godscroft.

he bore, called out to the left wing of the Scots, which he commanded, "Why stand ye still, to be shot from a distance? Follow me, and we shall soon come to handstrokes." Accordingly, they rushed furiously against the right wing of the English, who, commanded by Sir Magnus Redmain, advanced boldly to meet them. They encountered with great fury, and both leaders fell, Magnus Redmain being slain on the spot, and the Knight of Craigie-Wallace mortally wounded. The English, disconcerted by the loss of their great champion, Magnus, at length gave way. The Scots pressed furiously upon them, and as the little river Sark, which the English had passed at low water, was now filled by the advancing tide, many of the fugitives lost their lives. The victory, together with the spoils of the field, remained in possession of the Scots. The Earl of Northumberland escaped with difficulty, through the gallantry of one of his sons, who was made prisoner in covering his father's retreat.

The King, much pleased with this victory, gave great praise to the Earl of Douglas, and continued to employ his services as lieutenant-general of the kingdom.

This martial family of Douglas were as remarkable for the address with which they sustained the honour of their country in the tournaments and military sports of the age as in the field of battle. In 1449 a grand combat took place betwixt three renowned champions of Flanders, namely, Jacques de Lalain, Simon de Lalain, and Hervé Meriadet, and three Scottish knights, namely, James, brother of the Earl of Douglas, another James Douglas, brother to the Lord of Lochleven, and Sir John Ross of Halket. They fought in the presence of the King at Stirling, with lance, battle-axe, sword, and dagger. The Earl of Douglas himself attended his brother and kinsman with five thousand followers. The combat was to be waged to extremity; that is, the persons engaged were to kill each other if they could, although there was no personal enmity betwixt them, but, on the contrary, much mutual esteem and good-will. They only fought to show which of them was the bravest, and most skilful in the use of arms.

There was a space under the castle rock at Stirling which was used for such purposes. It was surrounded with a strong enclosure of wooden pales, and rich tents were pitched at each end for the convenience of the champions putting on their armour. Galleries were erected for the accommodation of the King and his nobles, while the ladies of the court in great numbers, and dressed as if for a theatre or ball-room, occupied a crag which commanded a view of the lists, still called the Ladies' Rock.

The combatants appeared at first in rich velvet dresses, and after having made their dutiful obeisances to the King, retired to their pavilions. They then sallied out in complete armour, and were knighted by the King. James Douglas and Jacques de Lalain rushed upon each other, and fought till all their weapons were broken, saving Douglas's dagger. The Flemish knight closing with his antagonist, and seizing his arm, Douglas could not strike, but they continued to wrestle fiercely together. The fight was also equal betwixt Simon de Lalain and Sir John Ross; they were neither of them skilful in warding blows, but struck at each other with great fury, till armour and weapons gave way, without either champion obtaining the advantage. James Douglas of Lochleven was less fortunate; Meriadet parried a thrust of the Scotsman's lance, and before Douglas could get his axe in hand, his antagonist struck him to the ground. Douglas, however, instantly sprung to his feet and renewed the conflict. But Meriadet, one of the most skilful and redoubted champions of his time, struck his antagonist a second time to the earth; and then, as the combat had become unequal, the King cast down his warder or truncheon, as a signal that the battle should cease. All the parties were highly praised for their valour, and nobly entertained by the King of Scotland.

Thus you see how gallantly the Douglases behaved themselves, both in war and in the military exercises of the time. It was unhappy for the country and themselves that their ambition and insubordination were at least equal to their courage and talents.

XXI

The Douglas Wars

1449-1460

W E mentioned that James II., in the early part of his reign, conferred on the Earl of Douglas the important post of lieutenant-general of Scotland. But that ambitious nobleman was soon disposed to extend his authority to independent power, and the King found it necessary to take from him the dangerous office with which he had entrusted him. Douglas retired to his own castle meditating revenge; whilst the King, on the other hand, looked around him for some fitting opportunity of diminishing the power of so formidable a rival.

Douglas was not long of showing his total contempt of the King's authority, and his power of acting for himself. One of his friends and followers, named Auchinleck, had been slain by the Lord Colville. The criminal certainly deserved punishment, but it ought to have been inflicted by the regular magistrates of the crown, not by the arbitrary pleasure of a private baron, however great and powerful. Douglas, however, took up the matter as a wrong done to himself, and revenged it by his own authority. He marched a large body of his forces against the Lord Colville, stormed his castle, and put every person within it to death. The King was unable to avenge this insult to his authority.

In like manner, Douglas connived at and encouraged some of his followers in Annandale to ravage and plunder the lands of Sir John Herries, a person of that country, eminently attached to the King. Herries, a man of high spirit and considerable power, retaliated, by wasting the lands of those who had thus injured him. He was defeated and made prisoner by Douglas, who caused him to be executed, although the King sent a positive order, enjoining him to forbear any injury to Herries's person. Soon after this, another audacious transaction occurred in the murder of Sir John Sandilands of Calder, a kinsman of the King, by Sir Patrick Thornton, a dependent of the house of Douglas; along with them were slain two knights, Sir James and Sir Allan Stewart, both of whom enjoyed the friendship and intimacy of the sovereign.

But a still more flagrant breach of law, and violation of all respect to the King's authority, happened in the case of Maclellan, the tutor, or guardian of the young lord of Bomby, ancestor of the Earls of Kirkcudbright. This was one of the few men of consequence in Galloway, who, defying the threats of the Earl of Douglas, had refused to join with him against the King. The Earl, incensed at his opposition, suddenly assaulted his castle, made him prisoner, and carried him to the strong fortress of Thrieve, in Galloway, situated on an island in the river Dee. The King took a particular interest in Maclellan's fate, the rather that he was petitioned to interfere in his favour by a personal favourite of his own. This was Sir Patrick Gray, the commander of the royal guard, a gentleman much in James's confidence, and constantly attending on his person, and who was Maclellan's near relative, being his uncle on the mother's side. In order to prevent Maclellan from sharing the fate of Colville and Herries, the King wrote a letter to the Earl of Douglas, entreating as a favour, rather than urging as a command, that he would deliver the person of the Tutor of Bomby, as Maclellan was usually entitled, into the hands of his relative, Sir Patrick Gray.

Sir Patrick himself went with the letter to the castle of Thrieve. Douglas received him just as he had arisen from dinner, and, with much apparent civility, declined to speak with Gray, on the occasion of his coming, until Sir Patrick also had dined, saying, "It was ill talking between a full man and a fasting." But this courtesy was only a pretence to gain time to do a very cruel and lawless action. Guessing that Sir Patrick Gray's visit respected the life of Maclellan, he resolved to hasten his execution before opening the King's letter. Thus, while he was feasting Sir Patrick with every appearance of hospitality, he caused his unhappy kinsman to be led out, and beheaded in the court-yard of the castle.

When dinner was over, Gray presented the King's letter, which Douglas received and read over with every testimony of profound respect. He then thanked Sir Patrick for the trouble he had taken in bringing him so gracious a letter from his sovereign, especially considering he was not at present on good terms with his Majesty. "And," he added, "the King's demand shall instantly be granted, the rather for your sake." The Earl then took Sir Patrick by the hand, and led him to the castle yard, where the body of Maclellan was still lying.

"Sir Patrick," said he, as his servants removed the bloody cloth which covered the body, "you have come a little too late. There lies your sister's son—but he wants the head. The body is, however, at your service."

"My lord," said Gray, suppressing his indignation, "if you have taken his head, you may dispose of the body as you will."

But, when he had mounted his horse, which he instantly called for, his resentment broke out, in spite of the dangerous situation in which he was placed:—

"My lord," said he, "if I live, you shall bitterly pay for this day's work."

So saying, he turned his horse and galloped off.

"To horse, and chase him!" said Douglas; and if Gray had not been well mounted, he would, in all probability, have shared the fate of his nephew. He was closely pursued till near Edinburgh, a space of fifty or sixty miles.

Besides these daring and open instances of contempt of the King's authority, Douglas entered into such alliances as plainly showed his determination to destroy entirely the royal government. He formed a league with the Earl of Crawford, called Earl Beardie, and sometimes, from the ferocity of his temper, the Tiger-Earl, who had great power in the counties of Angus, Perth, and Kincardine, and with the Earl of Ross, who possessed extensive and almost royal authority in the north of Scotland, by which these three powerful earls agreed that they should take each other's part in every quarrel, and against every man, the King himself not excepted.

James then plainly saw that some strong measures must be taken, yet it was not easy to determine what was to be done. The league between the three earls enabled them, if open war was attempted, to assemble a force superior to that of the crown. The King therefore, dissembled his resentment, and, under pretext of desiring an amicable conference and reconciliation, requested Douglas to come to the royal court at Stirling. The haughty Earl hesitated not to accept of this invitation, but before he actually did so, he demanded and obtained a protection, or safe conduct, under the great seal, pledging the King's promise that he should be permitted to come to the court and to return in safety. And the Earl was more confirmed in his purpose of waiting on the King, because he was given to understand that the Chancellor Crichton had retired from court in some disgrace; so that he imagined himself secure from the plots of that great enemy of his family.

Thus protected, as he thought, against personal danger, Douglas came to Stirling in the end of February 1452, where he found the King lodged in the castle of that place, which is situated upon a rock rising abruptly from the plain, at the upper end of the town, and only accessible by one gate, which is strongly defended. The numerous followers of Douglas were quartered in the town, but the Earl himself was admitted into the castle. One of his nearest confidents and most powerful allies, was James Hamilton of Cadyow, the head of the great house of Hamilton. This gentleman pressed forward to follow Douglas, as he entered the gate. But Livingston, who was in the castle with the King, thrust back Hamilton, who was his near relation, and struck him upon the face; and when Hamilton, greatly incensed, rushed on him, sword in hand, he repulsed him with a long lance, till the gates were shut against him. Sir James Hamilton was very angry at this usage at the time, but afterwards knew that Livingston acted a friendly part in excluding him from the danger into which Douglas was throwing himself.

The King received Douglas kindly, and, after some amicable expostulation with him upon his late conduct, all seemed friendship and cordiality betwixt James and his too-powerful subject. By invitation of James, Douglas dined with him on the day following. Supper was presented at seven o'clock, and after it was over, the King having led Douglas into another apartment, where only some of the privy council and of his bodyguard were in attendance, he introduced the subject of the Earl's bond with Ross and Crawford, and exhorted him to give up the engagement, as inconsistent with his allegiance and the quiet of the kingdom. Douglas declined to relinquish the treaty which he had formed. The King urged him more imperiously, and the Earl returned a haughty and positive refusal, upbraiding the King, at the same time, with maladministration of the public affairs. Then the King burst into a rage at his obstinacy, and exclaimed, "By Heaven, my lordy if *you* will not break the league, *this* shall." So saying, he, stabbed the Earl with his dagger first in the throat, and instantly after in the lower part of the body. Sir Patrick Gray, who had sworn revenge on Douglas for the execution of Maclellan, then struck the Earl on the head with a battle-axe; and others of the King's retinue showed their zeal by stabbing at the dying man with their knives and daggers. He expired without uttering a word, covered with twenty-six wounds. The corpse did not receive any Christian burial. At least, about forty years since a skeleton was found buried in the garden, just below the fatal window, which was, with much probability, conjectured to be the remains of the Earl of Douglas, who died thus strangely and unhappily by the hand of his sovereign.

This was a wicked and cruel action on the King's part; bad if it were done in hasty passion, and yet worse if James meditated the possibility of this violence from the beginning, and had determined to use force if Douglas should not yield to persuasion. The Earl had deserved punishment, perhaps even that of death, for many crimes against the state; but the King ought not to have slain him without form of trial, and in his own chamber, after decoying him thither under assurance that his person should be safe. Yet this assassination, like that of the Red Comyn at Dumfries, turned to the good of Scotland; for God, my dearest child, who is often pleased to bring good out of the follies and even the crimes of men rendered the death of Comyn the road to the freedom of Scotland, and that of this ambitious earl the cause of the downfall of the Douglas family, which had become too powerful for the peace of the kingdom.

The scene, however, opened very differently from the manner in which it was to end. There were in the town of Stirling four brethren of the murdered Douglas, who had come to wait on him to court. Upon hearing that their elder brother had died in the manner I have told you, they immediately acknowledged James, the eldest of the four, as his successor in the earldom. They then hastened each to the county where he had interest (for they were all great lords), and, collecting their friends and vassals, they returned to Stirling, dragging the safe-conduct, or passport, which had been granted to the Earl of Douglas, at the tail of a miserable cart-jade, in order to show their contempt for the King. They next, with the sound of five hundred horns and trumpets, proclaimed King James a false and perjured man. Afterwards they pillaged the town of Stirling, and, not thinking that enough, they sent back Hamilton of Cadyow to burn it to the ground. But the strength of the castle defied all their efforts; and after this bravado, the Douglases dispersed themselves to assemble a still larger body of forces.

So many great barons were engaged in alliance with the house of Douglas, that it is said to have been a question in the King's mind whether he should abide the conflict or fly to France, and leave the throne to the Earl. At this moment of extreme need James found a trusty counsellor in his cousin-german, Kennedy, Archbishop of St. Andrews, one of the wisest men of his time. The archbishop showed his advice in a sort of emblem or parable. He gave the King a bunch of arrows tied together with a thong of leather, and asked him to break them. The King said it was beyond his strength. "That may be the case, bound together as they are," replied the archbishop; "but if you undo the strap, and take the arrows one by one, you may easily break them all in succession. And thus, my liege, you ought in wisdom to deal with the insurgent nobility. If you attack them while they are united in one mind and purpose, they will be too strong for you; but if you can, by dealing with them separately, prevail on them to abandon their union, you may as easily master them one after the other, as you can break these arrows if you take each singly."

Acting upon this principle, the King made private representations to several of the nobility, to whom his agents found access, showing them that the rebellion of the Douglases would, if successful, render that family superior to all others in Scotland, and sink the rest of the peers into men of little consequence. Large gifts of lands, treasures, and honours, were liberally promised to those who, in this moment of extremity, should desert the Douglases and join the King's party. These large promises, and the secret dread of the great predominance of the Douglas family, drew to the King's side many of the nobles who had hitherto wavered betwixt their allegiance and their fear of the Earl.

Among these, the most distinguished was the Earl of Angus, who, although himself a Douglas, being a younger branch of that family, joined on this memorable occasion with the King against his kinsman, and gave rise to the saying that, "the Red Douglas (such was the complexion of the Angus family) had put down the black."

The great family of Gordon also declaring for the King, their chief, the Earl of Huntly, collected an army in the north, and marched south as far as Brechin to support the royal authority. Here he was encountered by the Tiger-Earl of Crawford, who had taken arms for the Douglas party, according to the fatal bond which had cost the Earl William his life. One of the chief leaders in Crawford's army was John Collasse of Bonnymoon (or Balnamoon), who commanded a gallant body of men, armed with bills and battle-axes, on whom the Earl greatly relied. But before the action, this John Collasse had asked Crawford to grant him certain lands, that lay convenient for him, and near his house, which the Earl refused to do. Collasse, incensed at the refusal, took an opportunity, when the battle was at the closest, to withdraw from the conflict; upon which Crawford's men, who had been on the point of gaining the victory, lost heart, and were defeated.

Other battles were fought in different parts of Scotland between the Douglases and their allies, and those noblemen and gentlemen who favoured the King. Much blood was spilt, and great mischief done to the country. Among other instances of the desolation of these civil wars, the Earl of Huntly burned one half of the town of Elgin, being that part which inclined to the Douglases, while he left standing the opposite part of the same street, which was inhabited by citizens attached to his own family. Hence the proverb, when a thing is imperfectly finished, that it is "Half done, as Elgin was burned."

Huntly, however, was afterwards surprised, and lost a considerable number of his followers in a morass, called Dunkinty, where they were attacked by Douglas, Earl of Murray. This gave rise to a jeering song, which ran thus:—

> "Where did you leave your men,
>   Thou Gordon so gay?
> In the bog of Dunkinty,
>   Mowing the hay."

In this period of calamity, famine and pestilence came to add to the desolation of the country, wasted by a civil war, which occasioned skirmishes, conflagrations, and slaughters, almost in every province of Scotland.

The royal party at length began to gain ground; for the Earl of Douglas seems to have been a man of less action and decision than was usual with those of his name and family.

The Earl of Crawford was one of those who first deserted him, and applied to the King for forgiveness and restoration to favour. He appeared before James in the most humble guise, in poor apparel, bareheaded and barefooted, like a condemned criminal; and throwing himself at the King's feet, he confessed his treasons, and entreated the royal mercy, on account of the loyalty of his ancestors and the sincerity of his repentance. The King, though he had many subjects of complaint against this powerful lord, and notwithstanding he had made a vow to destroy the Earl's castle of Finhaven, and to make the highest stone the lowest, nevertheless granted him a full pardon, and made him a visit at Finhaven, where he accomplished his vow, by getting to the top of the battlements, and throwing a small stone, which was lying loose there, down into the moat; thus, in one sense, making the highest stone in the house the lowest, though not by the demolition of the place. By this clemency the minds of the hostile nobles were conciliated, and many began to enter into terms of submission.

But the power of the Douglases remained still so great that there appeared little hope of the struggle being ended without a desperate battle. At length such an event seemed near approaching. The Earls of Orkney and Angus, acting for the King, had besieged Abercorn, a strong castle on the Firth of Forth, belonging to the Earl of Douglas. Douglas collected the whole strength which his family and allies could raise, amounting, it is said, to nearly forty thousand men, with which he advanced to raise the siege. The King, on the other hand, having assembled the whole forces of the north of Scotland, marched to meet him, at the head of an army somewhat superior in numbers to that of the Earl, but inferior in military discipline. Thus everything seemed to render a combat inevitable, the issue of which must have shown whether James Stewart or James Douglas was to wear the crown of Scotland. The small river of Carron divided the two armies.

But the intrigues of the Archbishop of St. Andrews had made a powerful impression upon many of the nobles who acted with Douglas, and there was a party among his followers who obeyed him more from fear than affection. Others, seeing a certain degree of hesitation in the Earl's resolutions, and a want of decision in his actions, began to doubt whether he was a leader fit to conduct so perilous an enterprise. Amongst these last was Sir James Hamilton of Cadyow, already mentioned, who commanded in Douglas's army three hundred horse, and as many infantry, all men of tried discipline and courage. The Archbishop

Kennedy was Hamilton's kinsman, and took advantage of their relationship to send a secret messenger to inform him that the King was well
disposed to pardon his rebellion, and to show him great favour, provided that he would, at that critical moment, set an example to the
insurgent nobility by renouncing the cause of Douglas, and returning to
the King's obedience. These arguments made considerable impression
on Hamilton, who, nevertheless, having been long the follower of the
Earl, was loath to desert his old friend in such an extremity.

On the next morning after this secret conference, the King sent a
herald to the camp of Douglas, charging the Earl to disperse his followers, on pain that he and his accomplices should be proclaimed traitors,
but at the same time promising forgiveness and rewards to all who
should leave his standard. Douglas made a mock of this summons; and
sounding his trumpets, and placing his men in order, marched stoutly
forward to encounter the King's army, who on their side left their camp
and advanced with displayed banners, as if to instant battle. It seems,
however, that the message of the herald had made some impression on
the followers of Douglas, and perhaps on the Earl himself, by render-
ing him doubtful of their adherence. He saw, or thought he saw, that
his troops were discouraged, and led them back into his camp, hoping
to inspire them with more confidence and zeal. But the movement had
a different effect; for no sooner had the Earl returned to his tent, than
Sir James Hamilton came to expostulate with him, and to require him
to say, whether he meant to fight or not, assuring him that every delay
was in favour of the King, and that the longer the Earl put off the day
of battle, the fewer men he would have to fight it with. Douglas
answered contemptuously to Hamilton, "That if he was afraid to stay,
he was welcome to go home." Hamilton took the Earl at his word, and,
leaving the camp of Douglas, went over to the King that very night.

The example was so generally followed, that the army of Douglas
seemed suddenly to disperse, like a dissolving snowball; and in the
morning not a hundred men were left in his silent and deserted camp,
excepting his own immediate dependents. He was obliged to fly to the
West Border, where his brothers and followers sustained a severe defeat
from the Scotts and other Borderers, near a place called Arkinholme, in
the valley of Esk. Archibald Douglas, Earl of Murray, one of the Earl's
brothers, falling in this battle, his head was cut off, and sent to the King,
then before Abercorn; another, Hugh, Earl of Ormond, was wounded
and made prisoner, and immediately executed, notwithstanding his

services at the battle of Sark. John, Lord Balvenie, the third brother, escaped into England, where the Earl also found a retreat. Thus the power of this great and predominant family, which seemed to stand so fair for possessing the crown, fell at length without any decisive struggle; and their greatness, which had been founded upon the loyalty and bravery of the Good Lord James, was destroyed by the rebellious and wavering conduct of the last earl.

That unfortunate nobleman remained nearly twenty years in England a banished man, and was almost forgotten in his own country, until the subsequent reign, when, in 1484, he was defeated and made prisoner, in a small incursion which he had attempted to make upon the frontiers of Annandale. He surrendered to a brother of Kirkpatrick, of Closeburn, who, in the Earl's better days, had been his own vassal, and who shed tears at seeing his old master in such a lamentable situation. Kirkpatrick even proposed to set him at liberty, and fly with him into England; but Douglas rejected this offer. "I am tired," he said, "of exile; and as there is a reward offered by the King, for my head, I had rather it were conferred on you, who were always faithful to me while I was faithful to myself, than on any one else." Kirkpatrick, however, acted kindly and generously. He secured the Earl in some secret abode, and did not deliver him up to the King until he had a promise of his life. Douglas was then ordained to be put into the abbey of Lindores, to which sentence he submitted calmly, only using a popular proverb, "He that cannot do better must be a monk." He lived in that convent only for four years, and with him, as the last of his family, expired the principal branch of those tremendous Earls of Douglas.

Other Scottish families arose upon the ruins of this mighty house, in consequence of the distribution made of their immense forfeited estates, to those who had assisted the King in suppressing their power. Amongst these the Earl of Angus, who, although kinsman to the Earl of Douglas, by siding with the King, received by far the greater share; to an amount, indeed, which enabled this shoot, as we shall see, to pursue the same ambitious course as that of their kinsfolk of the elder branch, although they neither rose to such high elevation, nor sunk into the same irreparable ruin, which was the lot of the original family.

Hamilton also rose into power on the fall of the Douglas. His opportune desertion of his kinsman at Abercorn was accounted good service, and was rewarded with large grants of land, and at last with the hand of the King's eldest daughter in marriage.

Sir Walter Scott of Kirkurd and Buccleuch likewise obtained great gifts of land for his clan's service and his own, at the battle of Arkinholme, and began that course of greatness which raised his family to the ducal dignity.

Such, my dear child, is the course of the world, in which the downfall of one great man or family is the means of advancing others; as a falling tree throws its seed upon the ground, and causes young plants to arise in its room.

The English did not make much war upon Scotland during this reign, being engaged at home with their dreadful civil quarrels of York and Lancaster. For the same reason, perhaps, the Scots had the advantage in such actions as took place.

Relieved from the rivalship of the Douglas, and from the pressure of constant war with England, James II. governed Scotland firmly. The kingdom enjoyed considerable tranquillity during the remainder of his reign; and his last Parliament was able to recommend to him the regular and firm execution of the laws, as to a prince who possessed the full means of discharging his kingly office, without resistance from evil doers or infringers of justice. This was in 1458. But only two years afterwards all these fair hopes were blighted.

The strong Border castle of Roxburgh had remained in the hands of the English ever since the fatal battle of Durham. The King was determined to recover this bulwark of the kingdom. Breaking through a truce which existed with England at the time, James summoned together the full force of his kingdom to accomplish this great enterprise. The nobles attended in numbers, and well accompanied, at the summons of a prince who was always respected, and generally successful in his military undertakings. Even Donald of the Isles proved himself a loyal and submissive vassal; and while he came with a force which showed his great authority, he placed it submissively at the disposal of his sovereign. His men were arrayed in the Highland fashion, with shirts of mail, two-handed swords, axes, and bows and arrows; and Donald offered, when the Scots should enter England, that he would march a mile in front of the King's host, and take upon himself the danger of the first onset. But James's first object was the siege of Roxburgh.

This strong castle was situated on an eminence near the junction of the Tweed and the Teviot; the waters of the Teviot, raised by a damhead or weir, flowed round the fortress, and its walls were as strong as the engineers of the time could raise. On former occasions it had been taken by stratagem, but James was now to proceed by a regular siege.

With this purpose he established a battery of such large clumsy cannon as were constructed at that time, upon the north side of the river Tweed. The siege had lasted some time, and the army began to be weary of the undertaking, when they received new spirit from the arrival of the Earl of Huntly with a gallant body of fresh troops. The King, out of joy at these succours, commanded his artillery to fire a volley upon the castle, and stood near the cannon himself, to mark the effect of the shot. The great guns of that period were awkwardly framed out of bars of iron, fastened together by hoops of the same metal, somewhat in the same manner in which barrels are now made. They were, therefore, far more liable to accidents than modern cannon, which are cast in one entire solid piece, and then bored hollow by a machine. One of these ill-made guns burst in going off. A fragment of iron broke James's thigh-bone, and killed him on the spot. Another splinter wounded the Earl of Angus. No other person sustained injury, though many stood around. Thus died James the Second of Scotland, in the twenty-ninth year of his age, after reigning twenty-four years.

This King did not possess the elegant accomplishments of his father; and the manner in which he slew the Earl of Douglas must be admitted as a stain upon his reputation. Yet he was, upon the whole, a good prince, and was greatly lamented by his subjects. A thorn-tree, in the Duke of Roxburghe's park at Fleurs, still shows the spot where he died.

XXII

James III.

1460-1488

UPON the lamentable death of James II., the army which lay before Roxburgh was greatly discouraged, and seemed about to raise the siege. But Mary, the widow of their slain monarch, appeared in their council of war, leading her eldest son, a child of eight years old, who was the successor to the crown, and spoke to them these gallant words: "Fy, my noble lords! think not now shamefully to give up an enterprise which is so bravely begun, or to abandon the revenge of this unhappy accident which has befallen before this ill-omened castle. Forward, my brave lords, and persevere in your undertaking; and never turn your backs till this siege is victoriously ended. Let it not be said that such brave champions needed to hear from a woman, and a widowed one, the courageous advice and comfort which she ought rather to receive from you!" The Scottish nobles received this heroic address with shouts of applause, and persevered in the siege of Roxburgh Castle, until the garrison, receiving no relief, were obliged to surrender the place through famine. The governor is stated to have been put to death, and in the animosity of the Scots against everything concerned with the death of their King, they levelled the walls of the castle with the ground, and returned victorious from an enterprise which had cost them so dear.

The minority of James III. was more prosperous than that of his father and grandfather. The affairs of state were guided by the experienced wisdom of Bishop Kennedy. Roxburgh was, as we have said, taken and destroyed. Berwick, during the dissensions of the civil wars of England, was surrendered to the Scots; and the dominions of the islands of Orkney and Zetland, which had hitherto belonged to the Kings of Norway, were acquired as the marriage portion of a Princess of Denmark and Norway, who was united in marriage to the King of Scotland.

These favourable circumstances were first interrupted by the death of Archbishop Kennedy; after which event one family, that of the Boyds, started into such a degree of temporary power as seemed to threaten the public tranquillity. The tutor of James III. was Gilbert Kennedy, a wise and grave man, who continued to regulate the studies of the King after the death of his brother the prelate, but unadvisedly called in to his assistance Sir Alexander, the brother of Lord Boyd, as one who was younger and fitter than himself to teach James military exercises. By means of this appointment, Sir Alexander, his brother Lord Boyd, and two of his sons, became so intimate with the King that they resolved to take him from under the management of Kennedy entirely. The court was then residing at Linlithgow, and the King, while abroad on a hunting party, was persuaded to direct his horse's head to Edinburgh, instead of returning. Kennedy, the tutor, hastened to oppose the King's desire, and seizing his horse by the bridle, wished to lead him back to Linlithgow. Alexander Boyd rushed forward, and striking with a huntingstaff the old man, who had deserved better usage at his hand, forced him to quit the King's rein, and accomplished his purpose of carrying James to Edinburgh, where he entered upon the administration of affairs, and having granted a solemn pardon to the Boyds for whatever violence had occurred in their proceedings, he employed them for a time as his chief ministers and favourites. Sir Thomas, one of Lord Boyd's sons, was honoured with the hand of the Princess Margaret, the King's eldest sister, and was created Earl of Arran. He deserved even this elevation by his personal accomplishments, if he approached the character given of him by an English gentleman. He is described as "the most courteous, gentle, wise, kind, companionable, and bounteous Earl of Arran;"—and again, as "a light, able-bodied, well-spoken man, a goodly archer, and a knight most devout, most perfect, and most true to his lady."

Notwithstanding the new Earl of Arran's accomplishments, the sudden rise of his family was followed by as sudden a fall. The King, either resenting the use which the Boyds had made of his favour, or changing his opinion of them from other causes, suddenly deprived the whole family of their offices, and caused them to be tried for the violence committed at Linlithgow, notwithstanding the pardon which he himself had granted. Sir Alexander Boyd was condemned and executed. Lord Boyd and his sons escaped, and died in exile. After the death of Sir Thomas (the Earl of Arran), the Princess Margaret was married to the Lord Hamilton, to whom she carried the estate and title of Arran.

It was after the fall of the Boyds that the King came to administer the government in person, and that the defects of his character began to appear. He was timorous, a great failing in a warlike age; and his cowardice made him suspicious of his nobility, and particularly of his two brothers. He was fond of money, and therefore did not use that generosity towards his powerful subjects which was necessary to secure their attachment; but, on the contrary, endeavoured to increase his private hoards of wealth by encroaching upon the rights both of clergy and laity, and thus made himself at once hated and contemptible. He was a lover of the fine arts, as they are called, of music and architecture; a disposition graceful in a monarch, if exhibited with due regard to his dignity. But he made architects and musicians his principal companions, excluding his nobility from the personal familiarity to which he admitted those whom the haughty barons of Scotland termed masons and fiddlers. Cochran, an architect, Rogers, a musician, Leonard, a smith, Hommel, a tailor, and Torphichen, a fencing-master, were his counsellers and companions. These habits of low society excited the hatred of the nobility, who began to make comparisons betwixt the King and his two brothers, the Dukes of Albany and Mar, greatly to the disadvantage of James.

These younger sons of James the Second were of appearance and manners such as were then thought most suited to their royal birth. This is the description of the Duke of Albany by an ancient Scottish author: He was well proportioned, and tall in stature, and comely in his countenance; that is to say, broad-faced, red-nosed, large-eared, and having a very awful countenance when it pleased him to speak with those who had displeased him. Mar was of a less stern temper, and gave great satisfaction to all who approached his person, by the mildness and gentleness of his manners. Both princes excelled in the military exercises of tilting, hunting, hawking, and other personal accomplishments, for which their brother, the King, was unfit, by taste, or from timidity, although they were in those times reckoned indispensable to a man of rank.

Perhaps some excuse for the King's fears may be found in the turbulent disposition of the Scottish nobles, who, like the Douglases and Boyds, often nourished schemes of ambition, which they endeavoured to gratify by exercising a control over the King's person. The following incident may serve to amuse you, among so many melancholy tales, and at the same time to show you the manners of the Scottish kings, and the fears which James entertained for the enterprises of the nobility.

About the year 1474 Lord Somerville being in attendance upon the King's court, James III. offered to come and visit him at his castle of Cowthally, near the town of Carnwath, where he then lived in all the rude hospitality of the time, for which this nobleman was peculiarly remarkable. It was his custom, when, being from home, he intended to return to the castle with a party of guests, merely to write the words, *Speates and raxes;* that is, spits and ranges; meaning by this hint that there should be a great quantity of food prepared, and that the spits and ranges, or framework on which they turn, should be put into employment. Even the visit of the King himself did not induce Lord Somerville to send any other than his usual intimation; only he repeated it three times, and despatched it to his castle by a special messenger. The paper was delivered to the Lady Somerville, who, having been lately married, was not quite accustomed to read her husband's handwriting, which probably was not very good; for in those times noblemen used the sword more than the pen. So the lady sent for the steward, and, after laying their heads together, instead of reading *Speates and raxes, speates and raxes, speates and raxes;* they made out the writing to be *Spears and jacks, spears and jacks, spears and jacks.* Jacks were a sort of leathern doublet, covered with plates of iron, worn as armour by horsemen of inferior rank. They concluded the meaning of these terrible words to be, that Lord Somerville was in some distress, or engaged in some quarrel in Edinburgh, and wanted assistance; so that, instead of killing cattle and preparing for a feast, they collected armed men together, and got ready for a fray. A party of two hundred horsemen were speedily assembled, and were trotting over the moors towards Edinburgh, when they observed a large company of gentlemen employed in the sport of hawking, on the side of Corsett-hill. This was the King and Lord Somerville, who were on their road to Cowthally, taking their sport as they went along. The appearance of a numerous body of armed men soon turned their game to earnest; and the King, who saw the Lord Somerville's banner at the head of the troop, concluded it was some rebellious enterprise against his person, and charged the baron with treason. Lord Somerville declared his innocence. "Yonder," said he, "are indeed my men and my banner, but I have no knowledge whatever of the cause that has brought them here. But if your grace will permit me to ride forward, I will soon see the cause of this disturbance. In the meantime, let my eldest son and heir remain as an hostage in your grace's power, and let him lose his head if I prove false to my duty." The King accordingly permitted Lord Somerville to ride towards his followers, when the matter was soon explained by those who commanded them. The mistake was then only subject of merriment; for the King, looking at the letter, protested he himself would have read it *Spears and jacks,* rather than *Speates and raxes.* When they came to Cowthally the lady was much out of countenance at the mistake. But the King greatly praised her for the despatch which she had used in raising men to assist her husband, and said he hoped she would always have as brave a band at his service when the King and kingdom required them. And thus everything went happily off.

It was natural that a prince of a timid, and at the same time a severe disposition, such as James III. seems to have had, should see with anxiety the hold which his brothers possessed over the hearts of his subjects; and the insinuations of the unworthy familiars of his private hours turned that anxiety and suspicion into deadly and implacable hatred. Various causes combined to induce the mean and obscure favourites of James to sow enmity betwixt him and his brothers. The Homes and Hepburns, families which had risen into additional power after the fall of the Douglases, had several private disputes with Albany concerning privileges and property belonging to the earldom of March, which had been conferred on him by his father. Albany was also Lord Warden of the east frontiers, and in that capacity had restrained and disobliged those powerful clans. To be revenged, they made interest with Robert Cochran, the King's principal adviser, and gave him, it is said, large bribes to put Albany out of credit with the King. Cochran's own interest suggested the same vile course; for he must have been sensible that Albany and Mar disapproved of the King's intimacy with him and his companions.

These unworthy favourites, therefore set themselves to fill the King's mind with apprehensions of dangers which were to arise to him from his brothers. They informed him that the Earl of Mar had consulted witches when and how the King should die, and that it had been answered that he should fall by means of his nearest relations. They brought to James also an astrologer, that is, a man who pretended to calculate future events by the motion of the stars, who told him that in Scotland a Lion should be killed by his own whelps. All these things wrought on the jealous and timid disposition of the King, so that he seized upon both his brethren. Albany was imprisoned in the castle of Edinburgh, but Mar's fate was instantly decided; the King caused him to be murdered by stifling him in a bath, or, as other historians say, by causing him to be bled to death. James committed this horrid crime in order to avoid dangers which were in a great measure imaginary; but we shall find that the death of his brother Mar rather endangered than added to his safety.

Albany was in danger of the same fate, but some of his friends in France or Scotland had formed a plan of rescuing him. A small sloop came into the roadstead of Leith, loaded with wine of Gascony, and two small barrels were sent up as a present to the imprisoned prince. The guard having suffered the casks to be carried to Albany's chamber, the duke, examining them in private, found that one of them contained a roll of wax, enclosing a letter, exhorting him to make his escape, and promising that the little vessel which brought the wine should be ready to receive him if he could gain the waterside. The letter conjured him to be speedy, as there was a purpose to behead him on the day following. A coil of ropes was also enclosed in the same cask, in order to enable him to effect his descent from the castle wall, and the precipice upon which it is built. There was a faithful attendant, his chamberlain, imprisoned with him in the same apartment, who promised to assist his master in this perilous undertaking. The first point was to secure the captain of the guard; for which purpose Albany invited that officer to sup with him, in order, as the Duke pretended, to taste the good wine which had been presented to him in the two casks. The captain accordingly, having placed his watches where he thought there was danger, came to the Duke's chamber, attended by three of his soldiers, and

partook of a collation. After supper, the Duke engaged him in playing at
tables and dice, until the captain, seated beside a hot fire, and plied with
wine by the chamberlain, began to grow drowsy, as did his attendants,
on whom the liquor had not been spared. Then the Duke of Albany, a
strong man and desperate, leapt from the table and stabbed the captain
with a whinger or dagger, so that he died on the spot. The like he did to
two of the captain's men, and the chamberlain despatched the other,
and threw their bodies on the fire. This was the more easily accomplished that the soldiers were intoxicated and stupefied. They then took
the keys from the captain's pocket, and, getting out upon the walls,
chose a retired corner, out of the watchman's sight, to make their perilous descent. The chamberlain tried to go down the rope first, but it
was too short, so that he fell and broke his thigh-bone. He then called to
his master to make the rope longer. Albany returned to his apartment,
and took the sheets from the bed, with which he lengthened the rope,
so that he descended the precipice in safety. He then got his chamberlain on his back, and conveyed him to a place of security, where he
might remain concealed till his hurt was cured, and went himself to the
sea side, when, upon the appointed signal, a boat came ashore and took
him off to the vessel, in which he sailed for France.

During the night, the guards, who knew that their officer was in
the Duke's apartment with three men, could not but suppose that all
was safe; but when daylight showed them the rope hanging from the
walls, they became alarmed, and hastened to the Duke's lodgings. Here
they found the body of one man stretched near the door, and the
corpses of the captain and other two lying upon the fire. The King was
much surprised at so strange an escape, and would give no credit to it
till he had examined the place with his own eyes.

The death of Mar, and the flight of Albany, increased the insolence
of King James's unworthy favourites. Robert Cochran, the mason, rose
into great power, and as every man's petition to the King came through
his hands, and he expected and received bribes to give his countenance,
he amassed so much wealth, that he was able in his turn to bribe the
King to confer on him the earldom of Mar, with the lands and revenues
of the deceased prince. All men were filled with indignation to see the
inheritance of the murdered earl, the son of the King of Scotland, conferred upon a mean upstart, like this Cochran. This unworthy favourite
was guilty of another piece of mal-administration, by mixing the silver
coin of the kingdom with brass and lead and thereby decreasing its real

value, while orders were given by proclamation to take it at the same rate as if it were composed of pure silver. The people refused to sell their corn and other commodities for this debased coin, which introduced great distress, confusion, and scarcity. Some one told Cochran, that this money should be called in, and good coin issued in its stead; but he was so confident of the currency of the Cochran-placks, as the people called them, that he said,—"The day I am hanged they may be called in; not sooner." This speech, which he made in jest, proved true in reality.

In the year 1482 the disputes with England had come to a great height, and Edward IV. made preparations to invade Scotland, principally in the hope of recovering the town of Berwick. He invited the Duke of Albany from France to join him in this undertaking, promising to place him on the Scottish throne instead of his brother. This was held out in order to take advantage of the unpopularity of King James, and the general disposition which manifested itself in Scotland in favour of Albany.

But, however discontented with their sovereign, the Scottish nation showed themselves in no way disposed to receive another king from the hands of the English. The Parliament assembled, and unanimously determined on war against Edward the Robber, for so they termed the King of England. To support this violent language, James ordered the whole array of the kingdom, that is, all the men who were bound to discharge military service, to assemble at the Borough-moor of Edinburgh, from whence they marched to Lauder, and encamped between the river Leader and the town, to the amount of fifty thousand men. But the great barons, who had there assembled with their followers, were less disposed to advance against the English than to correct the abuses of King James's administration.

Many of the nobility and barons held a secret council in the church of Lauder, where they enlarged upon the evils which Scotland sustained through the insolence and corruption of Cochran and his associates. While they were thus declaiming, Lord Gray requested their attention to a fable. "The mice," he said, "being much annoyed by the persecution of the cat, resolved that a bell should be hung about puss's neck, to give notice when she was coming. But though the measure was agreed to in full council, it could not be carried into effect, because no mouse had courage enough to undertake to tie the bell to the neck of the formidable enemy." This was as much as to intimate his opinion, that though the discontented nobles might make bold resolutions against the King's ministers, yet it would be difficult to find any one courageous enough to act upon them.

Archibald, Earl of Angus, a man of gigantic strength and intrepid courage, and head of that second family of Douglas whom I before mentioned, started up when Gray had done speaking. "I am he," he said, "who will bell the cat;" from which expression he was distinguished by the name of Bell-the-Cat to his dying day.

While thus engaged, a loud authoritative knocking was heard at the door of the church. This announced the arrival of Cochran, attended by a guard of three hundred men, attached to his own person, and all gaily dressed in his livery of white, with black facings, and armed with partisans. His own personal appearance corresponded with this magnificent attendance. He was attired in a riding suit of black velvet, and had round his neck a fine chain of gold, whilst a bugle-horn, tipped and mounted with gold, hung down by his side. His helmet was borne before him, richly inlaid with the same precious metal; even his tent and tent-cords were of silk, instead of ordinary materials. In this gallant guise, having learned there was some council holding among the nobility, he came to see what they were doing, and it was with this purpose that he knocked furiously at the door of the church. Sir Robert Douglas of Lochleven, who had the charge of watching the door, demanded who was there. When Cochran answered, "The Earl of Mar," the nobles greatly rejoiced at hearing he was come, to deliver himself, as it were, into their hands.

As Cochran entered the church, Angus, to make good his promise to bell the cat, met him, and rudely pulled the gold chain from his neck, saying, "A halter would better become him." Sir Robert Douglas, at the same time, snatched away his bugle-horn, saying, "Thou hast been a hunter of mischief too long."

"Is this jest or earnest, my lords?" said Cochran, more astonished than alarmed at this rude reception.

"It is sad earnest," said they, "and that thou and thy accomplices shall feel; for you have abused the King's favour towards you, and now you shall have your reward according to your deserts."

It does not appear that Cochran or his guards offered any resistance. A part of the nobility went next to the King's pavilion, and, while some engaged him in conversation, others seized upon Leonard, Hommel, Torphichen, and the rest, with Preston, one of the only two gentlemen amongst King James's minions, and hastily condemned them to instant death, as having misled the King, and misgoverned the kingdom. The only person who escaped was John Ramsay of Balmain, a youth of honourable birth, who clasped the King round the waist when he saw the others seized upon. Him the nobles spared, in respect of his youth, for he was not above sixteen years, and of the King's earnest intercession in his behalf. There was a loud acclamation among the troops, who contended with each other in offering their tent-ropes, and the halters of their horses, to be the means of executing these obnoxious ministers. Cochran, who was a man of audacity, and had first attracted the King's attention by his behaviour in a duel, did not lose his courage, though he displayed it in an absurd manner. He had the vanity to request that his hands might not be tied with a hempen rope, but with a silk cord, which he offered to furnish from the ropes of his pavilion; but this was only teaching his enemies how to give his feelings additional pain. They told him he was but a false thief, and should die with all manner of shame; and they were at pains to procure a hair-tether or halter, as still more ignominious than a rope of hemp. With this they hanged Cochran over the centre of the bridge of Lauder (now demolished), in the middle of his companions, who were suspended on each side of him. When the execution was finished, the lords returned to Edinburgh, where they resolved that the King should remain in the castle, under a gentle and respectful degree of restraint.

In the meantime the English obtained possession of Berwick, which important place was never again recovered by the Scots, though they continued to assert their claim to that bulwark of the eastern Marches. The English seemed disposed to prosecute their advantages; but the Scottish army having moved to Haddington to fight them, a peace was concluded, partly by the mediation of the Duke of Albany, who having seen the vanity of any hopes which the English had given him, and, laying aside his views upon the crown, appeared desirous to become the means of restoring peace to the country.

The Duke of Albany, and the celebrated Richard, Duke of Gloucester (afterwards Richard the Third), are said to have negotiated the terms of peace, as well between the King and his nobility as between France and England. They had a meeting at Edinburgh with the council of Scottish lords who had managed the affairs of the kingdom since the King's imprisonment. The council would pay no respect to the Duke of Gloucester, who, as an Englishman they justly thought, had

no right to interfere in the affairs of Scotland; but to the Duke of
Albany they showed much reverence, requesting to know what he
required at their hands.

"First of all," he said, "I desire that the King, my brother, be set at
liberty."

"My lord," said Archibald-Bell-the-Cat, who was chancellor, "that
shall be presently done, and the rather that you desire it. As to the
person who is with you (meaning the Duke of Gloucester), we know
him not; neither will we grant anything at his asking. But we know you
to be the King's brother, and nearest heir to his Grace after his infant
son. Therefore, we put the King's person at your disposal, trusting that
he will act by your advice in future, and govern the kingdom, so as not
to excite the discontent of the people, or render it necessary for us,
who are the nobles of Scotland, to act contrary to his pleasure."

James, being thus set at liberty, became, to appearance, so perfectly
reconciled with his brother, the Duke of Albany, that the two royal
brothers used the same chamber, the same table, and the same bed.
While the King attended to the buildings and amusements in which he
took pleasure, Albany administered the affairs of the kingdom, and, for
some time, with applause. But the ambition of his temper began again
to show itself; the nation became suspicious of his intimate connection
with the English, and just apprehensions were entertained that the
Duke aimed still at obtaining the crown by assistance of Richard III.,
now King of England. The Duke was, therefore, once more obliged to
fly into England, where he remained for some time, assisting the English against his countrymen. He was present at that skirmish in 1484
where the old Earl of Douglas was made prisoner, and only escaped by
the speed of his horse. Albany soon after retired into France, where he
formed a marriage with a daughter of the Earl of Boulogne, by whom
he had a son, John, afterwards Regent of Scotland in the days of
James V. Albany himself was wounded severely by the splinter of a
lance at one of the tournaments, or tilting-matches, which I have
described to you, and died in consequence. The fickleness with which
he changed from one side to another disappointed the high ideas
which had been formed of his character in youth.

Freed from his brother's superintendence, the King gradually sunk
back into those practices which had formerly cost him so dear. To prevent a renewal of the force put on his person, he made a rule that none
should appear armed in the royal presence except the King's Guard,

who were placed under the command of that same John Ramsay of Balmain, the only one of his former favourites who had been spared by Bell-the-Cat, and the other nobles, at the insurrection of Lauder bridge. This gave high offence in a country where to be without arms was accounted both unsafe and dishonourable.

The King's love of money also grew, as is often the case, more excessive as he advanced in years. He would hardly grant anything, whether as matter of favour or of right, without receiving some gift or gratuity. By this means he accumulated a quantity of treasure, which, considering the poverty of his kingdom, is absolutely marvellous. His "black chest," as his strong-box was popularly called, was brimful of gold and silver coins, besides quantities of plate and jewels. But while he hoarded these treasures, he was augmenting the discontent of both the nobility and people; and amid the universal sense of the King's weakness, and hatred of his avarice, a general rebellion was at length excited against him.

The King, among other magnificent establishments, had built a great hall, and a royal chapel, within the castle of Stirling, both of them specimens of finely ornamented Gothic architecture. He had also established a double choir of musicians and singing men in the chapel, designing that one complete band should attend him wherever he went, to perform Divine service before his person, while the other, as complete in every respect, should remain in daily attendance in the royal chapel.

As this establishment necessarily incurred considerable expense, James proposed to annex to the royal chapel the revenues of the priory of Coldinghame, in Berwickshire. This rich priory had its lands amongst the possessions of the Homes and the Hepburns, who had established it as a kind of right that the prior should be of one or other of these two families, in order to insure their being favourably treated in such bargains as either of them might have to make with the Church. When, therefore, these powerful clans understood that, instead of a Home or a Hepburn being named prior, the King intended to bestow the revenues of Coldinghame to maintain his royal chapel at Stirling, they became extremely indignant, and began to hold a secret correspondence, and form alliances, with all the discontented men in Scotland, and especially with Angus, and such other lords as, having been engaged in the affair of Lauder bridge, naturally entertained apprehensions that the King would, one day or other, find means of avenging himself for the slaughter of his favourites, and the restraint which had been imposed on his own person.

By the time that the King heard of this league against him, it had reached so great a head that everything seemed to be prepared for war, since the whole lords of the south of Scotland, who could collect their forces with a rapidity unknown elsewhere, were all in the field, and ready to act James, naturally timid, was induced to fly to the North. He fortified the castle of Stirling, commanded by Shaw of Fintrie, to whom he committed the custody of the prince his son, and heir-apparent, charging the governor neither to let any one enter the castle, nor permit any one to leave it, as he loved his honour and his life. Especially he commanded him to let no one have access to his son. His treasures James deposited in Edinburgh Castle; and having thus placed in safety, as he thought, the two things he loved best in the world, he hastened to the north country, where he was joined by the great lords and gentlemen on that side of the Forth; so that it seemed as if the south and the north parts of Scotland were about to fight against each other.

The King, in passing through Fife, visited James, the last Earl of Douglas, who had been compelled, as I have before told you, to become a monk in the abbey of Lindores. He offered him full reconciliation and forgiveness, if he would once more come out into the world, place himself at the head of his vassals, and, by the terror of his former authority, withdraw from the banners of the rebel peers such of the southland men as might still remember the fame of Douglas. But the views of the old Earl were turned towards another world, and he replied to the King—"Ah, sir, your Grace has kept me and your black casket so long under lock and key, that the time in which we might have done you good service is past and gone." In saying this, he alluded to the King's hoard of treasure, which, if he had spent in time, might have attached many to his person, as he, Douglas, when younger, could have raised men in his behalf; but now the period of getting aid from either source was passed away.

Meanwhile Angus, Home, Bothwell, and others of the insurgent nobility, determined, if possible, to get into their hands the person of the prince, resolving that, notwithstanding his being a child, they would avail themselves of his authority to oppose that of his father. Accordingly, they bribed, with a large sum of money, Shaw, the governor of Stirling Castle, to deliver the prince (afterwards James IV.) into their keeping. When they had thus obtained possession of Prince

James's person, they collected their army, and published proclamations in his name intimating that King James III. was bringing Englishmen into the country to assist in overturning its liberties, that he had sold the frontiers of Scotland to the Earl of Northumberland, and to the governor of Berwick, and declaring that they were united to dethrone a king whose intentions were so unkingly, and to place his son in his stead. These allegations were false; but the King was so unpopular that they were listened to and believed.

James, in the meantime, arrived before Stirling at the head of a considerable army, and passing to the gate of the castle, demanded entrance. But the governor refused to admit him. The King then eagerly asked for his son; to which the treacherous governor replied, that the lords had taken the Prince from him against his will. Then the poor King saw that he was deceived, and said in wrath, "False villain, thou hast betrayed me; but if I live, thou shalt be rewarded according to thy deserts!" If the King had not been thus treacherously deprived of the power of retiring into Stirling Castle, he might, by means of that fortress, have avoided a battle until more forces had come up to his assistance; and, in that case, might have overpowered the rebel lords, as his father did the Douglases before Abercorn. Yet having with him an army of nearly thirty thousand men, he moved boldly towards the insurgents. The Lord David Lindsay of the Byres, in particular, encouraged the King to advance. He had joined him with a thousand horse and three thousand footmen from the counties of Fife and Kinross; and now riding up to the King on a fiery gray horse, he lighted down, and entreated the King's acceptance of that noble animal, which, whether he had occasion to advance or retreat, would beat every other horse in Scotland, provided the King could keep his saddle.

The King upon this took courage, and advanced against the rebels, confident in his great superiority of numbers. The field of battle was not above a mile or two distant from that where Bruce had defeated the English on the glorious day of Bannockburn; but the fate of his descendant and successor was widely different.

The King's army was divided into three great bodies. Ten thousand Highlanders, under Huntly and Athole, led the van; ten thousand more, from the westland counties, were led by the Lords of Erskine, Graham, and Menteith. The King was to command the rear, in which the burghers sent by the different towns were stationed. The Earl of Crawford and Lord David Lindsay, with the men of Fife and Angus, had the right wing; Lord Ruthven commanded the left, with the people of Strathearn and Stormont.

The King, thus moving forward in order of battle, called for the horse which Lord David Lindsay had given him, that he might ride forward and observe the motions of the enemy. He saw them from an eminence advancing in three divisions, having about six thousand men in each. The Homes and Hepburns had the first division, with the men of the East Borders and of East Lothian. The next was composed of the Western Borderers, or men of Liddesdale and Annandale, with many from Galloway. The third division consisted of the rebel lords and their choicest followers, bringing with them the young Prince James, and displaying the broad banner of Scotland.

When the King beheld his own ensign unfurled against him, and knew that his son was in the hostile ranks, his heart, never very courageous, began altogether to fail him; for he remembered the prophecy, that he was to fall by his nearest of kin, and also what the astrologer had told him of the Scottish lion which was to be strangled by his own whelps. These idle fears so preyed on James's mind, that his alarm became visible to those around him, who conjured him to retire to a place of safety. But at that moment the battle began.

The Homes and Hepburns attacked the King's vanguard, but were repulsed by the Highlanders with volleys of arrows. On this the Borderers of Liddesdale and Annandale, who bore spears longer than those used in the other parts of Scotland, charged with the wild and furious cries, which they called their *slogan,* and bore down the royal forces opposed to them.

Surrounded by sights and sounds to which he was so little accustomed, James lost his remaining presence of mind, and turning his back, fled towards Stirling. But he was unable to manage the gray horse given him by Lord Lindsay, which, taking the bit in his teeth, ran full gallop downhill into a little hamlet, where was a mill, called Beaton's mill.[1] A woman had come out to draw water at the mill-dam, but, terrified at seeing a man in complete armour coming down towards her at full speed, she left her pitcher, and fled back into the mill. The sight of the pitcher frightened the King's horse, so that he swerved as he was about to leap the brook, and James, losing his seat, fell to the ground,

---

[1] "Beaton's mill—the house so called, from the name of the person who then possessed it, is still shown to the traveller as the place where the King was murdered; and the great antiquity and thickness of the walls corroborate the tradition."—Tytler.

where, being heavily armed and sorely bruised, he remained motionless. The people came out, took him into the mill, and laid him on a bed. Some time afterwards he recovered his senses; but feeling himself much hurt and very weak, he demanded the assistance of a priest. The miller's wife asked who he was, and he imprudently replied, "I was your King this morning." With equal imprudence the poor woman ran to the door, and called with loud exclamations for a priest to confess the King. "I am a priest," said an unknown person, who had just come up; "lead me to the King." When the stranger was brought into the presence of the unhappy monarch, he kneeled with apparent humility, and asked him, "Whether he was mortally wounded?" James replied, that his hurts were not mortal, if they were carefully looked to; but that, in the meantime, he desired to be confessed, and receive pardon of his sins from a priest, according to the fashion of the Catholic Church. "This shall presently give thee pardon!" answered the assassin; and, drawing a poniard, he stabbed the King four or five times to the very heart; then took the body on his back and departed, no man opposing him, and no man knowing what he did with the body.

Who this murderer was has never been discovered, nor whether he was really a priest or not. There were three persons, Lord Gray, Stirling of Keir, and one Borthwick, a priest, observed to pursue the King closely, and it was supposed that one or other of them did the bloody deed. It is remarkable that Gray was the son of that Sir Patrick, commonly called Cowe Gray, who assisted James II. to despatch Douglas in Stirling Castle. It would be a singular coincidence if the son of this active agent in Douglas's death should have been the actor in that of King James's son.

The battle did not last long after the King left the field, the royal party drawing off towards Stirling, and the victors returning to their camp. It is usually called the battle of Sauchie burn, and was fought upon the 18th of June 1488.

Thus died King James the Third, an unwise and unwarlike prince; although setting aside the murder of his brother the Earl of Mar his character is rather that of a weak and avaricious man than of a cruel and criminal King. His taste for the fine arts would have been becoming in a private person, though it was carried to a pitch which interfered with his duties as a sovereign. He fell, like most of his family, in the flower of his age, being only thirty-six years old.

XXIII

James IV.

1488-1502

THE fate of James III. was not known for some time. He had been a patron of naval affairs; and on the great revolt in which he perished, a brave sea officer, Sir Andrew Wood of Largo, was lying with a small squadron in the Firth of Forth, not far distant from the coast where the battle was fought. He had sent ashore his boats, and brought off several wounded men of the King's party, amongst whom it was supposed might be the King himself.

Anxious to ascertain this important point, the lords sent to Sir Andrew Wood to come on shore, and appear before their council. Wood agreed, on condition that two noblemen of distinction, Lords Seton and Fleming, should go on board his ships, and remain there as hostages for his safe return.

The brave seaman presented himself before the Council and the young King, in the town of Leith. As soon as the Prince saw Sir Andrew, who was a goodly person, and richly dressed, he went towards him, and said, "Sir, are you my father?"

"I am not your father," answered Wood, the tears falling from his eyes; "but I was your father's servant while he lived, and shall be so to lawful authority until the day I die."

The lords then asked what men they were who had come out of his ships, and again returned to them on the day of the battle of Sauchie.

"It was I and my brother," said Sir Andrew, undauntedly, "who were desirous to have bestowed our lives in the King's defence."

They then directly demanded of him, whether the King was on board his ships? To which Sir Andrew replied, with the same firmness, "He is not on board my vessels. I wish he had been there, as I should have taken care to have kept him safe from the traitors who have murdered him, and whom I trust to see hanged and drawn for their demerits."

These were bitter answers; but the lords were obliged to endure them, without attempting any revenge, for fear the seamen had retaliated upon Fleming and Seton. But when the gallant commander had returned on board his ship, they sent for the best officers in the town of Leith, and offered them a reward if they would attack Sir Andrew Wood and his two ships, and make him prisoner, to answer for his insolent conduct to the Council. But Captain Barton, one of the best mariners in Leith, replied to the proposal by informing the Council that though Sir Andrew had but two vessels, yet they were so well furnished with artillery, and he himself was so brave and skilful, that no ten ships in Scotland would be a match for him.

James IV. afterwards received Sir Andrew Wood into high favour; and he deserved it by his exploits. In 1490 a squadron of five English vessels came into the Forth, and plundered some Scottish merchant-ships. Sir Andrew sailed against them with his two ships, the *Flower,* and the *Yellow Carvel,* took the five English vessels, and making their crews and commanders prisoners, presented them to the King at Leith. Henry VII. of England was so much incensed at this defeat that he sent a stout sea-captain, called Stephen Bull, with three strong ships equipped on purpose, to take Sir Andrew Wood. They met him near the mouth of the Firth, and fought with the utmost courage on both sides, attending so much to the battle, and so little to anything else, that they let their ships drift with the tide; so that the action, which began off St. Abb's Head, ended in the Firth of Tay. At length Stephen Bull and his three ships were taken. Sir Andrew again presented the prisoners to the King, who sent them back to England, with a message to Henry VII, that he had as manly men in Scotland as there were in England, and therefore he desired he would send no more captains on such errands.

To return to the lords who had gained the victory at Sauchie. They took a resolution, which appears an act of daring effrontery. They resolved to try some of the principal persons who had assisted King James III. in the late civil commotion, as if in so doing they had committed treason against James IV., although the last was not, and could not be king, till after his father's death. They determined to begin with Lord David Lindsay of the Byres, a man well acquainted with military matters, but otherwise blunt and ignorant; so they thought it would be no difficult matter to get him to submit himself to the King's pleasure, when they proposed to take a fine in money from him, or perhaps confiscate some part of his lands. This they thought would encourage others to submit in like manner; and thus the conspirators proposed to enrich themselves, and to impoverish those who had been their enemies.

It was on the 10th of May 1489 that Lord David Lindsay was summoned before the Parliament, then sitting at Edinburgh, to defend himself against a charge of treason, which stated, "That he had come in arms to Sauchie with the King's father against the King himself, and had given the King's father a sword and good horse, counselling him to devour the King's grace here present."

Lord Lindsay knew nothing about the form of law affairs, but hearing himself repeatedly called upon to answer to this accusation, he started up, and told the nobles of the Parliament they were all villains and traitors themselves, and that he would prove them to be such with his sword. The late King, he said, had been cruelly murdered by villains, who had brought the Prince with them to be a pretext and colour for their enterprise, and that if he punish not you hastily for that murder, you will murder him when you think time, as you did his father. "And," said the stout old lord, addressing himself personally to the King, who was present in Parliament, "if your Grace's father were still living, I would fight for him to the death, and stand in no awe of these false lurdans" (that is villains), "Or, if your Grace had a son who should come in arms against you, I would take your part against his abettors, and fight in your cause against them, three men against six. Trust me, that though they cause your Grace to believe ill of me, I will prove in the end more faithful than any of them."

The Lord Chancellor, who felt the force of these words, tried to turn off their effect, by saying to the King, that Lord Lindsay was an old-fashioned man, ignorant of legal forms, and not able to speak reverently in his Grace's presence. "But," said he, "he will submit himself to your Grace's pleasure, and you must not be severe with him;" and, turning to the Lord David, he said, "It is best for you to submit to the King's will, and his Grace will be good to you."

Now you must know, that the Lord David had a brother-german, named Patrick Lindsay, who was as good a lawyer as Lord Lindsay was a soldier. The two brothers had been long upon bad terms; but when this Mr. Patrick saw the Chancellor's drift, he trod upon his elder brother's foot, to make him understand that he ought not to follow the advice given him, nor come into the King's will, which would be in fact confessing himself guilty. The Lord David, however, did not understand the hint. On the contrary, as he chanced to have a sore toe, the tread of his brother's foot was painful to him, so that be looked fiercely at him, and said, "Thou art too pert, thou loon, to stamp upon my foot—if it were out of the King's presence, I would strike thee upon the face."

But Mr. Patrick, without regarding his brother's causeless anger, fell on his knees before the assembled nobles, and besought that he might have leave to plead for his brother; "for," said he, "I see no man of law will undertake his cause for fear of displeasing the King's grace; and though, my lord, my brother and I have not been friends for many years, yet my heart will not suffer me to see the native house from which I am descended perish for want of assistance."

The King having granted Mr. Patrick Lindsay liberty of speech in his brother's behalf, he began by objecting to the King's sitting in judgment in a case in which he was himself a party, and had been an actor. "Wherefore," said Mr. Patrick, "we object to his presence to try this cause, in which, being a party, he ought not to be a judge. Therefore we require his Majesty, in God's name, to rise and leave the court, till the question be considered and decided." The Lord Chancellor and the lords, having conversed together, found that this request was reasonable. So the young King was obliged to retire into an inner apartment, which he resented as a species of public affront.

Mr. Patrick next endeavoured to procure favour, by entreating the lords who were about to hear the cause to judge it with impartiality, and as they would wish to be dealt with themselves were they in misfortune, and some party adverse to them possessed of power.

"Proceed, and answer to the accusation," said the Chancellor. "You shall have justice at our hands."

Then Mr. Patrick brought forward a defence in point of legal form, stating that the summons required that the Lord Lindsay should appear forty days after citation, whereas the forty days were now expired; so that he could not be legally compelled to answer to the accusation until summoned anew.

This was found good law; and Lord David Lindsay, and the other persons accused, were dismissed for the time, nor were any proceedings ever resumed against them.

Lord David, who had listened to the defences without understanding their meaning, was so delighted with the unexpected consequences of his brother's eloquence, that he broke out into the following rapturous acknowledgment of gratitude:—"Verily, brother, but you have fine piet words" (that is, magpie words). "I could not have believed, by Saint Mary, that ye had such words. Ye shall have the Mains of Kirkfother for your day's wage."

The King, on his side, threatened Mr. Patrick with a reward of a different kind, saying, "He would set him where he should not see his feet for twelve months." Accordingly, he was as good as his word, sending the successful advocate to be prisoner in the dungeon of the castle of Rothsay, in the island of Bute, where he lay for a whole year.

It is curious to find that the King's authority was so limited in one respect, and so arbitrary in another. For it appears that he was obliged to comply with Patrick Lindsay's remonstrance, and leave the seat of regal justice, when his jurisdiction was declined as that of a partial judge; whilst, on the other hand, he had the right, or at least the power, to inflict upon the objecting party a long and rigorous imprisonment, for discharging his duty towards his client.

James IV. was not long upon the throne ere his own reflections, and the remonstrances of some of the clergy, made him sensible that his accompanying the rebel lords against his father in the field of Sauchie was a very sinful action. He did not consider his own youth, nor the enticements of the lords, who had obtained possession of his person, as any sufficient excuse for having been, in some degree, accessory to his father's death, by appearing in arms against him. He deeply repented the crime, and, according to the doctrines of the Roman Catholic religion, endeavoured to atone for it by various acts of penance. Amongst other tokens of repentance, he caused to be made an iron belt, or girdle, which he wore constantly under his clothes; and every year of his life he added another link of an ounce or two to the weight of it, as if he desired that his penance should not be relaxed, but rather should increase, during all the days of his life.

It was, perhaps, in consequence of these feelings of remorse, that the King not only forgave that part of the nobility which had appeared on his father's side, and abstained from all further persecution against Lord Lindsay and others, but did all in his power to conciliate their affections, without losing those of the other party. The wealth of his father enabled him to be liberal to the nobles on both sides, and at the same time to maintain a more splendid appearance, in his court and royal state than had been practised by any of his predecessors. He was himself expert in all feats of exercise and arms, and encouraged the use of them, and the practice of tilts and tournaments in his presence, wherein he often took part himself. It was his frequent custom to make proclamation through his kingdom, that all lords and gentlemen who might desire to win honour should come to Edinburgh or Stirling, and exercise themselves in tilting with the lance, fighting with the battleaxe, the two-handed sword, shooting with the long bow, or any other warlike contention. He who did best in these encounters had his adversary's weapon delivered up to him, and the best tilter with the spear received from the King a lance with a head of pure gold.

The fame of these warlike sports—for sports they were accounted, though they often ended in sad and bloody earnest—brought knights from other parts of Europe to contend with those of Scotland; but, says the historian, with laudable partiality, there were none of them went unmatched, and few that were not overthrown.

We may mention, as an example, the combat in the lists betwixt a celebrated German knight, who came to Scotland in search of champions with whom to match himself in single fight, and whose challenge was accepted by Sir Patrick Hamilton, a brother of the Earl of Arran, and near kinsman to the King. They met gallantly with their lances at full gallop, and broke their spears without doing each other further injury. When they were furnished with fresh lances, they took a second course; but the Scottish knight's horse, being indifferently trained, swerved, and could by no endeavours of the rider be brought to encounter his adversary. Then Sir Patrick sprung from his saddle, and called to the German knight to do the same, saying, "A horse was a weak warrant to trust to when men had most to do." Then the German dismounted, and fought stoutly with Sir Patrick for the best part of an hour. At length Hamilton, by a blow of his sword, brought the foreigner on his knees, whereupon the King threw his hat into the lists, as a sign that the combat should cease. But the honour of the day remained with Sir Patrick Hamilton.

Besides being fond of martial exercises, James encouraged the arts, and prosecuted science, as it was then understood. He studied medicine and surgery, and appears to have been something of a chemist.

An experiment made under his direction shows at least the interest which James took in science, although he used a whimsical mode of gratifying his curiosity. Being desirous to know which was the primitive or original language, he caused a deaf and dumb woman to be transported to the solitary island of Inchkeith, with two infant children, devising thus to discover what language they would talk when they came to the age of speech. A Scottish historian, who tells the story, adds, with great simplicity, "Some say they spoke good Hebrew; for my part I know not, but from report." It is more likely they would scream like their dumb nurse, or bleat like the goats and sheep on the island.

The same historian gives a very pleasing picture of James IV.

There was great love, he says, betwixt the subjects and their sovereign, for the King was free from the vice of avarice, which was his father's failing.   Neither would he endure flatterers, cowards, or sycophants about his person, but ruled by the counsel of the most eminent nobles, and thus won the hearts of all men. He often went disguised among the common people, and asked them questions about the King and his measures, and thus learned the opinion which was entertained of him by his subjects.

He was also active in the discharge of his royal duties. His authority, as it was greater than that of any king who had reigned since the time of James I., was employed for the administration of justice, and the protection of every rank of his subjects, so that he was reverenced as well as beloved by all classes of his people. Scotland obtained, under his administration, a greater share of prosperity than she had yet enjoyed. She possessed some share of foreign trade, and the success of Sir Andrew Wood, together with the King's exertions in building vessels, made the country be respected, as having a considerable naval power.

These advantages were greatly increased by the unusually long continuance of the peace, or rather the truce, with England. Henry VII. had succeeded to the crown of that kingdom, after a dreadful series of civil strife; and being himself a wise and sagacious monarch, he was desirous to repair, by a long interval of repose and quiet, the great damage which the country had sustained by the wars of York and

Lancaster. He was the more disposed to peace with Scotland, that his own title to the throne of England was keenly disputed, and exposed him more than once to the risk of invasion and insurrection.

On the most memorable of those occasions, Scotland was for a short time engaged in the quarrel. A certain personage, calling himself Richard, Duke of York, second son of Edward IV., supposed to have been murdered in the Tower of London, laid claim to the crown which Henry VII. wore. On the part of Henry, this pretended prince was said to be a low-born Fleming, named Perkin Warbeck, trained up by the Duchess of Burgundy (sister of King Edward IV.), to play the part which he now assumed. But it is not, perhaps, even yet certain, whether he was the real person he called himself or an impostor. In 1496 he came to Scotland at the head of a gallant train of foreigners; and accompanied by about fifteen hundred men, and made the greatest offers to James IV., providing he would assist him in his claims against England. James does not appear to have doubted the adventurer's pretensions to the character which he assumed. He received him with favour and distinction, conferred on him the hand of Lady Catharine Gordon, daughter of the Earl of Huntly, the most beautiful woman in Scotland, and disposed himself to lend him assistance to ascend the English throne.

The Scottish King with this view entered Northumberland, and invited the people of that warlike country to join the ranks of the supposed prince. But the Northumbrians paid no attention to this invitation, and when the adventurer besought James to spare the country, the Scottish monarch answered with a sneer, that it was very kind of him to interfere in behalf of a people who did not seem at all disposed to acknowledge him. The English in 1497 revenged his inroad by an invasion of Berwickshire, in which they took a small castle, called Ayton. No other mischief was done on either side, for James gave up the cause of Perkin Warbeck, satisfied either that he had no right to the throne or that he had not a hold on the affections of any considerable party sufficient to make such a right good. The adventurer, abandoned by James, made afterwards an attempt to invade England from Cornwall, and, being made prisoner, was executed at Tyburn. His wife, who had faithfully attended him through all his misfortunes, fell into the hands of Henry VII., who assigned her a pension, and recommended her to the protection of his Queen. She was commonly called, from her grace and beauty, the White Rose of Scotland.

After this short war had been made up by a truce of seven years, Henry's wisdom was employed in converting that truce into a stable and lasting peace, which might, for a length of time at least, unite two nations whose mutual interest it was to remain friends, although circumstances had so long made them enemies. The grounds of the inveterate hostility between England and Scotland had been that unhappy claim of supremacy set up by Edward I., and persevered in by all his successors. This was a right which England would not abandon, and to which the Scots, by so many instances of determined resistance, had shown they would never submit. For more than a hundred years there had been no regular treaty of peace betwixt England and Scotland, except for the few years which succeeded the treaty of Northampton. During this long period, the kindred nations had been either engaged in the most inveterate wars, or reposing themselves under the protection of short and doubtful truces.

The wisdom of Henry VII. endeavoured to find a remedy for such great evils, by trying what the effects of gentle and friendly influence would avail, where the extremity of force had been employed without effect. The King of England agreed to give his daughter Margaret, a beautiful and accomplished princess, to James IV. in marriage. He offered to endow her with an ample fortune, and on that alliance was to be founded a close league of friendship between England and Scotland, the kings obliging themselves to assist each other against all the rest of the world. Unfortunately for both countries, but particularly so for Scotland, this peace, designed to be perpetual, did not last above ten years. Yet the good policy of Henry VII. bore fruit after a hundred years had passed away; and in consequence of the marriage of James IV. and the Princess Margaret, an end was put to all future national wars, by their great grandson, James VI. of Scotland and I. of England, becoming King of the whole island of Great Britain.

The claim of supremacy, asserted by England, is not mentioned in this treaty, which was signed on the 4th of January 1502; but as the monarchs treated with each other on equal terms, that claim, which had cost such oceans of Scottish and English blood, must be considered as having been then virtually abandoned.

This important marriage was celebrated with great pomp. The Earl of Surrey, a gallant English nobleman, had the charge to conduct the Princess Margaret to her new kingdom of Scotland. The King came to meet her at Newbattle Abbey, within six miles of Edinburgh. He was gallantly dressed in a jacket of crimson velvet, bordered with cloth of gold, and had hanging at his back his lure, as it is called, an implement which is used in hawking. He was distinguished by his strength and agility, leaping on his horse without putting his toe in the stirrup, and always riding full gallop, follow who could.

When he was about to enter Edinburgh with his new bride, he wished her to ride behind him, and made a gentleman mount to see whether his horse would carry double. But as his spirited charger was not broken for that purpose, the King got up before his bride on her palfrey, which was quieter, and so they rode through the town of Edinburgh in procession, in the same manner as you may now see a good farmer and his wife riding to church. There were shows prepared to receive them, all in the romantic taste of the age. Thus they found in their way a tent pitched, out of which came a knight armed at all points, with a lady bearing his bugle-horn. Suddenly another knight came up and took away the lady. Then the first knight followed him, and challenged him to fight. They drew swords accordingly, and fought before the King and Queen for their amusement, till the one struck the sword out of the other's hands, and then the King commanded the battle to cease. In this representation all was sport except the blows, and these were serious enough. Many other military spectacles were exhibited, tilts and tournaments in particular. James, calling himself the Savage Knight, appeared in a wild dress, accompanied by the fierce chiefs from the Borders and Highlands, who fought with each other till several were wounded and slain in these ferocious entertainments. It is said the King was not very sorry to see himself thus rid of these turbulent leaders, whose feuds and depredations contributed so often to the public disturbance.

The sports on occasion of the Queen's marriage, and indeed the whole festivities of King James's reign, and the style of living at his court, showed that the Scots, in his time, were a wealthier and a more elegant people than they had formerly been. James IV. was renowned, as we have seen, among foreign nations, for the splendour of his court, and for the honourable reception which he gave to strangers who visited his kingdom. And we shall see in the next chapter that his leisure was not entirely bestowed on sport and pastime, but that he also made wise laws for the benefit of the kingdom.

XXIV

The Battle of Flodden

1502-1513

DURING the season of tranquillity which followed the marriage of James and Margaret, we find that the King, with his Parliament, enacted many good laws for the improvement of the country. The Highlands and Islands were particularly attended to, because, as one of the acts of Parliament expressed it, they had become almost savage for want of justices and sheriffs. Magistrates were therefore appointed, and laws made for the government of those wild and unruly people.

Another most important act of Parliament permitted the King, and his nobles and barons, to let their land, not only for military service, but for a payment in money or in grain; a regulation which tended to introduce quiet peaceful farmers into lands occupied, but left uncultivated, by tenants of a military character. Regulations also took place for attendance on Parliament, and the representation of the different orders of society in that assembly. The possessors of lands were likewise called on to plant wood, and make enclosures, fishponds, and other improvements.

All these regulations show that the King had a sincere wish to benefit his subjects, and entertained liberal views of the mode of accomplishing that object. But the unfortunate country of Scotland was destined never to remain any long time in a state of peace or improvement; and accordingly towards the end of James's reign, events occurred which brought on a defeat still more calamitous than any which the kingdom had yet received.

While Henry VII., the father-in-law of James, continued to live, his wisdom made him very attentive to preserve the peace which had been established betwixt the two countries. His character was, indeed, far from being that of a generous prince, but he was a sagacious politician, and granted, from an enlightened view of his own interest, what perhaps he would otherwise have been illiberal enough to refuse. On this principle he made some allowance for the irritable pride of his son-in-law and his subjects, who were as proud as they were poor, and made it his study to remove all the petty causes of quarrel which arose from time to time. But when this wise and cautious monarch died, he was succeeded by his son Henry VIII., a prince of a bold, haughty, and furious disposition, impatient of control or contradiction, and rather desirous of war than willing to make any concessions for the sake of peace. James IV. and he resembled each other perhaps too nearly in temper to admit of their continuing intimate friends.

The military disposition of Henry chiefly directed him to an enterprise against France; and the King of France, on his part, desired much to renew the old alliance with Scotland, in order that the apprehension of an invasion from the Scottish frontiers might induce Henry to abandon his scheme of attacking France. He knew that the splendour in which King James lived had exhausted the treasures which his father had left behind him, and he concluded that the readiest way to make him his friend was to supply him with sums of money, which he could not otherwise have raised. Gold was also freely distributed amongst the counsellors and favourites of the Scottish King. This liberality showed to great advantage when compared with the very opposite conduct of the King of England, who delayed even to pay a legacy which had been left by Henry his father to his sister the Queen of Scotland.

Other circumstances of a different kind tended to create disagreements between England and Scotland. James had been extremely desirous to increase the strength of his kingdom by sea, and its commerce and Scotland presenting a great extent of sea-coast, and numerous harbours, had at this time a considerable trade. The royal navy, besides one vessel called the *Great Michael* supposed to be the largest in the world, and which, as an old author says, "cumbered all Scotland to get her fitted out for sea," consisted, it is said, of sixteen ships of war. The King paid particular attention to naval affairs, and seemed never more happy than when inspecting and exercising his little navy.

It chanced that one John Barton, a Scottish mariner, had been captured by the Portuguese, as far back as the year 1476. As the King of Portugal refused to make any amends, James granted the family of Barton letters of reprisals, that is, a warrant empowering them to take all Portuguese vessels which should come in their way, until their loss was made up. There were three brothers, all daring men, but especially the eldest, whose name was Andrew Barton. He had two strong ships, the larger called the *Lion,* the lesser the *Jenny Pirwen,* with which it would appear he cruised in the British Channel, stopping not only Portuguese vessels, but also English ships bound for Portugal. Complaints being made to King Henry, he fitted out two vessels, which were filled with chosen men, and placed under the command of Lord Thomas Howard and Sir Edward Howard, both sons to the Earl of Surrey. They found Barton and his vessels cruising in the Downs, being guided to the place by the captain of a merchant vessel whom Barton had plundered on the preceding day.

On approaching the enemy, the noble brothers showed no ensign of war, but put up a willow wand on their masts, as being the emblem of a trading vessel. But when the Scotsman attempted to make them bring to, the English threw out their flags and pennons, and fired a broadside of their ordnance. Barton then knew that he was engaged with the King of England's ships of war. Far from being dismayed at this, he engaged boldly, and, distinguished by his rich dress and bright armour, appeared on deck with a whistle of gold about his neck, suspended by a chain of the same precious metal, and encouraged his men to fight valiantly.

The fight was very obstinate. If we may believe a ballad of the time, Barton's ship was furnished with a peculiar contrivance, suspending large weights, or beams, from his yard-arms, to be dropped down upon the enemy when they should come alongside. To make use of this contrivance, it was necessary that a person should ascend the mainmast, or in naval language, go aloft. As the English apprehended much mischief from the consequences of this manoeuvre, Howard had stationed a Yorkshire gentleman, named Hustler, the best archer in the ship, with strict injunctions to shoot every one who should attempt to go aloft to let fall the beams of Barton's vessel. Two men were successively killed in the attempt, and Andrew Barton himself, confiding in the strong armour which he wore, began to ascend the mast. Lord Thomas Howard called out to the archer to shoot true, on peril of his life. "Were I to die for it," said Hustler, "I have but two arrows left." The first which he shot bounded from Barton's armour without hurting him; but as the Scottish mariner raised his arm to climb higher, the archer took aim where the armour afforded him no protection, and wounded him mortally through the arm-pit.

Barton descended from the mast. "Fight on," he said, "my brave hearts; I am a little wounded, but not slain. I will but rest a while, and then rise and fight again; meantime, stand fast by Saint Andrew's Cross," meaning the Scottish flag, or ensign. He encouraged his men with his whistle while the breath of life remained. At length the whistle was heard no longer, and the Howards, boarding the Scottish vessel, found that her daring captain was dead. They carried the *Lion* into the Thames, and it is remarkable that Barton's ship became the second man-of-war in the English navy. When the kings wanted to equip a fleet, they hired or pressed into their service merchant vessels, and put soldiers on board of them. The ship called the *Great Henry* was the first built especially for war, by the King as his own property,—this captured vessel was the second.

James IV. was highly incensed at this insult, as he termed it, on the flag of Scotland, and sent a herald to demand satisfaction. The King of England justified his conduct on the ground of Barton's being a pirate,—a charge which James could not justly deny; but he remained not the less heated and incensed against his brother-in-law. Another misfortune aggravated his resentment, though the subject of misunderstanding was of ancient date.

While Henry VII. was yet alive, Sir Robert Ker of Fairniehirst, chief of one branch of the clan of Ker, an officer of James's household, and a favourite of that monarch, held the office of warden on the Middle Marches of Scotland. In exercising this office with rather unusual strictness, he had given offence to some of the more turbulent English Borderers, who resolved to assassinate him. Three of these, namely Heron, called the Bastard, because a natural brother of Heron of Ford, with Starhed and Lilburn, surrounded the Scottish warden, at a meeting upon a day of truce, and killed him with their lances.

Henry VII., with the pacific policy which marked his proceedings towards Scotland, agreed to surrender the guilty persons. Lilburn was

given up to King James, and died in captivity; Starhed escaped for a
time, by flying into the interior parts of England; the Bastard Heron
caused it to be rumoured that he was dead of the plague, and made
himself be transported in a coffin, so that he passed unsuspected
through the party sent to arrest him, and skulked on the Borders, waiting for a quarrel between the kingdoms, which might make it safe for
him to show himself. Henry VII., anxious to satisfy James, arrested his
legitimate brother, and Heron of Ford was delivered up instead of the
Bastard. But when Henry VIII. and James were about to disagree, both
the Bastard Heron and Starhed began to show themselves more publicly. Starhed was soon disposed of, for Sir Andrew, commonly called
Dand Ker, the son of the murdered Sir Robert, sent two of his dependents, called Tait, to accomplish his vengeance upon the English Bor-
derer. They surprised and put him to death accordingly, and brought
his head to their patron, who exposed it publicly at the cross of Edinburgh, exulting in the revenge he had taken. But the Bastard Heron
continued to rove about the Border, and James IV. made the public
appearance of this criminal a subject of complaint against Henry VIII.,
who perhaps was not justly responsible for it.

While James was thus on bad terms with his brother-in-law,
France left no measures unattempted which could attach Scotland to
her side. Great sums of money were sent to secure the good-will of
those courtiers in whom James most confided. The Queen of France, a
young and beautiful princess, flattered James's taste for romantic gallantry by calling herself his mistress and lady-love, and conjuring him
to march three miles upon English ground for her sake. She sent him,
at the same time, a ring from her own finger; and her intercession was
so powerful, that James thought he could not in honour dispense with
her request. This fantastical spirit of chivalry was his own ruin, and
very nearly that of the kingdom also.

At length, in June or July 1513, Henry VIII. sailed to France with a
gallant army, where he formed the siege of Terouenne. James IV. now
took a decided step. He sent over his principal herald to the camp of
King Henry before Terouenne, summoning him in haughty terms to
abstain from aggressions against James's ally, the King of France, and
upbraiding him, at the same time, with the death of Barton, the
impunity of the Bastard Heron, the detention of the legacy of
Henry VII. to his daughter the Scottish Queen, and all the subjects of
quarrel which had occurred since the death of that monarch.

Henry VIII. answered this letter, which he justly considered as a declaration of war, with equal bitterness, treating the King of Scots as a perjured man, because be was about to break the peace which he had solemnly sworn to observe. His summons he rejected with scorn. "The King of Scotland was not," he said, "of sufficient importance to determine the quarrel between England and France." The Scottish herald returned with this message, but not in time to find his master alive.

James had not awaited the return of his embassy to commence hostilities. Lord Home, his lord high chamberlain, had made an incursion into England with an army of about three or four thousand men. They collected great booty; but marching carelessly and without order, fell into an ambush of the English Borderers, concealed among the tall broom by which Millfield Plain, near Wooler, was then covered. The Scots sustained a total defeat, and lost near a third of their numbers in slain and wounded. This was a bad commencement of the war.

Meanwhile James, contrary to the advice of his wisest counsellors, determined to invade England with a royal army. The Parliament were unwilling to go into the King's measures. The tranquillity of the country, ever since the peace with England, was recollected, and as the impolitic claim of the supremacy seemed to be abandoned, little remained to stir up the old animosity between the kingdoms. The King, however, was personally so much liked, that he obtained the consent of the Parliament to this fatal and unjust war; and orders were given to assemble all the array of the kingdom of Scotland upon the Borough-moor of Edinburgh, a wide common, in the midst of which the royal standard was displayed from a large stone, or fragment of rock, called the Harestone.

Various measures were even in this extremity resorted to for preventing the war. One or two of them seem to have been founded upon a knowledge that the King's temper was tinged with a superstitious melancholy, partly arising from constitutional habits, partly from the remorse which he always entertained for his accession to his father's death. It was to these feelings that the following scene was doubtless addressed:—

As the King was at his devotions in the church of Linlithgow, a figure, dressed in an azure-coloured robe, girt with a girdle, or sash of linen, having sandals on his feet, with long yellow hair, and a grave commanding countenance, suddenly appeared before him. This singular-looking person paid little or no respect to the royal presence, but pressing up to the desk at which the King was seated, leaned down on it with his arms, and addressed him with little reverence. He declared, that "his Mother laid her commands on James to forbear the journey which he purposed, seeing that neither he, nor any who went with him, would thrive in the undertaking." He also cautioned the King against frequenting the society of women, and using their counsel; "If thou dost," said he, "thou shalt be confounded and brought to shame."

These words spoken, the messenger escaped from among the courtiers so suddenly, that he seemed to disappear. There is no doubt that this person had been dressed up to represent Saint John, called in Scripture the adopted son of the Virgin Mary. The Roman Catholics believed in the possibility of the souls of departed saints and apostles appearing on earth, and many impostures are recorded in history of the same sort with that I have just told you.

Another story, not so well authenticated, says, that a proclamation was heard at the market-cross of Edinburgh, at the dead of night, summoning the King, by his name and titles, and many of his nobles and principal leaders, to appear before the tribunal of Pluto within the space of forty days. This also has the appearance of a stratagem, invented to deter the King from his expedition.

But neither these artifices, nor the advice and entreaty of Margaret, the Queen of Scotland, could deter James from his unhappy expedition. He was so well beloved that he soon assembled a great army, and placing himself at their head he entered England near the castle of Twisell on the 22d of August 1513. He speedily obtained possession of the Border fortresses of Norham, Wark, Etall, Ford, and others of less note, and collected a great spoil. Instead, however, of advancing with his army upon the country of England, which lay defenceless before him, the King is said to have trifled away his time with Lady Heron of Ford, a beautiful woman, who contrived to divert him from the prosecution of his expedition until the approach of an English army.

While James lay thus idle on the frontier, the Earl of Surrey, that same noble and gallant knight who had formerly escorted Queen Margaret to Scotland, now advanced at the head of an army of twenty-six thousand men. The Earl was joined by his son Thomas, the lord high admiral, with a large body of soldiers who had been disembarked at Newcastle. As the warlike inhabitants of the northern counties gathered fast to Surrey's standard, so, on the other hand, the Scots began to return home in great numbers; because, though according to the feudal laws, each man had brought with him provisions for forty days, these being now nearly expended, a scarcity began to be felt in James's host. Others went home to place their booty in safety.

Surrey, feeling himself the stronger party, became desirous to provoke the Scottish King to fight. He therefore sent James a message, defying him to battle; and the Lord Thomas Howard, at the same time, added a message, that as King James had often complained of the death of Andrew Barton, he, Lord Thomas, by whom that deed was done, was now ready to maintain it with his sword in the front of the fight. James returned for answer, that to meet the English in battle was so much his wish, that had the message of the Earl found him at Edinburgh, he would have laid aside all other business to have met him on a pitched field.

But the Scottish nobles entertained a very different opinion from their King. They held a council at which Lord Patrick Lindsay was made president, or chancellor. This was the same person who, in the beginning of the King's reign, had pleaded so well for his brother, to whose titles and estate he afterwards succeeded. He opened the discussion, by telling the council a parable of a rich merchant, who would needs go to play at dice with a common hazarder, or sharper, and stake a rose-noble of gold against a crooked halfpenny. "You, my lords," he said, "will be as unwise as the merchant, if you risk your King, whom I compare to a precious rose-noble, against the English general, who is but an old crooked churl, lying in a chariot. Though the English lose the day, they lose nothing but this old churl and a parcel of mechanics; whereas so many of our common people have gone home, that few are left with us but the prime of our nobility." He therefore gave it as his advice, that the King should withdraw from the army, for safety of his person, and that some brave nobleman should be named by the council, to command in the action. The council agreed to recommend this plan to the King.

But James, who desired to gain fame by his own military skill and prowess, suddenly broke in on the council, and told them, with much heat, that they should not put such a disgrace upon him. "I will fight with the English," he said, "though you had all sworn the contrary. You may shame yourselves by flight, but you shall not shame me; and as for Lord Patrick Lindsay, who has got the first vote, I vow, that when I return to Scotland, I will cause him to be hanged over his own gate."

In this rash and precipitate resolution to fight at all risks, the King was much supported by the French ambassador, De la Motte. This was remarked by one of our old acquaintances, the Earl of Angus, called Bell-the-Cat, who, though very old, had come out to the field with his sovereign. He charged the Frenchman with being willing to sacrifice the interests of Scotland to those of his own country, which required that the Scots and English should fight at all hazards; and Angus, like Lord Lindsay, alleged the difference between the parties, the English being many of them men but of mean rank, and the Scottish army being the flower of their nobility and gentry. Incensed at his opposition, James said to him scornfully, "Angus, if you are afraid, you may go home." The Earl, on receiving such an insult, left the camp that night; but his two sons remained, and fell in the fatal battle, with two hundred of the name of Douglas.

While King James was in this stubborn humour, the Earl of Surrey had advanced as far as Wooler, so that only four or five miles divided the armies. The English leader inquired anxiously for some guide who was acquainted with the country, which is intersected and divided by one or two large brooks, which unite to form the river Till, and is, besides, in part mountainous. A person well mounted, and completely armed, but having the visor of his helmet lowered, to conceal his face, rode up, and, dismounting, knelt down before the Earl, and offered to be his guide, if he might obtain pardon of an offence of which he had been guilty. The Earl assured him of his forgiveness, provided he had not committed treason against the King of England, or personally wronged any lady—crimes, which Surrey declared he would not pardon. "God forbid," said the cavalier, "that I should have been guilty of such shameful sin; I did but assist in killing a Scotsman who ruled our Borders too strictly, and often did wrong to Englishmen." So saying, he raised the visor of his helmet, which hid his face, and showed the countenance of the Bastard Heron, who had been a partner in the assassination of Sir Robert Ker, as you were told before. His appearance was most welcome to the Earl of Surrey, who readily pardoned him the death of a Scotsman at that moment, especially since he knew him to be as well acquainted with every pass and path on the eastern frontier as a life of constant incursion and depredation could make him.

The Scottish army had fixed their camp upon a hill called Flodden, which rises to close in, as it were, the extensive flat called Millfield

Plain. This eminence slopes steeply towards the plain, and there is an extended piece of level ground on the top, where the Scots might have drawn up their army, and awaited at great advantage the attack of the English. Surrey liked the idea of venturing an assault on that position so ill, that he resolved to try whether he could not prevail on the King to abandon it. He sent a herald to invite James to come down from the height, and join battle in the open plain of Millfield below—reminded him of the readiness with which he had accepted his former challenge—and hinted, that it was the opinion of the English chivalry assembled for battle, that any delay of the encounter would sound to the King's dishonour.

We have seen that James was sufficiently rash and imprudent, but his impetuosity did not reach to the pitch Surrey perhaps expected. He refused to receive the messenger into his presence, and returned for answer, that it was not such a message as it became an earl to send to a king.

Surrey, therefore, distressed for provisions, was obliged to resort to another mode of bringing the Scots to action. He moved northward, sweeping round the hill of Flodden, keeping out of the reach of the Scottish artillery, until, crossing the Till near Twisell Castle, he placed himself, with his whole army, betwixt James and his own kingdom. The King suffered him to make this flank movement without interruption, though it must have afforded repeated and advantageous opportunities for attack. But when he saw the English army interposed betwixt him and his dominions, he became alarmed lest he should be cut off from Scotland. In this apprehension he was confirmed by one Giles Musgrave, an Englishman, whose counsel he used upon the occasion, and who assured him, that if he did not descend and fight with the English army, the Earl of Surrey would enter Scotland, and lay waste the whole country. Stimulated by this apprehension, the King resolved to give signal for the fatal battle.

With this view the Scots set fire to their huts, and the other refuse and litter of their camp. The smoke spread along the side of the hill, and under its cover the army of King James descended the eminence, which is much less steep on the northern than the southern side, while the English advanced to meet them, both concealed from each other by the clouds of smoke.

The Scots descended in four strong columns, all marching parallel to each other, having a reserve of the Lothian men, commanded by

Earl Bothwell. The English were also divided into four bodies, with a reserve of cavalry led by Dacre.

The battle commenced at the hour of four in the afternoon. The first which encountered was the left wing of the Scots, commanded by the Earl of Huntly and Lord Home, which overpowered and threw into disorder the right wing of the English, under Sir Edmund Howard. Sir Edmund was beaten down, his standard taken, and he himself in danger of instant death, when he was relieved by the Bastard Heron, who came up at the head of a band of determined outlaws like himself, and extricated Howard. It is alleged against Lord Home by many Scottish writers, that he ought to have improved his advantage, by hastening to the support of the next division of the Scottish army. It is even pretended, that he replied to those who urged him to go to the assistance of the King, that "the man did well that day who stood and saved himself." But this seems invented, partly to criminate Home, and partly to account for the loss of the battle in some other way than by the superiority of the English. In reality, the English cavalry, under Dacre, which acted as a reserve, appear to have kept the victors in check; while Thomas Howard, the lord high admiral who commanded the second division of the English, bore down and routed the Scottish division commanded by Crawford and Montrose, who were both slain. Thus matters went on the Scottish left.

Upon the extreme right of James's army, a division of Highlanders, consisting of the clans of MacKenzie, MacLean, and others, commanded by the Earls of Lennox and Argyle, were so insufferably annoyed by the volleys of the English arrows, that they broke their ranks, and, in despite of the cries, entreaties, and signals of De la Motte, the French ambassador, who endeavoured to stop them, rushed tumultuously down hill, and being attacked at once in flank and rear by Sir Edward Stanley, with the men of Cheshire and Lancashire, were routed with great slaughter.

The only Scottish division which remains to be mentioned was commanded by James in person, and consisted of the choicest of his nobles and gentry, whose armour was so good, that the arrows made but slight impression upon them. They were all on foot—the King himself had parted with his horse. They engaged the Earl of Surrey, who opposed to them the division which he personally commanded. The Scots attacked with the greatest fury, and, for a time, had the better. Surrey's squadrons were disordered, his standard in great danger, Bothwell and the Scottish reserve were advancing, and the English seemed in some risk of losing the battle. But Stanley, who had defeated the Highlanders, came up on one flank of the King's division; the Admiral, who had conquered Crawford and Montrose, assailed them on the other. The Scots showed the most undaunted courage. Uniting themselves with the reserve under Bothwell, they formed into a circle, with their spears extended on every side, and fought obstinately. Bows being now useless, the English advanced on all sides with their bills, a huge weapon which made ghastly wounds. But they could not force the Scots either to break or retire, although the carnage among them was dreadful. James himself died amid his warlike peers and loyal gentry. He was twice wounded with arrows, and at length despatched with a bill. Night fell without the battle being absolutely decided, for the Scottish centre kept their ground, and Home and Dacre held each other at bay. But during the night, the remainder of the Scottish army drew off in silent despair from the bloody field, on which they left their King, and the flower of his nobility.

This great and decisive victory was gained by the Earl of Surrey on 9th September 1513. The victors had about five thousand men slain, the Scots twice that number at least. But the loss lay not so much in the number of the slain, as in their rank and quality. The English lost very few men of distinction. The Scots left on the field the King, two bishops, two mitred abbots, twelve earls, thirteen lords, and five eldest sons of peers. The number of gentlemen slain was beyond calculation;—there is scarcely a family of name in Scottish history who did not lose a relative there.

The Scots were much disposed to dispute the fact that James IV. had fallen on Flodden Field. Some said he had retired from the kingdom, and made a pilgrimage to Jerusalem. Others pretended that in the twilight, when the fight was nigh ended, four tall horsemen came into the field, having each a bunch of straw on the point of their spears, as a token for them to know each other by. They said these men mounted the King on a dun hackney, and that he was seen to cross the Tweed with them at night-fall. Nobody pretended to say what they did with him, but it was believed he was murdered in Home Castle; and I recollect, about forty years since, that there was a report, that in cleaning the draw-well of that ruinous fortress, the workmen found a skeleton wrapt in a bull's hide, and having a belt of iron round the waist. There was, however, no truth in this rumour. It was the absence of this

belt of iron which the Scots founded upon to prove that the body of
James could not have fallen into the hands of the English, since they
either had not that token to show, or did not produce it. They contended, therefore, that the body over which the enemy triumphed was
not that of James himself, but of one of his attendants, several of
whom, they said, were dressed in his armour.

But all these are idle fables, invented and believed because the
vulgar love what is mysterious, and the Scots readily gave credit to
what tended to deprive their enemies of so signal a trophy of victory.
The reports are contrary to common sense. Lord Home was the chamberlain of James IV., and high in his confidence. He had nothing whatever to gain by the King's death, and therefore we must acquit him of a
great crime, for which there could be no adequate motive. The consequence of James's death proved, in fact, to be the Earl's ruin, as we shall
see presently.

It seems true, that the King usually wore the belt of iron in token
of his repentance for his father's death, and the share he had in it. But it
is not unlikely that he would lay aside such a cumbrous article of
penance in a day of battle; or the English, when they despoiled his
person, may have thrown it aside as of no value. The body which the
English affirm to have been that of James was found on the field by
Lord Dacre, and carried by him to Berwick, and presented to Surrey.
Both of these lords knew James's person too well to be mistaken. The
body was also acknowledged by his two favourite attendants, Sir
William Scott and Sir John Forman, who wept at beholding it.

The fate of these relics were singular and degrading. They were
not committed to the tomb, for the Pope, being at that time in alliance
with England against France, had laid James under a sentence of
excommunication, so that no priest dared to pronounce the funeral
service over them. The royal corpse was therefore embalmed, and sent
to the Monastery of Sheen, in Surrey. It lay there till the Reformation,
when the monastery was given to the Duke of Suffolk; and after that
period, the body, which was lapped up in a sheet of lead, was suffered
to toss about the house like a piece of useless lumber. Stow, the historian, saw it flung into a waste room among old pieces of wood, lead,
and other rubbish. Some idle workmen, "for their foolish pleasure,"
says the same writer, "hewed off the head; and one Lancelot Young,
master-glazier to Queen Elizabeth, finding a sweet smell come from
thence, owing, doubtless, to the spices used for embalming the body,

carried the head home, and kept it for some time; but in the end, caused the sexton of Saint Michael's, Wood Street, to bury it in the charnel-house."

Such was the end of that King once so proud and powerful. The fatal battle of Flodden, in which he was slain, and his army destroyed, is justly considered as one of the most calamitous events in Scottish history.

XXV

The Queen Dowager

1513-1524

THE event of the defeat at Flodden threw all Scotland into a degree of mourning and despair which is not yet forgotten in the southern counties, on whom a great part of the loss fell, as their inhabitants, soldiers from situation and disposition, composed a considerable portion of the forces which remained with the King' s army, and suffered, of course, a great share in the slaughter which took place. The inhabitants of the smaller towns on the Border, as Selkirk, Hawick, Jedburgh, and others, were almost entirely cut off, and their songs and traditions preserve to this day the recollection of their sufferings and losses.

Not only a large proportion of the nobility and of the baronage, who had by right of birth the important task of distributing justice and maintaining order in their domains, but also the magistrates of the burghs, who, in general, had remained with the army, had fallen on the field; so that the country seemed to be left open to invasion and conquest, such as had taken place after the loss of the battles of Dunbar and Halidon Hill. Yet the firm courage of the Scottish people was displayed in its noblest colours in this formidable crisis;—all were ready to combat, and more disposed, even from the excess of the calamity, to resist than to yield to the fearful consequences which might have been expected.

Edinburgh, the metropolis, or capital city of Scotland, set a noble example of the conduct which should be adopted under a great national calamity. The provost, bailies, and magistracy of that city had been carried by their duty to the battle, in which most of them, with the burghers and citizens who followed their standard, had fallen with the King. A certain number of persons called *Presidents,* at the head of whom was George Towrs of Inverleith, had been left with a commission to discharge the duty of magistrates during the absence of those to whom the office actually belonged. The battle was fought, as we have said, on the 9th of September. On the 10th, being the succeeding day, the news reached Edinburgh, and George Towrs and the other presidents published on that day a proclamation, which would do honour to the annals of any country in Europe. The presidents must have known that all was lost, but they took every necessary precaution to prevent the public from yielding to a hasty and panic alarm, and to prepare with firmness the means of public defence.

"Whereas," says this remarkable proclamation, "news have arrived, which are yet uncertain, of misfortune which hath befallen the King and his army, we strictly command and charge all persons within the city to have their arms in readiness, and to be ready to assemble at the tolling of the common bell of the town, to repel any enemy who may seek to attack the city. We also discharge all women of the lower class, and vagabonds of every description, from appearing on the street to cry and make lamentations; and we command women of honest fame and character to pass to the churches, and pray for the King and his army, and for our neighbours; who are with the King's host." In this way the gallant George Towrs took measures at once for preventing the spreading of terror and confusion by frantic and useless lamentation, and for defence of the city, if need should arise. The simplicity of the order showed the courage and firmness of those who issued it under the astounding national calamity which had been sustained.

The Earl of Surrey did not, however, make any endeavour to invade Scotland, or to take any advantage of the great victory he had obtained, by attempting the conquest of that country. Experience had taught the English, that though it might be easy for them to overrun their northern neighbours, to ravage provinces, and to take castles and cities, yet that the obstinate valour of the Scots, and their love of

independence, had always, in the long run, found means of expelling
the invaders. With great moderation and wisdom, Henry, or his ministers, therefore, resolved rather to conciliate the friendship of the Scots,
by foregoing the immediate advantages which the victory of Flodden
afforded them, than to commence another invasion, which however
distressing to Scotland, was likely, as in the Bruce and Baliol wars, to
terminate in the English also sustaining great loss, and ultimately being
again driven out of the kingdom. The English counsellors remembered
that Margaret, the widow of James, was the sister of the King of England—that she must become Regent of the kingdom, and would naturally be a friend to her native country. They knew that the late war had
been undertaken by the King of Scotland against the wish of his
people; and with noble as well as wise policy, they endeavoured rather
to render Scotland once more a friendly power than, by invasion and
violence, to convert her into an irreconcilable enemy. The incursions
which followed the battle of Flodden extended only to the Borders; no
great attempt against Scotland was made, or apparently meditated.

Margaret, the Queen Dowager, became Regent of Scotland, and
guardian of the young King, James V., who, as had been too often the
case on former similar occasions, ascended the throne when a child of
not two years old.

But the authority of Margaret was greatly diminished, and her
character injured, by a hasty and imprudent marriage which she
formed with Douglas, Earl of Angus, the grandson of old Bell-the-Cat.
That celebrated person had not long survived the fatal battle of Flodden, in which both his sons had fallen. His grandson, the inheritor of
his great name, was a handsome youth, brave, high-born, and with all
the ambition of the old Douglases, as well as with much of their military talents. He was, however, young, rash, and inexperienced; and his
elevation to be the husband of the Queen Regent excited the jealousy
and emulation of all the other nobles of Scotland, who dreaded the
name and the power of the Douglas.

A peace now took place betwixt France and England, and Scotland
was included in the treaty; but this could hardly be termed fortunate,
considering the distracted state of the country, which, freed from English ravages, and no longer restrained by the royal authority, was left to
prosecute its domestic feuds and quarrels with the usual bloody animosity. The nation, or rather the nobles, disgusted with Margaret's
regency, chiefly on account of her marriage with Angus, and that young

lord's love of personal power, now thought of calling back into Scotland John, Duke of Albany, son of that Robert who was banished during the reign of James III. This nobleman was the nearest male relation of the King, being the cousin-german of his father. The Queen was by many considered as having forfeited the right of regency by her marriage, and Albany, on his arrival from France, was generally accepted in that character.

John, Duke of Albany, had been born and bred in France, where he had large estates by his mother, a daughter of the Earl of Boulogne; and he seems always to have preferred the interests of that kingdom to those of Scotland, with which he was only connected by hereditary descent. He was a weak and passionate man, taking up opinions too slightly, and driven out of his resolutions too easily. His courage may justly be suspected; and, if not quite a fool, he was certainly not the wise man whom Scotland required for a governor. He brought over with him, however, a large sum of money from France; and as his manners were pleasing, his birth high, and his pretensions great, he easily got the advantage over Queen Margaret, her husband the Earl of Angus, and other lords who favoured her interest.

After much internal disturbance, Queen Margaret was obliged altogether to retire from Scotland, and to seek refuge at her brother's court, where she bore a daughter, Lady Margaret Douglas, of whom you will hear more hereafter. In the meantime, her party in Scotland was still further weakened. Lord Home was one of her warmest supporters; this was the same nobleman who commanded the left wing at the battle of Flodden, and was victorious on that day, but exposed himself to suspicion by not giving assistance to the other divisions of the Scottish army. He and his brethren were enticed to Edinburgh, and seized upon, tried, and beheaded, upon accusations which are not known. This severity, however, was so far from confirming Albany's power, that it only excited terror and hatred; and his situation became so difficult, that to his friends in secret he expressed nothing but despair, and wished that he had broken his limbs when he first left his easy and quiet situation in France, to undertake the government of so distracted and unruly a country as Scotland. In fact, he accomplished a retreat to France, and during his absence, committed the wardenry of the Scottish frontiers to a brave French knight, the Chevalier de la Bastie, remarkable for the beauty of his person and the gallantry of his achievements, but destined, as we shall see, to a tragical fate.

The office of warden had belonged to the Lord Home; and his friends, numerous, powerful, and inhabiting the eastern frontier, to which the office belonged, were equally desirous to avenge the death of their chief, and to be freed from the dominion of a stranger like De la Bastie, the favourite of Albany, by whose authority Lord Home had been executed. Sir David Home of Wedderburn, one of the fiercest of the name, laid an ambush for the unfortunate warden, near Langton, in Berwickshire. De la Bastie, seeing his life aimed at, was compelled to fly, in the hope of gaining the castle of Dunbar; but near the town of Dunse his horse stuck fast in a morass. The pursuers came up and put him to death. Sir David Home knitted the head, by the long locks which the deceased wore, to the mane of his horse, rode with it in triumph to Home Castle, and placed it on a spear on the highest turret. The hair is said to be yet preserved in the charter chest of the family. By this cruel deed Wedderburn considered himself as doing a brave and gallant action in avenging the death of his chief and kinsman, by putting to death a friend and favourite of the Regent, although it does not appear that De la Bastie had the least concern in Lord Home's execution.

The decline of Albany's power enabled Queen Margaret and her husband to return to Scotland, leaving their infant daughter in the charge of her maternal uncle, King Henry. But after their return to their own country, the Queen Dowager quarrelled, to an irreconcilable pitch, with her husband Angus, who had seized upon her revenues, paid her little attention or respect, and otherwise gave her much cause for uneasiness. She at length separated from him, and endeavoured to procure a divorce, which she afterwards obtained. By this domestic discord, the power of Angus was considerably diminished; but he was still one of the first men in Scotland, and might have gained the complete government of the kingdom had not his power been counterbalanced by that of the Earl of Arran. This nobleman was the head of the great family of Hamilton; he was connected with the royal family by blood, and had such extensive possessions and lordships as enabled him, though inferior in personal qualities to the Earl of Angus, to dispute with that chief of the more modern Douglases the supreme administration. All, or almost all, the great men of Scotland were in league with one or other of these powerful earls; each of whom supported those who followed him, in right or wrong, and oppressed those who opposed him, without any form of justice, but merely at his own pleasure. In this distracted state of things, it was impossible for the meanest man in Scotland to obtain success in the best-founded suit, unless he was under the protection either of Angus or Arran, and to whichever he might attach himself, he was sure to become an object of hatred and suspicion to the other. Under pretence, also, of taking a side, and acting for the interests of their party, wicked and lawless men committed violences of every kind, burned, murdered, and plundered, and pretended that they did so in the cause of the Earl of Angus, or of his rival the Earl of Arran.

At length, on the 30th of April 1520, these two great factions of the Douglases and the Hamiltons came both to Edinburgh to attend a parliament, in which it was expected that the western noblemen would in general take part with Arran, while those of the east would side with Angus. One of the strongest supporters of Arran was the Archbishop of Glasgow, James Beaton, a man remarkable for talents, but unfortunately also for profligacy. He was at this time Chancellor of Scotland; and the Hamiltons met within his palace, situated at the bottom of Blackfriars Wynd, one of those narrow lanes which run down from the High Street of Edinburgh to the Cowgate. The Hamiltons finding themselves far the more numerous party, were deliberating upon a scheme of attacking the Douglases, and apprehending Angus. That Earl heard of their intentions, and sent his uncle, Gawain Douglas, Bishop of Dunkeld (a scholar and a poet), to remonstrate with Beaton, and to remind him, that it was his business as a churchman to preserve peace; Angus offering at the same time to withdraw out of the town, if he and his friends should be permitted to do so in safety. The Chancellor had, however, already assumed armour, which he wore under his rochet, or bishop's dress. As he laid his hand on his heart, and said, "Upon my conscience, I cannot help what is about to happen," the mail which he wore was heard to rattle. "Ha, my lord!" said the Bishop of Dunkeld, "I perceive that your conscience is not sound, as appears from its clatters!" And leaving him after this rebuke, he hastened back to his nephew, the Earl of Angus, to bid him defend himself like a man. "For me," he said, "I will go to my chamber and pray for you."

Angus collected his followers, and hastened, like a sagacious soldier, to occupy the High Street of the city. The inhabitants were his friends, and spears were handed out to such of the Douglases as had them not; which proved a great advantage, the Hamiltons having no weapons longer than their swords.

In the meantime Sir Patrick Hamilton, a wise and moderate man, brother to the Earl of Arran, strongly advised his brother not to come to blows; but a natural son of the Earl, Sir James Hamilton of Draphane, notorious for his fierce and cruel nature, exclaimed that Sir Patrick only spoke this "because he was afraid to fight in his friend's quarrel."

"Thou liest, false bastard!" said Sir Patrick; "I will fight this day where thou darest not be seen."

Immediately they all rushed towards the street, where the Douglases stood drawn up to receive them.

Now the Hamiltons, though very numerous, could only get at their enemies by thronging out of the little steep lanes which open into the High Street, the outlets of which the Douglases had barricaded with carts, barrels, and such like lumber. As the Hamiltons endeavoured to force their way, they were fiercely attacked by the Douglases with pikes and spears. A few who got out on the street were killed or routed. The Earl of Arran, and his son the bastard, were glad to mount upon a coal-horse, from which they threw the load, and escaped by flight. Sir Patrick Hamilton was killed, with many others; thus dying in a scuffle which he had done all in his power to prevent. The confusion was greatly increased by the sudden appearance of Sir David Home of Wedderburn, the fierce Border leader who slew De la Bastie. He came with a band of eight hundred horse to assist Angus, and finding the skirmish begun, made his way into the city by bursting open one of the gates with sledge-hammers. The Hamiltons fled out of the town in great confusion; and the consequences of this fray were such, that the citizens of Edinburgh called it *Clean-the-Causeway,* because the faction of Arran was, as it were, swept from the streets. This broil gave Angus a great advantage in his future disputes with Arran; but it exhibits a wild picture of the times, when such a conflict could be fought in the midst of a populous city.

A year after this, the Duke of Albany returned from France, to try to reassume the regency. He appears to have been encouraged to take this step by the King of France, who was desirous of recovering his influence in the Scottish councils, and who justly considered Angus as a friend of England. The Regent being successful in again taking up the reins of government, Angus was in his turn obliged to retire to France, where he spent his time so well that he returned much wiser and more experienced than he had been esteemed before his banishment. Albany, on the contrary, showed himself neither more prudent nor more prosperous than during his first government. He threatened much and did little. He broke the peace with England, and invaded that country with a large army; then made a dishonourable truce with Lord Dacre, who commanded on the English frontier, and finally retired without fighting, or doing anything to support the boasts which he had made. This mean and poor-spirited conduct excited the contempt of the Scottish nation, and the Duke found it necessary to retreat once more to France, that he might obtain money and forces to maintain himself in the regency, which he seemed to occupy rather for the advantage of that country than of Scotland.

The English, in the meanwhile, maintained the war which Albany had rekindled, by destructive and dangerous incursions on the Scottish frontiers; and that you may know how this fearful kind of warfare was conducted, I will give you some account of the storming of Jedburgh, which happened at this time.

Jedburgh was, after the castle and town of Roxburgh had been demolished, the principal town of the county. It was strongly walled, and inhabited by a class of citizens whom their neighbourbood to the English frontier made familiar with war. The town was also situated near those mountains in which the boldest of the Scottish Border clans had their abode.

The Earl of Surrey (son of him who had vanquished the Scots at Flodden, and who was now Duke of Norfolk) advanced from Berwick to Jedburgh in September 1523, with an army of about ten thousand men. The Border chieftains, on the Scottish frontier, could only oppose to this well-appointed army about fifteen or eighteen hundred of their followers; but they were such gallant soldiers, and so willing to engage in battle, that the brave English general, who had served in foreign countries as well as at home, declared he had never met their equal. "Could forty thousand such men be assembled," said Surrey, "it would be a dreadful enterprise to withstand them."[1] But the force of numbers prevailed, and the English carried the place by assault. There were six strong towers within the town, which continued their defence after the walls were surmounted. These were the residences of persons of rank, walled round, and capable of strong resistance. The abbey also was occupied by the Scots, and most fiercely defended. The battle

---

[1] "Surrey to Cardinal Wolsey—and who adds, 'I assure your grace I found the Scots, at this time, the boldest men and the hotest, that ever sawe any nacion.' The praise from Surrey is great, as he had often been employed on severe foreign service."—Pinkerton.

continued till late in the night, and the English had no way of completing the victory but by setting fire to the town; and even in this extremity, those who manned the towers and the abbey continued their defence. The next day Lord Dacre was despatched to attack the castle of Fairniehirst, within about three miles of Jedburgh, the feudal fortress of Sir Andrew Ker, a border chief, formerly mentioned. It was taken, but with great loss to the besiegers. In the evening Lord Dacre, contrary to Surrey's commands, chose to encamp with his cavalry without the limits of the camp which the latter had chosen. About eight at night, when the English leaders were at supper, and concluded all resistance over, Dacre's quarters were attacked, and his horses all cut loose. The terrified animals, upwards of fifteen hundred in number, came galloping down to Surrey's camp, where they were received with showers of arrows and volleys of musketry; for the English soldiers, alarmed by the noise, thought the Scots were storming their intrenchments, and shot off their shafts at hazard. Many of the horses ran into Jedburgh, which was still in flames, and were seized and carried off by the Scottish women, accustomed like their husbands to the management of these useful animals. The tumult was so great that the English imputed it to supernatural interference, and Surrey alleged that the devil was seen visibly six times during the confusion. Such was the credulity of the times; but the whole narrative may give you some notion of the obstinate defence of the Scots, and the horrors of a Border foray.

The Scots, on their side, were victorious in several severe actions, in one of which the Bastard Heron, who had contributed so much to Surrey's success at Flodden, was slain.

The young King of Scotland, though yet a boy, began to show tokens of ill-will towards the French and Albany. Some nobles asked him what should be done with the French, whom the Regent had left behind. "Give them," said James, "to Davie Home's keeping." Sir David Home, you must recollect, was the chieftain who put to death Albany's friend, De la Bastie, and knitted his head by the hair to his saddlebow.

Albany, however, returned again from France with great supplies of money, artillery, arms, and other provisions for continuing the war. These were furnished by France, because it was the interest of that country at all hazards to maintain the hostility between Scotland and England. The Regent once more, with a fine army, made an attack upon Norham, a castle on the English frontier; but when he had nearly gained this fortress, he suddenly, with his usual cowardice, left off the assault, on learning that Surrey was advancing to its relief. After this second dishonourable retreat, Albany left Scotland, detested and despised alike by the nobles and the common people, who felt that all his undertakings had ended in retreat and disgrace. In the month of May 1524 he took leave of Scotland, never to return.

XXVI

Angus, Buccleuch, Lennox, and Douglas

1524-1528

QUEEN Margaret, who hated her husband Angus, as I have told you, now combined with his enemy Arran to call James V., her son (though then only twelve years old), to the management of the public affairs; but the Earl of Angus, returning at this crisis from France, speedily obtained a superiority in the Scottish councils, and became the head of those nobles who desired to maintain a friendly alliance with England rather than to continue that league with France which had so often involved Scotland in quarrels with their powerful neighbour.

Margaret might have maintained her authority, for she was personally much beloved; but it was the fate or the folly of that Queen to form rash marriages. Like her brother Henry of England, who tired of his wives, Margaret seems to have been addicted to tire of her husbands; but she had not the power of cutting the heads from the spouses whom she desired to be rid of. Having obtained a divorce from Angus, she married a young man of little power and inferior rank, named Henry Stewart, a younger son of Lord Evandale. She lost her influence by that ill-advised measure. Angus, therefore, rose to the supreme authority in Scotland, obtained possession of the person of the King, transacted everything in the name of James, but by his own authority, and became in all respects the Regent of Scotland, though without assuming the name.

The talents of the Earl of Angus were equal to the charge he had assumed, and as he reconciled himself to his old rival the Earl of Arran, his power seemed founded on a sure basis. He was able to accomplish a treaty of peace with England, which was of great advantage to the kingdom. But, according to the fashion of the times, Angus was much too desirous to confer all the great offices, lands, and other advantages in the disposal of the crown, upon his own friends and adherents, to the exclusion of all the nobles and gentry, who had either taken part against him in the late struggle for power, or were not decidedly his partisans. The course of justice also was shamefully perverted, by the partiality of Angus for his friends, kinsmen, and adherents.

An old historian says, "That there dared no man strive at law with a Douglas, or yet with the adherent of a Douglas; for if he did, he was sure to get the worst of his law-suit. And," he adds, "although Angus travelled through the country under the pretence of punishing thieves, robbers, and murderers, there were no malefactors so great as those which rode in his own company."

The King, who was now fourteen years old, became disgusted with the sort of restraint in which Angus detained him, and desirous to free himself from his tutelage. His mother had doubtless a natural influence over him, and that likewise was exerted to the Earl's prejudice. The Earl of Lennox, a wise and intelligent nobleman, near in blood to the King, was also active in fostering his displeasure against the Douglases, and schemes began to be agitated for taking the person of the King out of the hands of Angus. But Angus was so well established in the government, that his authority could not be destroyed except by military force; and it was not easy to bring such to bear against one so powerful, and of such a martial character.

At length it seems to have been determined to employ the agency of Sir Walter Scott of Buccleuch, a man of great courage, and military talent, head of a numerous and powerful clan, and possessed of much influence on the Border. He had been once the friend of Angus, and had even scaled the walls of Edinburgh with a great body of his clan, in order to render the party of the Earl uppermost in that city. But of late he had attached himself to Lennox, by whose counsel he seems to have been guided in the enterprise which I am about to give you an account of.

Some excesses had taken place on the Border, probably by the con-nivance of Buccleuch, which induced Angus to march to Jedburgh, bringing the King in his company, lest he should have made his escape during his absence. He was joined by the clans of Home and Ker, both in league with him, and he had, besides, a considerable body of chosen attendants. Angus was returning from this expedition, and had passed the night at Melrose. The Kers and Homes had taken leave of the Earl, who with the King and his retinue had left Melrose, when a band of a thousand horsemen suddenly appeared on the side of an eminence called Halidon Hill, and, descending into the valley, interposed between the Earl and the bridge, by which he must pass the Tweed on his return northward.

"Sir," said Angus to the King, "yonder comes Buccleuch with the Border thieves of Teviotdale and Liddesdale, to interrupt your Grace's passage. I vow to God they shall either fight or fly. You shall halt upon this knoll with my brother George, while we drive off these banditti, and clear the road for your Grace."

The King made no answer, for in his heart he desired that Buc-cleuch's undertaking might be successful; but he dared not say so.

Angus, meantime, despatched a herald to charge Buccleuch to withdraw with his forces. Scott replied, "That he was come, according to the custom of the Borders, to show the King his clan and followers, and invite his Grace to dine at his house." To which he added, "That he knew the King's mind as well as Angus." The Earl advanced, and the Borderers, shouting their war-cry of Bellenden, immediately joined battle, and fought stoutly; but the Homes and Kers, who were at no great distance, returned on hearing the alarm, and coming through the little village of Darnick, set upon Buccleuch's men, and decided the fate of the day. The Border riders fled, but Buccleuch and his followers fought bravely in their retreat, and turning upon the Kers, slew several of them; in particular, Ker of Cessford, a chief of the name, who was killed by the lance of one of the Elliots, a retainer of Buccleuch. His death occasioned a deadly feud between the clans of Scott and Ker, which lasted for a century, and cost much blood. This skirmish took place on the 25th of July 1526. About eighty Scots were slain on the field of battle, and a sentence was pronounced against Buccleuch and many of his clan, as guilty of high treason. But after the King had shaken off the yoke of the Douglases, he went in person to Parliament to obtain the restoration of Buccleueh, who, he declared on his kingly word, had come to Melrose without any purpose of quarrel, but merely to pay his duty to his prince, and show him the number of his followers. In evidence of which the King affirmed that the said Wat was not clad in armour, in a leathern coat (a buff-coat, I suppose), with a black bonnet on his head. The family were restored to their estates accordingly; but Sir Walter Scott was long afterwards murdered by the Kers, at Edinburgh, in revenge of the death of the Laird of Cessford.

The Earl of Lennox being disappointed in procuring the King's release by means of Buccleuch, now resolved to attempt it in person. He received much encouragement from the Chancellor Beaton (distinguished at the skirmish called Clean-the-Causeway), from the Earl of Glencairn, and other noblemen, who saw with displeasure the Earl of Angus keeping the young King under restraint, and that all the administration of the kingdom centred in the Douglases. Lennox assembled an army of ten or twelve thousand men, and advanced upon Edinburgh from Stirling. Angus and Arran, who were still closely leagued together, encountered Lennox, with an inferior force, near the village of Newliston. The rumour that a battle was about to commence soon reached Edinburgh, when Sir George Douglas hastened to call out the citizens in arms, to support his brother, the Earl of Angus. The city bells were rung, trumpets were sounded, and the King himself was obliged to mount on horseback, to give countenance to the measures of the Douglases, whom in his soul he detested. James was so sensible of his situation, that he tried by every means in his power to delay the march of the forces which were mustered at Edinburgh. When they reached the village of Corstorphine, they heard the thunder of the guns; which inflamed the fierce impatience of George Douglas to reach the field of battle, and also increased the delays of the young King, who was in hopes Angus might be defeated before his brother could come up. Douglas, perceiving this, addressed the King in language which James never forgot nor forgave;—"Your Grace need not think to escape us," said this fierce warrior; "if our enemies had hold of you on one side, and we on the other, we would tear you to pieces ere we would let you go."

Tidings now came from the field of battle that Lennox had been defeated, and that Angus had gained the victory. The young King, dismayed at the news, now urged his attendants to gallop forward, as much as he had formerly desired them to hang back. He charged them to prevent slaughter, and save lives, especially that of Lennox. Sir Andrew Wood, one of the King's cup-bearers, arrived in the field of battle time enough to save the Earl of Glencairn, who, protected by some strong ground, was still fighting gallantly, though he had scarce thirty men left alive; and Wood contrived to convey him safe out of the field. But Lennox, about whose safety the King was so anxious, was already no more. He had been slain, in cold blood, by that bloodthirsty man, Sir James Hamilton of Draphane, who took him from the Laird of Pardivan, to whom he had surrendered himself. This deed seemed to flow from the brutal nature of the perpetrator, who took such a pleasure in shedding blood that he slashed with his own hand the faces of many of the prisoners. Arran, the father of this ferocious man, bitterly lamented the fate of Lennox, who was his nephew. He was found mourning beside the body, over which he had spread his scarlet cloak. "The hardiest, stoutest, and wisest man that Scotland bore," he said, "lies here slain."

After these two victories, the Earl of Angus seemed to be so firmly established in power that his followers set no bounds to their presumption, and his enemies were obliged to fly and hide themselves. Chancellor Beaton, disguised as a shepherd, fed sheep on Bogrian-knowe, until he made his peace with the Earls of Angus and Arran, by great gifts, both in money and in church lands. Angus established around the King's person a guard of a hundred men of his own choice, commanded by Douglas of Parkhead; he made his brother George, whom James detested, Master of the Royal Household; and Archibald of Kilspindie, his uncle, Lord Treasurer of the Realm. But the close restraint in which the King found himself only increased his eager desire to be rid of all the Douglases together. Force having failed in two instances, James had recourse to stratagem.

He prevailed on his mother, Queen Margaret, to yield up to him the castle of Stirling, which was her jointure-house, and secretly to put it into the hands of a governor whom he could trust. This was done with much caution. Thus prepared with a place of refuge, James watched with anxiety an opportunity of flying to it; and he conducted himself with such apparent confidence towards Angus, that the Douglases were lulled into security, and concluded that the King was reconciled to his state of bondage, and had despaired of making his escape.

James was then residing at Falkland, a royal palace conveniently situated for hunting and hawking, in which he seemed to take great pleasure. The Earl of Angus at this period left the court for Lothian, where he had some urgent business—Archibald Douglas of Kilspindie went to Dundee, to visit a lady to whom he was attached—and George Douglas had gone to St. Andrews to extort some further advantages from Chancellor Beaton, who was now archbishop of that see, and primate of Scotland. There was thus none of the Douglases left about the King's person except Parkhead, with his guard of one hundred men, in whose vigilance the others confided.

The King thought the time favourable for his escape. To lay all suspicion asleep, he pretended he was to rise next morning at an early hour, for the purpose of hunting the stag. Douglas of Parkhead, suspecting nothing, retired to bed after placing his watch. But the King was no sooner in his private chamber than he called a trusty page, named John Hart:—"Jockie," said he, "dost thou love me?"

"Better than myself," answered the domestic.

"And will you risk anything for me?"

"My life, with pleasure," said John Hart.

The King then explained his purpose, and dressing himself in the attire of a groom, he went with Hart to the stable, as if for the purpose of getting the horses ready for the next day's hunt. The guards, deceived by their appearance, gave them no interruption. At the stables three good horses were saddled and in readiness, under charge of a yeoman, or groom, whom the King had entrusted with his design.

James mounted with his two servants, and galloped, during the whole night, as eager as a bird just escaped from a cage. At daylight he reached the bridge of Stirling, which was the only mode of passing the river Forth, except by boats. It was defended by gates, which the King, after passing through them, ordered to be closed, and directed the passage to be watched. He was a weary man when he reached Stirling Castle, where he was joyfully received by the governor, whom his mother had placed in that strong fortress. The drawbridges were raised, the portcullises dropt, guards set, and every measure of defence and precaution resorted to. But the King was so much afraid of again falling into the hands of the Douglases, that, tired as he was, he would not go to sleep until the keys of the castle were placed in his own keeping, and laid underneath his pillow.

In the morning there was great alarm at Falkland. Sir George Douglas had returned thither, on the night of the King's departure, about eleven o'clock. On his arrival, he inquired after the King, and was answered by the porter as well as the watchmen upon guard that he was sleeping in his chamber, as he intended to hunt early in the morning.

Sir George therefore retired to rest in full security. But the next morning he learned different tidings. One Peter Carmichael, bailie of Abernethy, knocked at the door of his chamber, and asked him if he knew "what the King was doing that morning?"

"He is in his chamber asleep," said Sir George.

"You are mistaken," answered Carmichael; "he passed the bridge of Stirling this last night."

On hearing this, Douglas started up in haste, went to the King's chamber, and knocked for admittance. When no answer was returned, he caused the door to be forced, and when he found the apartment empty, he cried, "Treason!—The King is gone, and none knows whither." Then he sent post to his brother, the Earl of Angus, and despatched messengers in every direction, to seek the King, and to assemble the Douglases.

When the truth became known, the adherents of Angus rode in a body to Stirling; but the King was so far from desiring to receive them, that he threatened, by sound of trumpet, to declare any of the name of Douglas a traitor who should approach within twelve miles of his person, or who should presume to meddle with the administration of government. Some of the Douglases inclined to resist this proclamation; but the Earl of Angus and his brother resolved to obey it, and withdrew to Linlithgow.

Soon afterwards, the King assembled around him the numerous nobility who envied the power of Angus and Arran, or had suffered injuries, at their hands; and, in open parliament, accused them of treason, declaring that he had never been sure of his life all the while that he was in their power. A sentence of forfeiture was, therefore, passed against the Earl of Angus, and he was driven into exile, with all his friends and kinsmen. And thus the Red Douglases of the house of Angus, shared almost the same fate with the Black Douglases, of the elder branch of that mighty house; with this difference, that as they had never risen so high, so they did not fall so irretrievably; for the Earl of Angus lived to return and enjoy his estates in Scotland, where he again played a distinguished part. But this was not till after the death of James V., who retained, during his whole life, an implacable resentment against the Douglases and never permitted one of the name to settle in Scotland while he lived.

James persevered in this resolution even under circumstances which rendered his unrelenting resentment ungenerous. Archibald

Douglas of Kilspindie, the Earl of Angus's uncle, had been a personal favourite of the King before the disgrace of his family. He was so much recommended to James by his great strength, manly appearance, and skill in every kind of warlike exercise, that he was wont to call him his Graysteil, after the name of a champion in a romance then popular. Archibald, becoming rather an old man, and tired of his exile in England, resolved to try the King's mercy. He thought that as they had been so well acquainted formerly, and as he had never offended James personally, he might find favour from their old intimacy. He therefore threw himself in the King's way one day as he returned from hunting in the park at Stirling. It was several years since James had seen him, but he knew him at a great distance, by his firm and stately step, and said, "Yonder is my Graysteil, Archibald of Kilspindie." But when they met, he showed no appearance of recognising his old servant. Douglas turned, and still hoping to obtain a glance of favourable recollection, ran along by the King's side; and although James trotted his horse hard against the hill, and Douglas wore a heavy shirt of mail under his clothes, for fear of assassination, yet Graysteil was at the castle gate as soon as the King. James passed him, and entered the castle; but Douglas, exhausted with exertion, sat down at the gate and asked for a cup of wine. The hatred of the King against the name of Douglas was so well known, that no domestic about the court dared procure for the old warrior even this trifling refreshment. The King blamed, indeed, his servants for their discourtesy, and even said, that but for his oath never to employ a Douglas he would have received Archibald of Kilspindie into his service, as he had formerly known him a man of great ability. Yet he sent his commands to his poor Graysteil to retire to France, where be died heart-broken soon afterwards. Even Henry VIII. of England, himself of an unforgiving temper, blamed the implacability of James on this occasion, and quoted an old proverb,—

"A King's face
Should give grace."

XXVII

James V.

1528-1540

FREED from the stern control of the Douglas family, James V. now began to exercise the government in person, and displayed most of the qualities of a wise and good prince. He was handsome in his person, and resembled his father in the fondness for military exercises, and the spirit of chivalrous honour which James IV. loved to display. He also inherited his father's love of justice, and his desire to establish and enforce wise and equal laws, which should protect the weak against the oppression of the great. It was easy enough to make laws, but to put them in vigorous exercise was of much greater difficulty; and in his attempt to accomplish this laudable purpose, James often incurred the ill-will of the more powerful nobles. He was a well-educated and accomplished man; and like his ancestor, James I., was a poet and a musician. He had, however, his defects. He avoided his father's failing of profusion, having no hoarded treasures to employ on pomp and show; but he rather fell into the opposite fault, being of a temper too parsimonious; and though he loved state and display, he endeavoured to gratify that taste as economically as possible, so that he has been censured as rather close and covetous. He was also, though the foibles seem inconsistent, fond of pleasure, and disposed to too much indulgence. It must be added, that when provoked, he was unrelenting even to cruelty; for which he had some apology, considering the ferocity of the subjects over whom he reigned. But, on the whole, James V. was an amiable man, and a good sovereign.

His first care was to bring the Borders of Scotland to some degree of order. These, as you were formerly told, were inhabited by tribes of men, forming each a different clan, as they were called, and obeying no orders, save those which were given by their chiefs. These chiefs were supposed to represent the first founder of the name, or family. The attachment of the clansmen to the chief was very great: indeed, they paid respect to no one else. In this the Borderers agreed with the Highlanders, as also in their love of plunder, and neglect of the general laws of the country. But the Border men wore no tartan dress, and served almost always on horseback, whereas the Highlanders acted always on foot. You will also remember that the Borderers spoke the Scottish language, and not the Gaelic tongue used by the mountaineers.

The situation of these clans on the frontiers exposed them to constant war; so that they thought of nothing else but of collecting bands of their followers together, and making incursions, without much distinction, on the English, on the Lowland (or inland) Scots, or upon each other. They paid little respect either to times of truce or treaties of peace, but exercised their depredations without regard to either, and often occasioned wars betwixt England and Scotland which would not otherwise have taken place.

It is said of a considerable family on the Borders, that when they had consumed all the cattle about the castle, a pair of spurs was placed on the table in a covered dish, as a hint that they must ride out and fetch more. The chiefs and leading men told down their daughters' portions according to the plunder which they were able to collect in the course of a Michaelmas moon, when its prolonged light allowed them opportunity for their freebooting excursions. They were very brave in battle, but in time of peace they were a pest to their Scottish neighbours. As their insolence had risen to a high pitch after the field of Flodden had thrown the country into confusion, James V. resolved to take very severe measures against them.

His first step was to secure the persons of the principal chieftains by whom these disorders were privately encouraged. The Earl of Bothwell, the Lord Home, Lord Maxwell, Scott of Buccleuch, Ker of Fairniehirst, and other powerful chiefs, who might have opposed the

King's purposes, were seized, and imprisoned in separate fortresses in the inland country.

James then assembled an army, in which warlike purposes were united with those of silvan sport; for he ordered all the gentlemen in the wild districts which he intended to visit to bring in their best dogs, as if his only purpose had been to hunt the deer in those desolate regions. This was intended to prevent the Borderers from taking the alarm, in which case they would have retreated into their mountains and fast-nesses, from whence it would have been difficult to dislodge them.

These men had indeed no distinct idea of the offences which they had committed, and consequently no apprehension of the King's dis-pleasure against them. The laws had been so long silent in that remote and disorderly country, that the outrages which were practised by the strong against the weak seemed to the perpetrators the natural course of society, and to present nothing that was worthy of punishment.

Thus, as the King, in the beginning of his expedition, suddenly approached the castle of Piers Cockburn of Henderland, that baron was in the act of providing a great entertainment to welcome him, when James caused him to be suddenly seized on, and executed. Adam Scott of Tushielaw, called the King of the Border, met the same fate. But an event of greater importance was the fate of John Armstrong of Gilnockie, near Langholm.

This freebooting chief had risen to great consequence, and the whole neighbouring district of England paid him *black mail,* that is, a sort of tribute, in consideration of which he forbore plundering them. He had a high idea of his own importance, and seems to have been unconscious of having merited any severe usage at the King's hands. On the contrary, he came to meet his sovereign at a place about ten miles from Hawick, called Carlinrigg chapel, richly dressed, and having with him twenty-four gentlemen, his constant retinue, as well attired as himself. The King, incensed to see a freebooter so gallantly equipped, commanded him instantly to be led to execution, saying, "What wants this knave, save a crown, to be as magnificent as a king?" John Armstrong made great offers for his life, offering to maintain him-self, with forty men, ready to serve the King at a moment's notice, at his own expense; engaging never to hurt or injure any Scottish subject, as indeed had never been his practice; and undertaking that there was not a man in England, of whatever degree, duke, earl, lord, or baron, but he would engage, within a short time, to present him to the King, dead or alive. But when the King would listen to none of his offers, the robber chief said very proudly, "I am but a fool to ask grace at a grace-less face; but had I guessed you would have used me thus, I would have kept the Border-side, in despite of the King of England and you both; for I well know that King Henry would give the weight of my best horse in gold to know that I am sentenced to die this day."

John Armstrong was led to execution, with all his men, and hanged without mercy. The people of the inland counties were glad to be rid of him; but on the Borders he was both missed and mourned, as a brave warrior, and a stout man-at-arms against England.

Such were the effects of the terror struck by these general executions, that James was said to have made "the rush bush keep the cow;" that is to say, that even in this lawless part of the country, men dared no longer make free with property, and cattle might remain on their pastures unwatched. James was also enabled to draw profit from the lands which the crown possessed near the Borders, and is said to have had ten thousand sheep at one time grazing in Ettrick Forest, under the keeping of one Andrew Bell, who gave the King as good an account of the profits of the flock as if they had been grazing in the bounds of Fife, then the most civilised part of Scotland.

On the other hand, the Borders of Scotland were greatly weakened by the destruction of so many brave men, who, notwithstanding their lawless course of life, were true defenders of their country; and there is reason to censure the extent to which James carried his severity, as being to a certain degree impolitic, and beyond doubt cruel and excessive.

In the like manner James proceeded against the Highland chiefs; and by executions, forfeitures, and other severe measures, he brought the Northern mountaineers, as he had already done those of the South, into comparative subjection. He then set at liberty the Border chiefs, and others whom he had imprisoned, lest they should have offered any hindrance to the course of his justice.

As these fiery chieftains, after this severe chastisement, could no longer as formerly attack each other's castles and lands, they were forced to vent their deadly animosities in duels, which were frequently fought in the King's presence, his royal permission being first obtained. Thus Douglas of Drumlanrig and Charteris of Amisfield did battle together in presence of the King, each having accused the other of high treason. They fought on foot with huge two-handed swords. Drumlanrig was somewhat blind, or short-sighted, and being in great fury,

struck about him without seeing where he hit, and the Laird of Amisfield was not more successful, for his sword broke in the encounter;
upon this, the King caused the battle to cease, and the combatants
were with difficulty separated. Thus the King gratified these unruly
barons, by permitting them to fight in his own presence, in order to
induce them to remain at peace elsewhere.

James V. had a custom of going about the country disguised as a
private person, in order that he might hear complaints which might
not otherwise reach his ears, and perhaps, that he might enjoy amusements which he could not have partaken of in his avowed royal character. This is also said to have been a custom of James IV., his father,
and several adventures are related of what befell them on such occasions. One or two of these narratives may help to enliven our story.

When James V. travelled in disguise, he used a name which was
known only to some of his principal nobility and attendants. He was
called the Goodman (the tenant, that is) of Ballengiech. Ballengiech is a
steep pass which leads down behind the castle of Stirling. Once upon a
time, when the court was feasting in Stirling, the King sent for some
venison from the neighbouring hills. The deer were killed, and put on
horses' backs, to be transported to Stirling. Unluckily they had to pass
the castle gates of Arnpryor, belonging to a chief of the Buchanans,
who chanced to have a considerable number of guests with him. It was
late, and the company were rather short of victuals, though they had
more than enough of liquor. The chief, seeing so much fat venison
passing his very door, seized on it; and to the expostulations of the
keepers, who told him it belonged to King James, he answered insolently, that if James was King in Scotland, he, Buchanan, was King in
Kippen; being the name of the district in which the castle of Arnpryor
lay. On hearing what had happened, the King got on horseback, and
rode instantly from Stirling to Buchanan's house, where he found a
strong fierce-looking Highlander, with an axe on his shoulder, standing
sentinel at the door. This grim warder refused the King admittance,
saying, that the laird of Arnpryor was at dinner, and would not be disturbed. "Yet go up to the company, my good friend," said the King,
"and tell him that the Goodman of Ballengiech is come to feast with the
King of Kippen." The porter went grumbling into the house, and told
his master that there was a fellow with a red beard at the gate, who
called himself the Goodman of Ballengiech, who said he was come to
dine with the King of Kippen. As soon as Buchanan heard these words,

he knew that the King was come in person, and hastened down to kneel at James's feet, and to ask forgiveness for his insolent behaviour. But the King, who only meant to give him a fright, forgave him freely, and, going into the castle, feasted on his own venison which Buchanan had intercepted. Buchanan of Arnpryor was ever afterwards called the King of Kippen.

Upon another occasion, King James, being alone and in disguise, fell into a quarrel with some gypsies, or other vagrants, and was assaulted by four or five of them. This chanced to be very near the bridge of Cramond; so the King got on the bridge, which, as it was high and narrow, enabled him to defend himself with his sword against the number of persons by whom he was attacked. There was a poor man thrashing corn in a barn near by, who came out on hearing the noise of the scuffle, and seeing one man defending himself against numbers, gallantly took the King's part with his flail, to such good purpose that the gypsies were obliged to fly. The husbandman then took the King into the barn, brought him a towel and water to wash the blood from his face and hands, and finally walked with him a little way towards Edinburgh, in case he should be again attacked. On the way, the King asked his companion what and who he was. The labourer answered, that his name was John Howieson, and that he was a bondsman on the farm of Braehead, near Cramond, which belonged to the King of Scotland. James then asked the poor man if there was any wish in the world which he would particularly desire should be gratified; and honest John confessed he should think himself the happiest man in Scotland were he but proprietor of the farm on which he wrought as a labourer. He then asked the King, in turn, who *he* was; and James replied, as usual, that he was the Goodman of Ballengiech, a poor man who had a small appointment about the palace; but he added, that if John Howieson would come to see him on the next Sunday, he would endeavour to repay his manful assistance, and, at least, give him the pleasure of seeing the royal apartments.

John put on his best clothes, as you may suppose, and appearing at a postern gate of the palace, inquired for the Goodman of Ballengiech. The King had given orders that he should be admitted; and John found his friend, the goodman, in the same disguise which he had formerly worn. The King, still preserving the character of an inferior officer of the household, conducted John Howieson from one apartment of the palace to another, and was amused with his wonder and his remarks. At length James asked his visitor if he should like to see the King; to which John replied, nothing would delight him so much, if he could do so without giving offence. The Goodman of Ballengiech, of course, undertook that the King would not be angry, "But," said John, "how am I to know his Grace from the nobles who will be all about him?"—"Easily," replied his companion; "all the others will be uncovered—the King alone will wear his hat or bonnet."

So speaking, King James introduced the countryman into a great hall, which was filled by the nobility and officers of the crown. John was a little frightened, and drew close to his attendant; but was still unable to distinguish the King. "I told you that you should know him by his wearing his hat," said the conductor. "Then," said John, after he had again looked round the room, "it must be either you or me, for all but us two are bare-headed."

The King laughed at John's fancy; and that the good yeoman might have occasion for mirth also, he made him a present of the farm of Braehead, which he had wished so much to possess, on condition that John Howieson, or his successors, should be ready to present a ewer and basin for the King to wash his hands, when his Majesty should come to Holyrood Palace, or should pass the bridge of Cramond. Accordingly, in the year 1822, when George IV. came to Scotland, the descendant[1] of John Howieson of Braehead, who still possesses the estate which was given to his ancestor, appeared at a solemn festival, and offered his Majesty water from a silver ewer, that he might perform the service by which he held his lands.

James V. was very fond of hunting, and, when he pursued that amusement in the Highlands, he used to wear the peculiar dress of that country, having a long and wide Highland shirt, and a jacket of tartan velvet, with plaid hose, and everything else corresponding. The accounts for these are in the books of his chamberlain, still preserved.

On one occasion, when the King had an ambassador of the Pope along with him, with various foreigners of distinction, they were splendidly entertained by the Earl of Athole in a huge and singular rustic palace. It was built of timber, in the midst of a great meadow, and surrounded by moats, or fosses, full of the most delicate fish. It was enclosed and defended by towers, as if it had been a regular castle, and had within it many apartments, which were decked with

---

[1] William Howieson Crawford, Esq., of Braehead and Crawford-land.

flowers and branches, so that in treading them one seemed to be in a garden. Here were all kinds of game, and other provisions in abundance, with many cooks to make them ready, and plenty of the most costly spices and wines. The Italian ambassador was greatly surprised to see, amongst rocks and wildernesses, which seemed to be the very extremity of the world, such good lodging and so magnificent an entertainment. But what surprised him most of all, was to see the Highlanders set fire to the wooden castle as soon as the hunting was over, and the King in the act of departing. "Such is the constant practice of our Highlanders," said James to the ambassador; "however well they may be lodged over night, they always burn their lodging before they leave it." By this the King intimated the predatory and lawless habits displayed by these mountaineers.

The reign of James V. was not alone distinguished by his personal adventures and pastimes, but is honourably remembered on account of wise laws made for the government of his people, and for restraining the crimes and violence which were frequently practised among them; especially those of assassination, burning of houses and driving of cattle, the usual and ready means by which powerful chiefs avenged themselves of their feudal enemies.

For the decision of civil questions, James V. invented and instituted what is called the College of Justice, being the Supreme Court of Scotland in civil affairs. It consisted of fourteen judges (half clergy, half laity), and a president, who heard and decided causes. A certain number of learned men trained to understand the laws, were appointed to the task of pleading the causes of such as had lawsuits before these judges, who constituted what is popularly termed the Court of Session. These men were called advocates; and this was the first establishment of a body, regularly educated to the law, which has ever since been regarded in Scotland as an honourable profession, and has produced many great men.

James V. used great diligence in improving his navy, and undertook what was, at the time, rather a perilous task, to sail in person round Scotland, and cause an accurate survey to be made of the various coasts, bays, and islands, harbours, and roadsteads of his kingdom, many of which had been unknown to his predecessors, even by name.

This active and patriotic prince ordered the mineral wealth of Scotland to be also inquired into. He obtained miners from Germany, who extracted both silver and gold from the mines of Leadhills, in the upper part of Clydesdale. The gold was of fine quality, and found in quantity sufficient to supply metal for a very elegant gold coin, which, bearing on one side the head of James V. wearing a bonnet, has been thence called the Bonnet-piece. It is said, that upon one occasion the King invited the ambassadors of Spain, France, and other foreign countries, to hunt with him in Crawford Moor, the district in which lie the mines I have just mentioned. They dined in the castle of Crawford, a rude old fortress. The King made some apology for the dinner, which was composed of the game they had killed during the hunting and hawking of the day, but he assured his guests that the dessert would make them some amends, as he had given directions that it should consist of the finest fruits which the country afforded. The foreigners looked at each other in surprise, on hearing the King talk of fruits being produced amidst the black moors and barren mountains around them. But the dessert made its appearance in the shape of a number of covered saucers, one of which was placed before each guest, and being examined was found full of gold bonnet-pieces, which they were desired to accept as the fruit produced by the mountains of Crawford Moor. This new sort of dessert was no doubt as acceptable as the most delicate fruits of a southern climate. The mines of the country are now wrought only for lead, of which they produce still a very large quantity.

Although, as we have mentioned, James was a good economist, he did not neglect the cultivation of the fine arts. He rebuilt the palace of Linlithgow, which is on a most magnificent plan, and made additions to that of Stirling. He encouraged several excellent poets and learned men, and his usual course of life appears to have been joyous and happy. He was himself a poet of some skill, and he permitted great freedom to the rhymers of his time, in addressing verses to him, some of which conveyed severe censure of his government, and others satires on his foibles.

James also encouraged the sciences, but was deceived by a foreigner, who pretended to have knowledge of the art of making gold. This person, however, who was either crack-brained, or an impostor, destroyed his own credit by the fabrication of a pair of wings, with which he proposed to fly from the top of Stirling Castle. He actually made the attempt, but as his pinions would not work easily, he fell down the precipice and broke his thigh-bone.

As the kingdom of Scotland, except during a very short and indecisive war with England, remained at peace till near the end of James's reign, and as that monarch was a wise and active prince, it might have been hoped that he at least would have escaped the misfortunes which seemed to haunt the name of Stewart. But a great change, which took place at this period, led James V. into a predicament, as unhappy as attended any of his ancestors.

XXVIII

The Stirrings of Reformation

1536-1542

YOU remember, my dear child, that James V. was nephew to Henry VIII. of England, being a son of Margaret, sister of that monarch. This connection, and perhaps the policy of Henry, who was aware that it was better for both countries that they should remain at peace, prevented for several years the renewal of the destructive wars between the two divisions of the island. The good understanding would probably have been still more complete, had it not been for the great and general change in religious matters called in history the Reformation. I must give you some idea of the nature of this alteration, otherwise you cannot understand the consequences to which it led.

After the death of our blessed Saviour Jesus Christ, the doctrine which he preached was planted in Rome, the principal city of the great Roman empire, by the Apostle Peter, as it is said, whom the Catholics, therefore, term the first Bishop of Rome. In process of time, the bishops of Rome, who succeeded, as they said, the apostle in his office, claimed an authority over all others in Christendom. Good and well-meaning persons, in their reverence for the religion which they had adopted, admitted these pretensions without much scrutiny. As the Christian religion was more widely received, the emperors and kings who embraced it thought to distinguish their piety by heaping benefits on the Church, and on the bishops of Rome in particular, who at length obtained great lands and demesnes as temporal princes; while, in their character of clergymen, they assumed the title of Popes, and the full and exclusive authority over all other clergymen in the Christian world. As the people of those times were extremely ignorant, any little knowledge which remained was to be found among the clergy, who had some leisure to study; while the laity, that is all men who were not clergymen, learned little excepting to tilt, fight, and feast. The popes of Rome, having established themselves as heads of the Church, went on by degrees, introducing into the simple and beautiful system delivered to us in the Gospel, other doctrines, many of them inconsistent with, or contradictory of, pure Christianity, and all of them tending to extend the power of the priests over the minds and consciences of other men. It was not difficult for the popes to make these alterations. For as they asserted that they were the visible successors of Saint Peter, they pretended that they were as infallible as the apostle himself, and that all that they published in their ordinances, which they called Bulls, must be believed by all Christians, as much as if the same had been enjoined in the Holy Scripture itself. We shall notice two or three of these innovations.

Some good men, in an early age of Christianity, had withdrawn from the world to worship God in desert and desolate places. They wrought for their bread, gave alms to the poor, spent their leisure in the exercise of devotion, and were justly respected. But by degrees, as well-meaning persons bestowed great sums to support associations of such holy men, bequeathed lands to the monasteries or convents in which they lived, and made them wealthy, the Monks, as they were called, departed from the simplicity of their order, and neglected the virtues which they undertook to practise. Besides, by the extravagant endowments of these convents, great sums of money and large estates were employed in maintaining a useless set of men, who, under pretence of performing devotional exercises, withdrew themselves from the business of the world, and from all domestic duties. Hence, though there continued to be amongst the monks many good, pious, and learned men, idleness and luxury invaded many of the institutions, and corrupted both their doctrines and their morals.

The worship also of saints, for which Scripture gives us no warrant whatever, was introduced in those ignorant times. It is natural we should respect the memory of any remarkably good man, and that we should value anything which has belonged to him. The error lay in carrying this natural veneration to extremity—in worshipping the relics of a saintly character, such as locks of hair, bones, articles of clothing, and other trumpery, and in believing that such things are capable of curing sickness, or of working other miracles shocking to common sense. Yet the Roman Church opened the way to this absurdity, and imputed to these relics, which were often a mere imposture, the power, which God alone possesses, of altering those laws of nature which his wisdom has appointed. The popes also encouraged and enjoined the worship of saints, that is, the souls of holy men deceased, as a sort of subordinate deities, whose intercession may avail us before the throne of God, although the Gospel has expressly declared that our Lord Jesus Christ is our only Mediator. And in virtue of this opinion, not only were the Virgin Mary, the apostles, and almost every other person mentioned in the Gospels, erected by the Roman Catholics into the office of intercessors with the Deity, but many others who never existed were canonised, as it was called, that is, declared by the Pope to be saints, and had altars and churches dedicated to them. Pictures also and statues, representing these alleged holy persons, were exhibited in churches, and received the worship which ought not, according to the second commandment, to be rendered to any idol or graven image.

Other doctrines there were, about fasting on particular days, and abstaining from particular kinds of food, all of which were gradually introduced into the Roman Catholic faith, though contrary to the Gospel.

But the most important innovation, and that by which the priests made most money, was the belief that the Church, or, in other words, the priest, had the power of pardoning such sins as were confessed to him, upon the culprit's discharging such penance as the priest imposed on him. Every one was, therefore, obliged to confess himself to a priest, if he hoped to have his sins pardoned; and the priest enjoined certain kinds of penance, more or less severe, according to the circumstances of the offence. But, in general, these penances might be excused, provided a corresponding sum of money were paid to the Church, which possessed thus a perpetual and most lucrative source of income, which was yet more increased by the belief in Purgatory.

We have no right, from Scripture, to believe in the existence of any intermediate state betwixt that of happiness, which we call Heaven, to which good men have access immediately after death, or that called Hell, being the place of eternal punishment, to which the wicked are consigned with the devil and his angels. But the Catholic priests imagined the intervention of an intermediate state, called Purgatory. They supposed that many, or indeed that most people, were not of such piety as to deserve immediate admission into a state of eternal happiness, until they should have sustained a certain portion of punishment; but yet were not so wicked as to deserve instant and eternal condemnation. For the benefit of these, they invented the intermediate situation of Purgatory, a place of punishment to which almost every one, not doomed to Hell itself, was consigned for a greater or less period, in proportion to his sins, before admission into a state of happiness. But here lay the stress of the doctrine. The power was in the Church to obtain pardon, by prayer, for the souls who were in Purgatory, and to have the gates of that place of torture opened for their departure sooner than would otherwise have taken place. Men, therefore, whose consciences told them that they deserved a long abode in this place of punishment, left liberal sums to the Church to have prayers said for the behoof of their souls. Children, in like manner, procured masses (that is, a particular sort of devotional worship practised by Catholics) to be said for the souls of their deceased parents. Widows did the same for their departed husbands—husbands for their wives. All these masses and prayers could only be obtained by money, and all this money went to the priests.

But the pope and his clergy carried the matter still farther; and not only sold, as they pretended, the forgiveness of Heaven, to those who had committed sins, but also granted them (always for money) a liberty to break through the laws of God and the Church. These licences were called indulgences, because those who purchased them were indulged in the privilege of committing irregularities and vices, without being supposed answerable to the Divine wrath.

To support this extraordinary fabric of superstition, the Pope assumed the most extensive powers, even to the length of depriving kings of their thrones, by his sentence of excommunication, which declared their subjects free from their oath of allegiance, and at liberty to rise up against their sovereign and put him to death. At other times the Pope took it upon him to give the kingdoms of the excommunicated prince to some ambitious neighbour. The rule of the Church of Rome was as severe against inferior persons as against princes. If a layman read the Bible, he was accounted guilty of a great offence; for the priests well knew that a perusal of the sacred Scriptures would open men's eyes to their extravagant pretensions. If an individual presumed to disbelieve any of the doctrines which the Church of Rome taught, or to entertain any which were inconsistent with these doctrines, he was tried as a heretic, and subjected to the horrid punishment of being burnt alive; and this penalty was inflicted without mercy for the slightest expressions approaching to what the Papists called heresy.

This extraordinary and tyrannical power over men's consciences was usurped during those ages of European history which are called dark, because men were at that period without the light of learning and information. But the discovery of the art of printing began, in the fifteenth century, to enlighten men's minds. The Bible, which had been locked up in the hands of the clergy, then became open to all, and was generally read; and wise and good men in Germany and Switzerland made it their study to expose the errors and corruptions of the see of Rome. The doctrine of saint-worship was shown to be idolatrous—that of pardons and indulgences, a foul encouragement to vice—that of Purgatory, a cunning means of extorting money—and the pretensions of the Pope to infallibility, a blasphemous assumption of the attributes proper to God alone. These new opinions were termed the doctrines of the Reformers, and those who embraced them became gradually more and more numerous. The Roman Catholic priests attempted to defend the tenets of their church by argument: but as that was found difficult, they endeavoured, in most countries of Europe, to enforce them by violence. But the Reformers found protection in various parts of Germany. Their numbers seemed to increase rather than diminish, and to promise a great revolution in the Christian world.

Henry VIII., the King of England, was possessed of some learning, and had a great disposition to show it in this controversy. Being in the earlier part of his reign, sincerely attached to the Church of Rome, he wrote a book in defence of its doctrines, against Martin Luther, one of the principal reformers. The Pope was so much gratified by this display of zeal, that he conferred on the King the appellation of Defender of the Faith; a title which Henry's successors continue to retain, although in a very different sense from that in which it was granted.

Now Henry, you must know, was married to a very good princess, named Catherine, who was a daughter of the King of Spain, and sister to the Emperor of Germany. She had been in her youth, contracted to Henry's elder brother Arthur; but that prince dying, and Henry becoming heir of the throne, his union with Catherine had taken place. They had lived long together, and Catherine had borne a daughter, Mary, who was the natural heir-apparent of the English crown. But at length Henry VIII. fell deeply in love with a beautiful young woman, named Ann Boleyn, a maid of honour in the Queen's retinue, and he became extremely desirous to get rid of Queen Catherine, and marry this young lady. For this purpose he applied to the Pope, in order to obtain a divorce from the good Queen, under pretence of her having been contracted to his elder brother before he was married to her. This, he alleged, seemed to him like marrying his brother's wife, and therefore he desired that the Pope would dissolve a marriage which, as he alleged, gave much pain to his conscience. The truth was, that his conscience would have given him very little disturbance, had he not wanted to marry another, a younger and more beautiful woman.

The Pope would have, probably, been willing enough to gratify Henry's desire, at least his predecessors had granted greater favours to men of less consequence; but then Catherine was the sister of Charles V., who was at once Emperor of Germany and King of Spain, and one of the wisest as well as the most powerful princes in Christendom. The Pope, who depended much on Charles's assistance for checking the Reformation, dared not give him the great offence which would have been occasioned by encouraging his sister's divorce. His holiness, therefore, evaded giving a precise answer to the King of England from day to day, week to week, and year to year. But this led to a danger which the Pope had not foreseen.

Henry VIII., a hot, fiery, and impatient prince as ever lived, finding that the Pope was trifling with him, resolved to shake off his authority entirely. For this purpose he denied the authority of the Pope in England, and declared that he himself was the only Head of the English Church, and that the Bishop of Rome had nothing to do with him or his dominions. Many of the bishops and clergymen of the English Church adopted the reformed doctrines, and all disowned the supreme rule, hitherto ascribed to the Pope.

But the greatest blow to the papal authority was the dissolution of the monasteries, or religious houses, as they were called. The King seized on the convents, and the lands granted for their endowment, and, distributing the wealth of the convents among the great men of his court, broke up for ever those great establishments, and placed an insurmountable obstacle in the way of the Catholic religion being restored, after the interest of so many persons had been concerned in its being excluded.

The motive of Henry VIII.'s conduct was by no means praiseworthy, but it produced the most important and salutary consequences; as England was for ever afterwards, except during the short reign of his eldest daughter, freed from all dependence upon the Pope, and from the superstitious doctrines of the Roman Catholic religion.

Now here, returning to Scottish history, you must understand that one of Henry's principal wishes was to prevail upon his nephew, the young King of Scotland, to make the same alteration of religion in his country, which had been introduced into England. Henry, if we can believe the Scottish historians, made James the most splendid offers, to induce him to follow this course. He proposed to give him the hand of his daughter Mary in marriage, and to create him Duke of York; and, with a view to the establishment of a lasting peace between the countries, he earnestly desired a personal meeting with his nephew in the north of England.

There is reason to believe that James was, at one period, somewhat inclined to the reformed doctrines; at least, he encouraged a Scottish poet, called Sir David Lindsay of the Mount, and also the celebrated scholar, George Buchanan, in composing some severe satires against the corruptions of the Roman Catholic religion; but the King was, notwithstanding, by no means disposed altogether to fall off from the Church of Rome. He dreaded the power of England, and the rough, violent, and boisterous manners of Henry, who disgusted his nephew by the imprudent violence with which he pressed him to imitate his steps. But, in particular, James found the necessity of adhering to the Roman Catholic faith, from the skill, intelligence, and learning of the clergy, which rendered them far more fit to hold offices of state, and to assist him in administering the public business, than the Scottish nobility, who were at once profoundly ignorant, and fierce, arrogant, and ambitious in the highest degree.

The Archbishop Beaton, already mentioned, and his nephew David Beaton, who was afterwards made a cardinal, rose high in James's favour and, no doubt, the influence which they possessed over the King's mind was exerted to prevent his following the example of his uncle Henry in religious affairs.

The same influence might also induce him to seek an alliance with France, rather than with England; for it was natural that the Catholic clergy, with whom James advised, should discountenance, by every means in their power, any approaches to an intimate alliance with Henry, the mortal enemy of the Papal See. James V. accordingly visited France, and obtained the hand of Magdalen, the daughter of Francis I., with a large portion. Much joy was expressed at the landing of this princess at Leith, and she was received with as great splendour and demonstration of welcome as the poverty of the country would permit. But the young Queen was in a bad state of health, and died within forty days after her marriage.

After the death of this princess, the King, still inclining to the French alliance, married Mary of Guise, daughter of the Duke of Guise, thus connecting himself with a family, proud, ambitious, and attached, in the most bigoted degree, to the Catholic cause. This connection served, no doubt, to increase James's disinclination to any changes in the established Church.

But whatever were the sentiments of the sovereign, those of the subjects were gradually tending more and more towards a reformation of religion. Scotland at this time possessed several men of learning who had studied abroad, and had there learned and embraced the doctrines of the great reformer Calvin. They brought with them, on their return, copies of the Holy Scripture, and could give a full account of the controversy between the Protestants, as they are now called, and the Roman Catholic Church. Many among the Scots, both of higher and lower rank, became converts to the new faith.

The Popish ministers and counsellors of the King ventured to have recourse to violence, in order to counteract these results. Several persons were seized upon, tried before the spiritual courts of the Bishop of St. Andrews, and condemned to the flames. The modesty and decency with which these men behaved on their trials, and the patience with which they underwent the tortures of a cruel death, protesting at the same time their belief in the doctrines for which they had been condemned to the stake, made the strongest impression on the beholders, and increased the confidence of those who had embraced the tenets of the Reformers. Stricter and more cruel laws were made against heresy. Even the disputing the power of the Pope was punished with death; yet the Reformation seemed to gain ground in proportion to every effort to check it.

The favours which the King extended to the Catholic clergy led the Scottish nobility to look upon them with jealousy, and increased their inclination towards the Protestant doctrines. The wealth of the abbeys and convents, also, tempted many of the nobles and gentry, who hoped to have a share of the church lands, in case of these institutions being dissolved, as in England. And although there were, doubtless, good men as well as bad among the monks, yet the indolent, and even debauched lives of many of the order, rendered them, generally, odious and contemptible to the common people.

The popular discontent was increased by an accident which took place in the year 1537. A matron of the highest rank, Jane Douglas, sister of the banished Earl of Angus, widow of John Lyon, Lord of Glamis, and wife of Archibald Campbell of Kepneith, was accused of having practised against the life of James, by the imaginary crime of witchcraft, and the more formidable means of poison. Her purpose was alleged to be the restoration of the Douglases to Scotland, and to their estates and influence in that country. This lady was burnt alive on the Castle-hill of Edinburgh and the spectators, filled with pity for her youth and beauty, and surprised at the courage with which she endured the sentence, did not fail to impute her execution less to any real crime than to the King's deep-rooted hatred against the house of Douglas. Another capital punishment, though inflicted on an object of general dislike, served to confirm the opinion entertained of James's severity, not to say cruelty, of disposition. We have mentioned Sir James Hamilton of Draphane, called the Bastard of Arran, as distinguished on account of the ferocity of his disposition, and the murders which he committed in cold blood. This man had been made sheriff of Ayr, and had received other favours from the King's hand. Notwithstanding, he was suddenly accused of treason by a cousin and namesake of his own; and on that sole testimony, condemned and executed. Upon this occasion also, public opinion charged James with having proceeded without sufficient evidence of guilt.

In the meantime, Henry continued to press the King of Scotland, by letters and negotiations, to enter unto common measures with him against the Catholic clergy. He remonstrated with his nephew upon his preferring to improve his royal revenue by means of herds and flocks, which he represented as an unprincely practice, saying, that if he wanted money, he, his kind uncle, would let him have what sums he pleased; or, that the wealth of the Catholic convents and monasteries was a fund which lay at his command whenever he liked to seize it. Lastly, the English ambassador, Sir Ralph Sadler, insisted, as directed by his instructions, upon the evil doctrines and vicious lives of the clergy, against whom he urged the King to take violent measures.

Much of this message was calculated to affront James, yet he answered temperately. He acknowledged that he preferred living on his own revenue, such as it was, to becoming dependent upon another king, even though that king was his uncle. He had no pretext or motive, he said, to seize the possessions of the clergy, because they were always ready to advance him money when he had need of it. Those among them who led vicious lives, he would not fail, he added, to correct severely; but he did not consider it as just to punish the whole body for the faults of a few. In conclusion, King James suffered a doubtful promise to be extracted from him that he would meet Henry at York, if the affairs of his kingdom would permit.

The King of Scotland was now brought to a puzzling alternative, being either obliged to comply with his uncle's wishes, break off his alliance with France, and introduce the Reformed religion into his dominions, or, by adhering to France and to the Catholic faith, to run all the hazards of a war with England. The churchmen exercised their full authority over the mind of James at this crisis. The gold of France was not spared to determine his resolution; and it may be supposed that the young Queen, so nearly connected with the Catholic house of Guise, gave her influence to the same party. James at length determined to disappoint his uncle; and after the haughty Henry had remained six days at York, in the expectation of meeting him, he excused himself by some frivolous apology. Henry was, as might have been expected, mortally offended, and prepared for war.

A fierce and ruinous war immediately commenced. Henry sent numerous forces to ravage the Scottish Border. James obtained success in the first considerable action, to his very great satisfaction, and prepared for more decisive hostility. He assembled the array of his kingdom, and marched from Edinburgh as far as Fala, on his way to the Border, when tidings arrived, 1st November 1542, that the English general had withdrawn his forces within the English frontier. On this news, the Scottish nobles, who, with their vassals, had joined the royal standard intimated to their sovereign that, though they had taken up arms to save the country from invasion, yet they considered the war with England as an impolitic measure, and only undertaken to gratify the clergy; and that, therefore, the English having retired, they were determined not to advance one foot into the enemy's country. One Border chieftain alone offered with his retinue to follow the King wherever he chose to lead. This was John Scott of Thirlstane, whom James rewarded with an addition to his paternal coat-of-arms, with a bunch of spears for the crest, and the motto, "*Ready, aye Ready.*"

James, finding himself thus generally thwarted and deserted by the nobility, returned to Edinburgh, dishonoured before his people, and in the deepest dejection of mind.

To retaliate the inroads of the English, and wipe out the memory of Fala Moss, the King resolved that an army of ten thousand men should invade England on the Western Border; and he imprudently sent with them his peculiar favourite, Oliver Sinclair, who shared with the priests the unpopularity of the English war, and was highly obnoxious to the nobility, as one of those who engrossed the royal favour to their prejudice.

The army had just entered English ground, at a place called Solway Moss, when this Oliver Sinclair was raised upon the soldiers' shields to read to the army a commission, which, it was afterwards said, named Lord Maxwell commander of the expedition. But no one doubted at the time that Oliver Sinclair had himself been proclaimed commander-in-chief; and as he was generally disliked and despised, the army instantly fell into a state of extreme confusion. Four or five hundred English Borderers, commanded by Thomas Dacre and John Musgrave, perceived this fluctuation, and charged the numerous squadrons of the invading army. The Scots fled without even attempting to fight. Numbers of noblemen and persons of note suffered themselves to be made prisoners rather than face the displeasure of their disappointed sovereign.

The unfortunate James had lately been assailed by various calamities. The death of his two sons, and the disgrace of the defection at Fala, had made a deep impression on his mind, and haunted him even in the visions of the night. He dreamed he saw the fierce Sir James Hamilton, whom he had caused to be put to death upon slight evidence, approach him with a drawn sword, the bloody shade said, "Cruel tyrant, thou hast unjustly murdered me, who was indeed barbarous to other men, but always faithful and true to thee; wherefore now shalt thou have thy deserved punishment." So saying, it seemed to him as if Sir James Hamilton cut off first one arm and then another, and then left him, threatening to come back soon and cut his head off. Such a dream was very likely to arise in the King's mind, perturbed as it was by misfortunes, and even perhaps internally reproaching himself for Sir James Hamilton's death. But to James the striking off his arms appeared to allude to the death of his two sons, and he became convinced that the ultimate threats of the vision presaged his own death.

The disgraceful news of the battle, or rather the rout of Solway, filled up the measure of the King's despair and desolation. He shut himself up in the palace of Falkland, and refused to listen to any consolation. A burning fever, the consequence of his grief and shame, seized on the unfortunate monarch. They brought him tidings that his wife had given birth to a daughter; but he only replied, "Is it so?" reflecting on the alliance which had placed the Stewart family on the throne; "then God's will be done. It came with a lass, and it will go with a lass." With these words, presaging the extinction of his house, he made a signal of adieu to his courtiers, spoke little more, but turned his face to the wall, and died of the most melancholy of all diseases, a broken heart. He was scarcely thirty-one years old; in the very prime, therefore, of life. If he had not suffered the counsels of the Catholic priests to hurry him into a war with England, James V. might have been as fortunate a prince as his many good qualities and talents deserved.

KINGS OF SCOTLAND

Dep. indicates *deposed*—Ab. *abdicated*—Res. *resigned*—d. *daughter*

Name	Parentage	Marriage	Accession (A.D.)	Death (A.D.)	Reign (Yrs.)	Children
Duncan I.	Crinan, Abbot of Dunkeld, and Beatrice, d. of Malcolm II.	With the sister of Seward, Earl of Northumberland.	1034	1039	6	1. Malcolm Canmore; 2. Donald Bane.
Macbeth.	Finlegh, Thane of Ross and Doada, d. of Malcolm II.	The Lady Gruach, granddaughter of Kenneth IV.	1039	1056	17	
Malcolm III. (Canmore.)	Duncan I.	Margaret of England.	1057	1093	36	1. Edward; 2. Ethelred; 3. Edmund; 4. EDGAR; 5. ALEXANDER; 6. DAVID; 7. Matilda; 8. Mary.
Donald Bane.	Duncan I.		1093	1094	1	
Duncan II.	Grandson of Malcolm III.	Ethreda, daughter of Gosspatric.	1094	1095	1	William.
Donald (restored).			1095	Dep 1097	2	Madach, 1st Earl of Athole.
Edgar.	Malcolm III.		1097	1107	10	
Alexander I.	Malcolm III.	Sibilla, natural d. of Henry I. of England.	1107	1124	18	
David I.	Malcolm III.	Matilda, d. of Waltheof, Earl of Northumberland.	1124	1153	30	Henry[1].
Malcolm IV.	Henry, son of David I. and Ada, d. of the Earl of Warrne and Surrey.		1153	1165	13	
William the Lion.	The same.	Ermengarde, d. of Viscount Beaumont.	1165	1214	49	1. ALEXANDER; 2. Margaret; 3. Isabella; 4. Marjory.
Alexander II.	William.	I. Joan, d. of King John of England, no issue; II. Mary of Picardy.	1214	1249	35	ALEXANDER.

[1] Prince Henry who died before his father, 12th June 1152, married Ada, d. of Earl of Warrene and Surrey. Issue: 1. Malcolm; 2. William, afterwards Kings; 3. David, Earl of Huntington, and three daughters.

271

Name	Parentage	Marriage	Accession (A.D.)	Death (A.D.)	Reign (Yrs.)	Children
Alexander III.	Alexander II.	I. Margaret, d. of King Henry III. of England, issue; II. Joleta, d. of the Count de Dreux, no issue.	1249	1286	37	1. Alexander; 2. David; 3. Margaret.
Margaret.	Eric, King of Norway, and Margaret, d. of Alexander III.		1286	1290	5	
Interregnum.					2	
John Baliol.	John Baliol of Barnard Castle, and Devorgoil, gr. d. of David, Earl of Huntington, gr. son of David I. Marriage: Isabella, d. of John de Warren, Earl of Surrey.	Isabella, d. of John de Warren, Earl of Surrey.	1292	Res. 1296 died 1314	4	1. Edward; 2. Henry.
Interregnum.					10	
Robert I. The Bruce.	The grandson of Bruce, Baliol's competitor.	I. Isabella, d. of Donald, tenth Earl of Mar; II. Elizabeth, d. of the Earl of Ulster.	1306	1329	24	I. Marjory. II. 1. DAVID; 2. Margaret; 3. Matilda; 4. Elizabeth.
David II.	Robert Bruce.	I. Johanna, d. of King Edward II. of England; II. Margaret, d. of Sir J. Logie.	1329	1371	42	

HOUSE OF STEWART

Name	Parentage	Marriage	Accession (A.D.)	Death (A.D.)	Reign (Yrs.)	Children
Robert II.	Walter, Steward of Scotland, and Marjory, d. of Robert Bruce.	I. Elizabeth, d. of Sir Adam More of Rowallan; II. Euphemia, d. of the Earl of Ross.	1371	1390	19	I. 1. John, afterwards named ROBERT; 2. Walter; 3. Robert; 4. Alexander; and six daughters. II. 1. David; 2. Walter; and four daughters.
Robert III.	Robert II.	Annabella, d. of Sir John Drummond of Stobhall.	1390	1406	17	1. David, Duke of Rothsay; 2. James; and three daughters.
Regencies of the Dukes of Albany, 1406 to 1424			1406	1424	18	
James I.	Robert III.	Joanna, d. of John, Duke of Somerset, gr. Grandson of King Edward III.	1424	1437	13	1. JAMES; and five daughters.
James II.	James I.	Mary, d. of Arnold, Duke of Guelderland.	1437	1460	24	1. JAMES; 2. Alexander; 3. John; 4. Mary; 5. Margaret.

Name	Parentage	Marriage	Accession (A.D.)	Death (A.D.)	Reign (Yrs.)	Children
James III.	James II.	Margaret of Denmark.	1460	1488	28	1. JAMES; 2. James, Marquis of Ormond; 3. John, Earl of Mar.
James IV.	James III.	Margaret, d. of King Henry VII. of England.	1488	1513	26	1. JAMES; 2. Alexander.
James V.	James IV.	I. Magdalen, d. of King Francis I. of France; II. Mary, d. of the Duke of Guise.	1513	1542	29	MARY.
Regency.			1542	1561	19	
Mary.	James V.	I. Francis, son of King Henry II. of France; II. Henry, Lord Darnley; III. Hepburn, E. of Bothwell.	1561 Res. 1567	1587	6	JAMES.
James VI.	Mary.	Anne of Denmark.	1567		36	
Union of the Crowns. James VI. now James. I. of England.			1603	1625	22	1. Henry; 2. CHARLES; 3. Elizabeth.
Charles I.	James VI.	Henrietta of France.	1625	1649	24	1. CHARLES; 2. JAMES; 3. Henry; 4. Mary; 5. Elizabeth; 6. Henrietta.
Charles II.	Charles I.	Catherine of Portugal.	1649		2	
The Commonwealth			1651	1660	9	
Charles II. restored.			1660	1685	25	
James VII. and II. of England[1].	Charles I.	I. Anne Hyde, d. of the Earl of Clarendon; II. Mary of Este.	1685	Abd. 1688	4	I. 1. MARY; 2. ANNE. II. James, afterwards known as the Pretender.
William III. and	Prince of Orange	Mary, d. of King James VII.	1689	M. 1694	6	
Mary	James VII.	William, Prince of Orange.	—	W. 1701	13	
Anne.	James VII.	Prince George of Denmark.	1701	1714	14	

[1] The last Sovereign of the House of Stewart, in the male line.

Name	Parentage	Marriage	Accession (A.D.)	Death (A.D.)	Reign (Yrs.)	Children
Union of Parliaments (1707)						
George I.	Sophia, grand d. of James VI.	Sophia, d. of the Duke of Zell.	1714	1727	13	1. GEORGE; 2. Sophia.
George II.	George I.	Caroline of Anspach.	1727	1760	34	1. Frederick, father of George III.; 2. William, Duke of Cumberland; and five daughters.

INDEX

275